SIMPLE SOUS VIDE

200 MODERN RECIPES MADE EASY

JASON LOGSDON

CASTLE POINT BOOKS

NEW YORK

www.castlepointbooks.com
www.stmartins.com

The Castle Point Books trademark is owned by Castle Point Publications, LLC.
Castle Point books are published and distributed by St. Martin's Press.

ISBN 978-1-250-16359-2 (paper over board)
ISBN 978-1-250-16360-8 (ebook)

Photography by Jason Logsdon and used by permission from Shutterstock.com
Cover photo used by permission from iStock.com

Our books may be purchased in bulk for promotional, educational, or business use.
Please contact your local bookseller or the Macmillan Corporate and Premium Sales Department
at 1-800-221-7945, extension 5442, or by e-mail at MacmillanSpecialMarkets@macmillan.com.

First Edition: January 2018

10 9 8 7 6 5 4 3 2 1

For Mom and Dad,
Thanks for helping me get
to where I am today.

Love,
Jason

CONTENTS

INTRODUCTION

Sous vide is becoming more and more popular, and for good reason. It's a convenient method of cooking that results in perfectly cooked food almost every time. Most sous vide preparations follow the same general process.

The first step is to prepare your food by trimming it, shaping it, and seasoning it. This is very similar to most traditional cooking methods. You can use many of the same seasonings with sous vide, including spice rubs, many herbs, and salt and pepper. Some people omit the salt and pepper for longer cooking times, but I tend to always use it before sous viding food. The only seasonings to stay away from are aromatics like raw garlic and onion since they will not break down during the lower temperatures used for meat.

The second step is to determine the time and temperature at which you want to cook your food. This information should be given in a sous vide recipe, or you can learn to figure it out using the explanations I give later in this book. Once the time and temperature are determined, you then heat water to that temperature, usually using a sous vide machine.

The next step is to seal your food in plastic. This is done with either a vacuum sealer or by using Ziploc brand freezer bags. Once sealed, the bags are placed in the heated water and cooked for the desired amount of time. After the sous vide cooking is done, the food is removed from the bags, patted dry, then quickly seared to give it a flavorful crust. At that point it is ready to be finished off with any sauces or sides before serving to friends and family.

That's all that there is to the sous vide process, though I will take you through some of the specifics in the rest of the book.

SAFETY

Sous vide is a new method of cooking and of thinking about cooking, so there has been a lot of focus on how to safely use it. While it seems there are special safety concerns with sous vide, almost all these concerns apply to traditional cooking as well; most people just don't follow them in their daily cooking. Taking time to understand sous vide safety will not only ensure you use sous vide correctly but also will make your usual methods of cooking safer.

Danger Zone

In my opinion, the most important piece of cooking-safety knowledge is to understand how bacteria and other pathogens react to temperature. The bacteria we are concerned with generally thrive from around 40°F (4.4°C) to 126°F (52.2°C). They stop growing, but don't really start dying quickly until around 130°F (54.4°C).

This temperature range of 40°F (4.4°C)

to 126°F (52.2°C) is often called the "danger zone," and most food scientists recommend making sure that food is only in this span for no more than 2 to 4 hours. Some government recommendations suggest that 140°F (60°C) should be the upper limit of the danger zone, but this is based on a built-in level of error for restaurants not on the actual growth and death of the pathogens.

If you want to be safe using sous vide, or almost any type of cooking, just remember that food shouldn't be held at temperatures between 40°F (4.4°C) and 130°F (54.4°C) for more than a few hours. Cooking meat at lower than 125°F (51.2°C) is basically the equivalent of letting it sit for several hours on your counter. It's fine for a little while, but after that it starts to get dangerous.

Safety is More Than Temperature

One of the most common misconceptions in cooking is that temperature equals safety. People have been taught that pork or chicken has to be cooked to a certain temperature to be safe. This is really only half the story; the missing component in this equation is time.

A piece of raw chicken heated to 140°F (60°C) and held at this temperature for 30 minutes is actually just as safe as one heated to 165°F (73.8°C). The reason the government suggests such a high temperature is that the pathogens are killed instantly at that temperature, but the same levels of pasteurization (killing of the unsafe bacteria) occur at much lower temperatures when the food is held there over longer periods of time. Using sous vide allows you to take advantage of this, and, as we explore later, this ability to cook food at lower temperatures results in much moister food.

The pasteurization time and temperature recommendations in this book are based on reducing the amount of dangerous pathogens to acceptable levels. The US Government suggests these recommendations should kill all but one in one million, or one in ten million, of the pathogens, depending on the pathogen type.

Plastic Safety

A big concern that is fairly unique to sous vide is whether or not cooking in plastic is safe. In this matter I turn to the experts, and almost all food scientists have stated that food-safe, BPA-free plastic does not pose any risk at low temperatures. If you have concerns, I highly recommend you read the associated literature and make your own informed conclusions.

Safety is a pretty big subject, so for a more detailed look at the topics, including links to several experts' discussions of the danger zone and of pasteurization, you can view my safety article on AFMEasy.com/SSafety.

TIME

Time is the first of the two main components of sous vide cooking. Time comes into play in several diverse ways during the cooking process, but the length of time you apply heat to your food will accomplish the following three things:

Heats the Food

The simplest way to cook food is to apply heat to it just long enough for it to get to a pleasant temperature. This is how we usually cook steak and tender vegetables. Knowing how long it takes to heat your food is very important, especially in traditional cooking, since keeping your steak on the grill for too long results in overcooking.

The process of proper heating becomes much easier with sous vide because the food is cooked at the temperature at which you want to eat it, so there is no worry about overcooking. This gives you a much wider range of time within which the food will remain perfectly cooked. In fact, you will see that almost all the recipes in this book have a range noted for the sous vide cooking time, and within this range the food will always taste great.

A tender cut of beef, pork, or lamb that is being sous vided will heat through in a set amount of time. A general guide is that out of the refrigerator, a 1-inch-thick piece will heat through in 1 hour and 15 minutes, a 1½-inch-thick piece in 2 hours and 20 minutes, and a 2-inch-thick piece in 3 hours and 35 minutes. If the meat is frozen, you can increase the times by about 50 percent. For practical purposes, it doesn't really matter what temperature you are heating it to, as the difference in timing is very small.

Makes the Food Safe

As discussed in the safety section, another huge consideration of time that most people don't realize is that the cooking time makes the food safe to eat. Most food becomes safe to eat when it is heated to a specific temperature for a specific amount of time. So even though you could cook a chicken breast until just heated through, it probably wouldn't be safe to eat at that point. However, it will become safe to eat if you hold it at that temperature for long enough.

Some foods almost always need to be pasteurized, like chicken and poultry, but all foods can be pasteurized, and many people always pasteurize their food as an added precaution. Even though most steaks are safe to eat when they are unpasteurized, you never know when bacteria may have been introduced into the meat via a knife or meat tenderizer used at the market. It is also worth mentioning that for immuno-compromised individuals, such as the elderly or pregnant women, it is best to pasteurize all food.

The length of time it takes to pasteurize food depends on the type of food, its thickness, and the cooking temperature. A 1-inch-thick chicken breast will be pasteurized when cooked at 136°F (58°C) for 2 hours and 20 minutes, 140°F (60°C) for 1 hour and 40 minutes, or 149°F (65°C) for 1 hour. A 1-inch-thick steak or pork chop will be pasteurized when cooked at 131°F (55°C) for 2 hours and 45 minutes, 135°F (57°C) for 1 hour and 50 minutes, or 140°F (60°C) for 1 hour and 20 minutes.

For more information about cooking by thickness, including detailed timing charts, please view my free online article at AFMEasy.com/SThick.

Tenderizes the Food

The final reason for heating food is to tenderize it. You can heat a chuck roast in a few hours, and even pasteurize it pretty quickly, but it will still be tough and unpleasant to eat. If you hold it at the proper temperature for long enough; however, it will eventually become tender.

There are a lot of variables that go into how long certain foods must be cooked to tenderize them, but the two most important variables are the type of food and the cooking temperature.

Some meats such as beef tenderloin or chicken breast are already tender when raw and therefore just need to be heated through.

A sirloin steak or flank steak is tough, so these meats benefit from additional cooking time to break them down. A chuck roast or lamb shank is very tough and therefore needs an even longer cooking time.

As the temperature is increased, the speed at which the food is tenderized increases greatly. So a chuck roast might take 36 to 60 hours to tenderize at 131°F (55°C), 18 to 24 hours at 156°F (68.8°C), and 12 to 18 hours at 176°F (80°C). And if you traditionally braise it around 200°F (93.3°C), it might be done in several hours.

As mentioned previously, the recipes in this book provide a time range for when the food is done. For tougher cuts of meat, like a chuck roast, it is important to remember that it will be well cooked anywhere within that range. It is similar to ordering a steak medium rare, as we don't usually concern ourselves if it is cooked to 131°F (55°C) or 133°F (56.1°C); it will still be good at either temperature.

TEMPERATURE

Temperature is arguably the most important factor in cooking, and it has a dramatic impact on food. Once you understand how temperature affects food, you will be able to consistently make great meals.

Effects of Temperature on Meat

As meat is heated, various things happen causing it to change. Taking advantage of these changes is where sous vide can shine.

As meat heats, it starts to tenderize as it breaks down. However, as the temperature rises, the proteins also contract and squeeze moisture out of the meat. The hotter the meat gets, the faster this happens, which is why meat becomes drier at higher temperatures. Then, past a certain temperature, the collagen in the meat starts to break down, further tenderizing it. Balancing the two processes to achieve your ideal texture and moistness is the key to creating amazing food.

In sous vide, you can choose a specific temperature at which to cook your food, so it is helpful to look at the specific ranges where these changes happen. From about 120°F (48.9°C) to 140°F (60°C), meat begins to tenderize and lose moisture. The higher the temperature, the faster this process happens, though the moisture loss happens very quickly compared to the tenderizing effects.

From about 141°F (60.5°C) to 155°F (68.3°C), the moisture loss increases dramatically with little gain in tenderizing power. Most foods do not benefit from being cooked in this temperature range, with the exceptions being perhaps chicken breast or pork chops at the low end of the range and chicken thighs in the middle of the range.

Above the range of 156°F (68.9°C) to 160°F (71.1°C), meat begins to again tenderize much more quickly as the collagen breaks down. The higher the temperature, the more quickly and more efficiently the breakdown occurs, and the resulting textures will be different at different temperatures.

Some of the most common temperature ranges are:

- Medium-rare beef: 130°F to 139°F (54.4°C to 59.4°C)

- Medium beef: 140°F to145°F (60°C to 62.8°C)

- Traditional "braised" beef: 156°F to 175°F (68.8°C to 79.4°C)

- Moist tender pork: 135°F to 145°F (57.2°C to 62.8°C)

- Traditional tender pork: 145°F to 155°F (62.8°C to 68.3°C)

- Traditional "braised" pork: 156°F to 175°F (68.8°C to 79.4°C)

- Extra-rare chicken breast: 136°F to139°F (57.7°C to 59.4°C)

- Traditional chicken breast: 140°F to150°F (60°C to 65.6°C)

- Mi-cuit fish: 104°F (40°C)

- Traditional fish: 122°F to 132°F (50°C to 55.5°C)

Gourmia Sous Vide 140

For a much more detailed look at time and temperatures, including recommendations for specific cuts of meat, I recommend my free online time and temperature charts found at AFMEasy.com/STimes.

Effects of Temperature on Vegetables

Sous viding vegetables is much less complicated than meat. In general, vegetables are always cooked at a minimum of 183°F (83.9°C) because the pectin contained in them within begins to break down at this temperature. Higher temperatures will cook the vegetables more quickly, but they all will have the same texture in the end. Lower temperatures will not tenderize many vegetables at all, no matter how long they are cooked sous vide.

HEATING WATER

Now that you have a better understanding of how critical temperature is to the sous vide process, both from a safety and a texture

Sansaire Classic Circulator

perspective, you can see why a good sous vide machine is so important.

There are several approaches to maintaining the water's temperature, but the most convenient approach is to purchase a dedicated sous vide machine. These come in many different styles, but the most popular and least expensive is currently a "wand" or "stick" sous vide circulator. These are shaped like a tube and sit in a container of water, evenly heating and circulating the water while the food cooks.

There are currently several good options for newer machines that can be found for less than $150. I maintain an updated list of the current sous vide machines with detailed reviews and benchmark tests at AFMEasy. com/SMachines.

It is possible to do sous vide on a stove with a carefully monitored pot, or in a beer cooler, but it takes much more effort for anything longer than a short cooking time. Using a dedicated sous vide circulator allows you to really "set it and forget it" since it will do all the heat monitoring on its own. For many of the longer cooking times, a dedicated machine is a requirement.

SEALING

One of the distinguishing factors of sous vide is the food is usually sealed in plastic before it is cooked. Many people are under the mistaken impression that the food has to be vacuum sealed, probably because "sous vide" means "under pressure." However, having an actual vacuum isn't that important. The main reason for removing the air from the bag is just to ensure close contact with the water so the heat will be readily exchanged, so any method that removes the majority of the air will be sufficient.

There are several different options for sealing your sous vide bags:

Ziploc-Brand Freezer Bags

For most cooks new to sous vide, the most convenient method of sealing is to simply use Ziploc-brand freezer bags. These bags are inexpensive and easy to find. They work pretty well with sous vide, especially for cooking times that are short and at low temperatures. Just place the meat in the bag in one layer and seal all but one corner of the bag. Then, place the bag into the water (except for the open corner); the water pressure will squeeze all the air out. Seal the exposed corner and you are ready to start cooking.

Edge Vacuum Sealers

The next step up from Ziploc bags is to use edge vacuum sealers. There are several companies that make these, including FoodSaver and several sous-vide machine manufacturers. These machines work well to remove the majority of the air, which is also nice if you store a

Oliso Vacuum Sealer

lot of food in the freezer. However, they do not work well when liquids are contained within the bags. The bags can also be expensive.

Chamber Vacuum Sealers

The highest level of sealing is chambered vacuum sealers. These machines remove all air from the bags by pulling a strong vacuum. They also work well with liquids, and with many you can control the strength of the vacuum. The machines are much more expensive, but the bags are less expensive than the other methods, which can lead to savings over time. They are also great for preserving food, especially in the freezer.

SEARING

One of the most flavorful parts of cooked meat is the crispy, crunchy crust that forms on the outside. Sous vide excels at perfectly cooking the inside of food, but it does nothing to create this amazing crust. This means that once the food is cooked, you still need to sear the outside to maximize its flavor.

The most important point to remember when searing is to thoroughly dry off the food once it is removed from the bag. Any moisture remaining will result in a subpar sear and over-cooked food; you can use paper towels or dish clothes to dry the food thoroughly.

If you want a better sear with less risk of overcooking, you can briefly chill your food before searing it. Before you remove it from the sous vide bag, place it in an ice-water bath for 5 to 10 minutes to cool. This will give you more time to develop the sear before the internal temperature rises.

There are several ways to sear your food, depending on what you are trying to accomplish and how your kitchen is set up:

In a Pan

The simplest way to sear your food is in a heavy pan on the stove top. Heat a few tablespoons of oil in a pan until the oil is piping hot (but not burning), then add the meat. Cook until it just starts to brown, 1 to 2 minutes per side.

Using a Torch

One of the more convenient ways to sear your food is to use a blow torch. These can be found in most hardware stores for under $40, and they are great at searing food without over-cooking it. Most larger hardware torches work well, but I usually recommend the Bernzomatic TS8000BT or the Iwatani Torch. Smaller crème brûlée or pastry torches will not work because they do not have enough power. To use the torch, dry off the food then slowly pass the lit torch back and forth across the outside until the food is seared.

Grilling

Depending on the flavor profile of your final dish, finishing on the grill is a great way to add smokiness to your food. Just crank the grill up as hot as it goes, dry off your meat, then throw it on the grill for 1 to 2 minutes per side.

Using an Oven and Broiler

If there are a lot of nooks and crannies to your food, or if it is a rounded cut, then finishing it in a very hot oven or under the broiler is often a good choice. This method tends to overcook the food more than other methods but it works well for larger cuts of meat, such as roasts or brisket. You can also use it with traditionally BBQed foods to add a bark to the outside of the meat after it has been sous vided.

CHAPTER ONE

SALADS

FLAT IRON STEAK SALAD with RASPBERRIES and TOMATOES

COOKS: **131°F (55°C) for 4 to 10 hours** · PREP: **15 minutes** · SERVES: **2**

FOR THE STEAK

1 pound flat iron steak

1 teaspoon fresh thyme leaves

1/2 teaspoon garlic powder

Salt and freshly ground black pepper

FOR THE DRESSING

2 tablespoons raspberry or raspberry–champagne vinegar

1 tablespoon orange juice

1 shallot, diced

2 tablespoons honey

5 tablespoons olive oil

TO ASSEMBLE

Mixed baby greens or the lettuce of your choice

1 red bell pepper, diced

12 cherry tomatoes, halved

1/2 cup fresh raspberries or mixed berries

3 radishes, sliced

2 tablespoons roasted pumpkin seeds

This is a nice and light steak salad that will fill you up without making you feel stuffed. The fresh berries give the salad it a nice sweet-and-sour note to counteract the richness of the steak. I like to grill the steak after the sous vide for additional bold flavors to the salad, but it can be pan seared if you prefer.

This salad uses a subtle raspberry vinaigrette, but any light dressing on hand will do. If you can't find raspberry vinegar, use white or red wine vinegar instead.

PREPARE THE STEAK

Preheat a water bath to 131°F (55°C).

Season the steak with salt and pepper then sprinkle it with the thyme and garlic powder. Place the steak in the sous vide bag then seal the bag. Place the bag in the water bath and cook for 4 to 10 hours.

PREPARE THE DRESSING

In a small bowl, stir together the vinegar, orange juice, shallot, and honey. While whisking, slowly drizzle in the oil just until the mixture comes together. Season with salt and pepper.

TO ASSEMBLE

Take the steak out of the sous vide bag and pat the steak dry. Sear the steak until just browned, 1 to 2 minutes per side. Remove the steak from the heat and slice it into short strips.

Assemble the salad by placing the lettuce on plates. Top with the bell pepper, tomatoes, raspberries, and radishes. Drizzle the vinaigrette on to the salad, and add the strips of steak on top. Top with the pumpkin seeds and serve.

RAISIN-MINT SALAD
with LEG of LAMB

COOKS: **131°F (55°C) for 2 to 3 hours** · PREP: **15 minutes** · SERVES: **4**

In Middle Eastern cooking, lamb is often paired with mint, yogurt, and raisins. Raisin-Mint Salad with Leg of Lamb combines all of these components into a flavorful and hearty salad. The lamb is cooked just long enough to heat through then is briefly seared for additional color and flavor. The lamb pairs great with the yogurt, mint, and raisin dressing.

PREPARE THE LEG OF LAMB

Preheat a water bath to 131°F (55°C).

Season the lamb with salt and pepper and place it in a sous vide bag. Add the thyme and rosemary then seal the bag. Place the bag in the water bath and cook for 2 to 3 hours.

PREPARE THE DRESSING

Put the yogurt, mint, and raisins into a blender and blend until smooth. Add the lemon juice, season with salt and pepper, and process briefly to combine. With the blender still running, slowly drizzle in the oil and process just until the mixture is smooth.

TO ASSEMBLE

Take the lamb out of the sous vide bag and pat the lamb dry. Sear the lamb on a very hot grill or in a hot pan just until browned, 1 to 2 minutes per side. Remove the lamb from the heat and slice it into strips. Place the mixed greens on individual plates and top with the lamb slices and tomato. Drizzle the raisin-mint dressing over the top. Sprinkle with the walnuts and feta cheese and serve.

FOR THE LEG OF LAMB

1 pound lamb leg, whole or in pieces

4 sprigs thyme

2 sprigs rosemary

Salt and freshly ground black pepper

FOR THE DRESSING

1 cup plain yogurt

$1/2$ cup fresh mint leaves

$1/2$ cup golden raisins

2 tablespoons fresh lemon juice

$1/2$ cup olive oil

TO ASSEMBLE

Mixed greens

1 tomato, diced

$1/4$ cup walnuts

$1/4$ cup crumbled feta

CHICKEN CAESAR SALAD

COOKS: **141°F (60.5°C) for 2 to 4 hours** · PREP: **15 minutes** · SERVES: **6**

FOR THE CHICKEN

1 teaspoon garlic powder

1 teaspoon paprika

1/2 teaspoon ground cumin

2 to 3 chicken breasts

Salt and freshly ground
  black pepper

FOR THE DRESSING

1 egg yolk

2 anchovy fillets

2 teaspoons Dijon mustard

1 teaspoon minced garlic

3 tablespoons fresh lemon
  juice

1/2 cup olive oil

TO ASSEMBLE

1 head romaine lettuce,
  coarsely chopped

1/2 cup freshly grated
  Parmesan cheese

2 cups croutons

Fresh cracked black pepper

Caesar salad is a flavorful and refreshing salad that is made more hardy with the addition of seared chicken. You can also easily make fresh croutons by dicing bread, drizzling it with olive oil and garlic powder, then toasting it. If you worry about the raw egg, you can pasteurize it by holding it at a temperature of 135°F (57.2°C) for 75 minutes before adding it to the salad.

PREPARE THE CHICKEN

Preheat a water bath to 141°F (60.5°C).

In a small bowl, combine the spices. Season the chicken breasts with salt and pepper then sprinkle them with the spice mixture. Place the chicken breasts in a sous vide bag then seal the bag. Place the bag in the water bath and cook for 2 to 4 hours.

PREPARE THE DRESSING

Place the egg yolk, fillets, Dijon, garlic, and lemon juice in a food processor and process until thoroughly combined. With the food processor still running, slowly drizzle in the oil and process until the mixture is smooth. Season with salt and pepper.

TO ASSEMBLE

Take the chicken out of the sous bag and pat the chicken dry. Sear the chicken over high heat in a hot pan until just browned, 1 to 2 minutes per side. Remove the chicken from the heat and slice it.

Place the lettuce in a large bowl. Add enough dressing to coat the leaves then toss the lettuce until evenly coated. Place the coated lettuce on individual plates. Top with the chicken, Parmesan, and croutons. Crack some fresh pepper on top and serve.

CHICKEN CHIPOTLE CAESAR SALAD

COOKS: **141°F (60.5°C) for 2 to 4 hours** · PREP: **15 minutes** · SERVES: **6**

The chipotle pepper adds a nice kick to classic Caesar dressing. You can add the chipotle to the dressing a little at a time to make sure the dressing is not too spicy for you. If you worry about the raw egg, you can pasteurize it by holding it at a temperature of 135°F (57.2°C) for 75 minutes before adding it to the salad.

PREPARE THE CHICKEN

Preheat a water bath to 141°F (60.5°C).

In a small bowl, combine the spices. Season the chicken breasts with salt and pepper then sprinkle them with the spice mixture. Place the chicken in a sous vide bag then seal the bag. Place the bag in the water bath and cook for 2 to 4 hours.

PREPARE THE DRESSING

Place the egg yolks, fillets, garlic, Dijon, chipotle pepper, and lemon juice in a food processor and process until thoroughly combined. With the food processor still running, slowly drizzle in the oil and process until the mixture is smooth. Season with salt and pepper.

TO ASSEMBLE

Take the chicken out of the sous vide bag and pat the chicken dry. Sear the chicken over high heat in a hot pan until just browned, 1 to 2 minutes per side. Remove the chicken from the heat and slice it.

Place the lettuce in a large bowl. Add enough dressing to lightly coat the leaves, then toss the lettuce until evenly coated. Place the lettuce on individual plates. Top with the chicken, Parmesan, and croutons. Crack some fresh pepper on top and serve.

FOR THE CHICKEN

1 teaspoon garlic powder

1/2 teaspoon ground coriander

1/2 teaspoon ground cumin

1/4 teaspoon ground ancho pepper

2 to 3 chicken breasts

Salt and freshly ground black pepper

FOR THE DRESSING

1 egg yolk

2 anchovy fillets

2 teaspoons minced garlic

1 teaspoon Dijon mustard

1 chipotle pepper in adobo

3 tablespoons fresh lemon juice

1/2 cup olive oil

TO ASSEMBLE

1 head romaine lettuce, coarsely chopped

1/2 cup freshly grated Parmesan cheese

2 cups croutons

Fresh cracked black pepper

GRILLED CHICKEN SALAD
with HONEY MUSTARD

COOKS: **141°F (60.5°C) for 2 to 4 hours** · PREP: **20 minutes** · SERVES: **6**

FOR THE CHICKEN

1 teaspoon garlic powder

1 teaspoon ground coriander

1/2 teaspoon ground cumin

4 chicken breasts

Salt and freshly ground black pepper

FOR THE DRESSING

1/2 cup mayonnaise

2 tablespoons olive oil

2 tablespoons honey mustard

1 tablespoon fresh lemon juice

TO ASSEMBLE

Mixed greens

Radishes, sliced

Yellow bell peppers, cut into strips

Fresh blueberries

Sunflower seeds

Grilled Chicken Salad with Honey Mustard is a nice and light option. You can use any garnishes you prefer, but here we use radishes, bell pepper, sunflower seeds, and fresh blueberries to add sweetness and crunch. I also like this salad with fresh snap peas or green beans. For a more savory salad, you can add a few roasted garlic cloves to the dressing and mash them in well.

PREPARE THE CHICKEN

Preheat a water bath to 141°F (60.5°C).

In a small bowl, combine the spices. Season the chicken breasts with salt and pepper then sprinkle them with the spice mixture. Place the chicken breasts in a sous vide bag then seal the bag. Place the bag in the water bath and cook for 2 to 4 hours.

PREPARE THE DRESSING

In a bowl, whisk together all the dressing ingredients until thoroughly combined. Season with salt and pepper.

TO ASSEMBLE

Preheat a grill to very hot.

Take the chicken out of the sous vide bag and pat the chicken dry. Sear the chicken over high heat on the grill, 1 to 2 minutes per side.

Place the mixed greens in a bowl and top with the radishes and bell peppers. Drizzle with the dressing, then add the chicken, blueberries, and sunflower seeds and serve.

CURRIED CHICKEN SALAD

COOKS: **141°F (60.5°C) for 2 to 4 hours** · PREP: **15 minutes** · SERVES: **4**

A good chicken salad is one of my favorite meals. If you add some fruit chutney to the salad it bumps up the flavors and, when combined with a little curry powder on the chicken, you will have an excellent and easy-to-make meal! If you have leftovers, this also works awesome on a sandwich!

PREPARE THE CHICKEN

Preheat a water bath to 141°F (60.5°C).

Season the chicken breasts with salt and pepper then sprinkle them with the curry powder. Place the chicken breasts in a sous vide bag. Place the bag in the water bath and cook for 2 to 4 hours.

PREPARE THE DRESSING

In a large serving bowl whisk together all the dressing ingredients until thoroughly combined.

PREPARE THE SALAD

Take the chicken out of the water bath and pat it dry. Shred or chop it into bite-size pieces. Combine the chicken, celery, carrots, tarragon, basil, grapes, and pears in a bowl and add the dressing. Stir to evenly coat the ingredients.

TO ASSEMBLE

Place several lettuce leaves in a bowl and spoon on some of the chicken salad. Top with the cashews and serve.

FOR THE CHICKEN

4 chicken breasts

2 teaspoons curry powder

Salt and freshly ground black pepper

FOR THE DRESSING

2 teaspoons curry powder

2 tablespoons mayonnaise

$1/3$ cup fruit chutney

$1/4$ cup olive oil

1 tablespoon fresh lemon juice

$1/2$ teaspoon pepper

$1/2$ teaspoon salt

FOR THE SALAD

1 celery stalk, diced

2 carrots, peeled and diced

$1/8$ cup fresh tarragon leaves, minced

$1/8$ cup fresh basil leaves, minced

1 cup seedless grapes, halved

1 cup diced pears

TO ASSEMBLE

Bibb lettuce

$1/2$ cup cashews

BACON CHIPOTLE RANCH SALAD with CHICKEN

COOKS: **141°F (60.5°C) for 2 to 4 hours** · PREP: **15 minutes** · SERVES: **4**

Ranch dressing is already flavorful, but blending bacon and chipotle chiles into it makes it even more incredibly tasty. The chipotles can be very hot, so you might want to add them in slowly, tasting the dressing after adding each one until you reach the heat level you like. This salad also works well with turkey or steak.

FOR THE CHICKEN

1 teaspoon garlic powder

1 teaspoon onion powder

1 teaspoon paprika

1 pound chicken breasts

Salt and freshly ground black pepper

FOR THE DRESSING

2 cups ranch dressing

1 to 2 chipotle chiles in adobo, or to taste

4 strips cooked bacon

TO ASSEMBLE

Mixed greens or the lettuce of your choice

1 orange bell pepper, cut into strips

1 tomato, diced

8 baby bella or white button mushrooms, sliced

Cheddar cheese, shredded

Sunflower seeds

PREPARE THE CHICKEN

Preheat a water bath to 141°F (60.5°C).

In a small bowl, combine the spices. Season the chicken breasts with salt and pepper then sprinkle them with the spice mixture. Place the chicken breasts in a sous vide bag then seal the bag. Place the bag in the water bath and cook for 2 to 4 hours.

PREPARE THE DRESSING

Place all the dressing ingredients in a food processor and process until thoroughly combined.

TO ASSEMBLE

Take the chicken breasts out of the sous vide bag and pat them dry. Sear the chicken breasts for 1 to 2 minutes per side, just until browned. Remove from the heat and slice.

Place the lettuce in bowls and top with the bell pepper, tomato, and mushrooms. Add the dressing, top with the chicken, cheese, and sunflower seeds, and serve.

AVOCADO and TURKEY SALAD

COOKS: **141°F (60.5°C) for 2 to 4 hours** · PREP: **15 minutes** · SERVES: **4**

Avocado and Turkey Salad is a light option, with the bite of the arugula offset by the richness of the avocado while pairing well with the mild turkey. This salad is great for a whole meal, especially if you serve it with warm rolls or a fresh baguette. I give instructions for a lemon vinaigrette, but you can use any dressing you like; the salad also goes great with honey mustard or Italian dressing.

PREPARE THE TURKEY

Preheat a water bath to 141°F (60.5°C).

In a small bowl, combine the spices. Season the turkey breast fillets with salt and pepper then sprinkle them with the spice mixture. Place the fillets in a sous vide bag then seal the bag. Place the bag in the water bath and cook for 2 to 4 hours.

PREPARE THE LEMON VINAIGRETTE

Combine the lemon juice and garlic in a bowl, add some salt and pepper, and let sit for a few minutes. Slowly whisk in the oil until the mixture thickens.

TO ASSEMBLE

Take the turkey breasts out of the sous vide bag and pat them dry. Sear the breasts on a very hot grill or in a hot pan, about 1 minute per side. Remove the breasts from the heat and cut them into strips.

Place the arugula in a serving bowl and add enough vinaigrette to lightly cover it, tossing to coat. Top the arugula with the avocado slices and the strips of turkey. Spoon a bit more dressing over them and season with salt and pepper. Using a vegetable peeler, shave strips of Parmesan over the top and serve.

FOR THE TURKEY

1 teaspoon paprika

1 teaspoon onion powder

$1/2$ teaspoon chipotle pepper powder

2 pounds turkey breast or fillets

Salt and freshly ground black pepper

FOR THE LEMON VINAIGRETTE

2 tablespoons fresh lemon juice

2 cloves garlic, minced

$1/3$ cup olive oil

TO ASSEMBLE

Arugula or baby spinach

2 avocados, sliced

Parmigiano-Reggiano cheese, for shaving

PESTO SALAD with BACON and TURKEY

COOKS: **141°F (60.5°C) for 2 to 4 hours** · PREP: **15 minutes** · SERVES: **4**

FOR THE TURKEY

1/2 teaspoon garlic powder

1/2 teaspoon onion powder

1/2 teaspoon dried basil

1/2 teaspoon dried oregano

2 turkey breasts or fillets, halved

Salt and freshly ground black pepper

FOR THE CROUTONS

1/2 loaf of bread, preferably a baguette or sourdough

3 tablespoons olive oil

2 teaspoons minced garlic

1 tablespoon dried basil

TO ASSEMBLE

5 bacon strips, cut lengthwise 1/2 inch wide

1/4 cup mayonnaise

5 tablespoons pesto

Bibb lettuce

1/2 pint cherry tomatoes, halved

Pesto Salad with Bacon and Turkey is a very flavorful meal, getting a lot of complex flavors from the pesto and the homemade croutons. It's hearty enough to be served as a main course but light enough to enjoy during the day for a healthy lunch.

PREPARE THE TURKEY

Preheat a water bath to 141°F (60.5°C).

In a small bowl, combine the spices and then season the turkey. Place the turkey breasts in a sous vide bag then seal the bag. Place the bag in the water bath and cook for 2 to 4 hours.

PREPARE THE CROUTONS

Preheat the oven to 350°F (176.7°C). Cut the loaf of bread into 1/2- to 1-inch cubes. Toss the cubes with the oil, garlic, basil, salt, and pepper. Place the cubes on a baking sheet with raised sides and toast them in the oven for 10 to 15 minutes. The cubes should be slightly crispy and browned but still soft on the inside. Remove from the oven and set aside.

TO ASSEMBLE

Fry the bacon in a pan over medium heat until the fat is rendered and the bacon is crisp. Remove from the heat and drain the bacon on paper towels.

Remove the turkey breasts from the water bath and pat them dry. Sear the breasts on a very hot grill or in a hot pan, about 1 minute per side. Remove the breasts from the heat and cut them into strips.

Whisk together the mayonnaise and pesto in a bowl. Place the lettuce leaves on a plate and top with the turkey. Spoon the desired amount of pesto on the turkey. Top with the tomatoes, croutons, and bacon strips and serve.

DUCK and ORANGE SALAD

COOKS: **131°F (55°C) for 2 to 4 hours** · PREP: **10 minutes** · SERVES: **4**

I enjoy the pairing of rich and fatty duck with sweet and acidic oranges. Duck and Orange Salad is a simple salad that comes together quickly but is full of flavor. The dressing also works well with pork or steak, though I especially like it with chicken thighs.

PREPARE THE DUCK

Preheat a water bath to 131°F (55°C).

Season the duck breasts with salt, pepper, and garlic powder. Place the duck in a sous vide bag with the orange zest then seal the bag. Place the bag in the water bath and cook for 2 to 4 hours.

PREPARE THE VINAIGRETTE

In a small bowl, stir together the orange juice, mustard, vinegar, and honey. While whisking, slowly drizzle in the oil, just until the mixture comes together.

TO ASSEMBLE

Remove the duck breasts from the sous vide bag and pat them dry. Sear the breasts in a pan over high heat, 1 to 2 minutes per side. Remove the breasts from the heat and slice them into $1/2$-inch-thick-slices.

Divide the mixed greens among individual bowls or plates. Top with the bell pepper and orange sections. Add the duck slices and spoon the vinaigrette on top. Add the pecans and serve.

FOR THE DUCK

4 duck breasts

1 teaspoon garlic powder

1 teaspoon orange zest

Salt and freshly ground black pepper

FOR THE VINAIGRETTE

1 cup orange juice

$1/2$ teaspoon mustard

2 tablespoons red wine vinegar

1 tablespoon honey

$1/2$ cup olive oil

TO ASSEMBLE

Mixed greens

1 sweet red bell pepper, diced

1 large orange, separated into sections

$1/2$ cup pecans

DUCK BREAST and CHERRY SALAD

COOKS: **131°F (55°C) for 2 to 4 hours** · PREP: **20 minutes** · SERVES: **4**

FOR THE DUCK

2 duck breasts

1 tablespoon Chinese five-spice powder

Salt and freshly ground black pepper

FOR THE VINAIGRETTE

3 tablespoons apple cider vinegar

1 tablespoon honey

6 cherries, pitted

6 tablespoons olive oil

TO ASSEMBLE

Mixed greens

Cherries, pitted

Cherry tomatoes, halved

Walnut halves

Duck and cherries are a classic pairing because their flavors blend so well together. The vinaigrette helps to cut the fattiness from the duck while the cherries add sweetness. I often serve this salad with a fresh baguette and a ricotta cheese spread to round out the full meal.

PREPARE THE DUCK

Preheat a water bath to 131°F (55°C).

Sprinkle the duck breasts with the Chinese five-spice powder then season them with salt and pepper. Place the duck breasts in a sous vide bag then seal the bag. Place the bag in the water bath and cook for 2 to 4 hours.

PREPARE THE VINAIGRETTE

Place the vinegar, honey, and cherries in a blender and process until smooth. With the blender still running, slowly drizzle in the oil and process until the mixture is smooth. Season with salt and pepper.

TO ASSEMBLE

Remove the duck breasts from the sous vide bag and pat them dry. Lightly salt the breasts then quickly sear them until the outside has browned and the fat has begun to render. Cut the breasts into strips.

Place the mixed greens in a bowl and add the strips of duck. Top with the cherries, walnuts, and tomatoes then drizzle with the vinaigrette and serve.

CORN and MANGO SALAD WITH SHRIMP

COOKS: **130°F (54.4°C) for 15 to 45 minutes** · PREP: **15 minutes** · SERVES. **4**

Sous vide shrimp is always plump and juicy, with none of the rubberiness you can find in the pan-fried version. Combining the shrimp with a sweet, spicy, and bold salad pumps up the flavor level a ton. The sweet mango and corn combines with the jalapeño for bright bursts of flavor. You can use more or less jalapeños, depending on how spicy you like your food.

This salad would also be great with a white fish, such as cod, swordfish, or grouper. Even chicken breasts are a great option.

PREPARE THE SHRIMP

Preheat a water bath to 130°F (54.4°C).

In a small bowl, combine the spices. Season the shrimp with salt and pepper then sprinkle them with the spice mixture. Place the shrimp in a sous vide bag with the butter and seal. Let the shrimp sit for 30 minutes for the dry brine to take effect then place the bag in the water bath and cook for 15 to 45 minutes.

PREPARE THE SALAD

Whisk together the vinegar and oil in a large bowl. Add the corn, jalapeños, bell pepper, and mango, and stir to thoroughly combine. Season with salt and pepper.

TO ASSEMBLE

Place the lettuce in individual bowls and add the corn mixture. Place the cherry tomatoes on top of the salad. Take the shrimp out of the sous vide bag and add them to the top of the salads. Top with the basil and lemon zest and then serve.

FOR THE SHRIMP

1 teaspoon paprika

1 teaspoon ancho chile powder or chile powder of your choice

1 pound shrimp, shelled and deveined

2 tablespoons salted butter

Salt and freshly ground black pepper

FOR THE SALAD

1 tablespoon white wine vinegar

2 tablespoons olive oil

2 cups cooked corn kernels

2 jalapeño chilies, seeded and diced

1 red bell pepper, diced

1 mango, diced

TO ASSEMBLE

1 handful red and green lettuce

12 cherry tomatoes, halved

1 handful fresh basil leaves, chopped

1 tablespoon grated lemon zest

CAESAR SALAD with BLACKENED GROUPER

COOKS: **130°F (54.4°C) for 15 to 40 minutes** · PREP: **20 minutes** · SERVES: **4**

FOR THE GROUPER

$1/2$ teaspoon ground cumin

$1/2$ teaspoon garlic powder

$1/2$ teaspoon onion powder

$1/2$ teaspoon ground coriander

$1/4$ teaspoon cayenne pepper, or to taste

1 pound grouper, cut into 4 portions

1 tablespoon unsalted butter

Salt and freshly ground black pepper

FOR THE DRESSING

1 egg yolk

2 anchovy fillets

2 teaspoons Dijon mustard

1 teaspoon minced garlic

3 tablespoons lemon juice

$1/2$ cup olive oil

TO ASSEMBLE

1 head romaine lettuce, coarsely chopped

$1/2$ cup freshly grated Parmesan cheese

2 cups croutons

Fresh cracked black pepper

I first had a similar dish at the Lazy Flamingo in Bokeelia, Florida. This dish takes a traditional Caesar salad and tops it off with blackened grouper. It is also very good with any white, mild fish–or even chicken. I give instructions for a homemade Caesar dressing, but you can also use your favorite bottle of Caesar dressing to save time. If you worry about the raw egg, you can pasteurize it by holding it at a temperature of 135°F (57.2°C) for 75 minutes before adding it to the salad.

PREPARE THE GROUPER

Preheat a water bath to 130°F (54.4°C).

In a small bowl, combine the spices. Season the grouper with salt and pepper then sprinkle it with the spice mixture. Place the grouper in a sous vide bag with the butter then seal the bag. Place the bag in the water bath and cook for 15 to 40 minutes.

PREPARE THE DRESSING

Place the egg yolk, anchovies, Dijon, garlic, and lemon juice into a food processor and process until thoroughly mixed. With the food processor still running, slowly drizzle in the oil and process until the mixture is smooth. Season with salt and pepper.

TO ASSEMBLE

Take the grouper out of the bag and pat it dry. Sear the grouper over high heat in a hot pan until just browned, about 1 minute per side.

Place the lettuce in a large bowl. Add some dressing and toss the lettuce to evenly coat it. Place the coated lettuce on individual plates. Top with the grouper, Parmesan, and croutons. Crack some fresh pepper on top and serve.

CHAPTER TWO

SANDWICHES and BURGERS

FRENCH DIP SANDWICHES

COOKS: **131°F (55°C) for 1 to 2 days** · PREP: **15 minutes** · SERVES: **4 to 6**

FOR THE ROAST

1 tablespoon garlic powder

2 teaspoons onion powder

1 teaspoon ancho chile powder or chile powder of your choice

1 teaspoon dried sage

1/2 teaspoon ground cloves

1/4 teaspoon ground cinnamon

1/4 teaspoon ground nutmeg

2 pounds top round roast

Salt and freshly ground black pepper

TO ASSEMBLE

8 to 12 slices Swiss cheese

4 to 6 hoagie rolls or small baguettes

4 to 6 dill pickles

French dip sandwiches are a classic deli food, and they are very easy to make at home using sous vide. Adding all the spices to the sous vide process helps to flavor an otherwise occasionally bland cut of meat. Once the meat is cooked for several days, it is seared and thinly sliced. I like to pile the slices on a hoagie roll with melted Swiss cheese but you can serve it however you prefer. Many people enjoy thinly sliced red onion on it. For a more refined presentation, you can bring the sous vide juices to a boil and skim the fat off the top before serving with the sandwiches.

PREPARE THE ROAST

Preheat a water bath to 131°F (55°C).

In a small bowl, combine the spices. Season the roast with salt and pepper then cover it with the spice mixture. Place the roast in a sous vide bag then seal the bag. Place the bag in the water bath and cook for 1 to 2 days.

TO ASSEMBLE

Heat a pan over medium-high heat.

Take the roast out of the sous vide bag, reserving the juice in the bag, and pat the roast dry. Quickly sear the roast in the pan until just browned, 1 to 2 minutes per side. Remove the roast from the heat and place it on a cutting board. Slice the meat as thinly as possible.

Place the cheese on the rolls and toast them in an oven or toaster oven until the cheese melts and the buns begin to brown. Remove the rolls from the oven and pile the roast beef on top. Pour the reserved juices from the sous vide bag into ramekins or small bowls for dipping and serve with the pickles.

CORNED BEEF REUBENS

COOKS: **135°F (57.2°C) for 1 to 3 days** · PREP: **10 minutes** · SERVES: **4**

Corned beef cooked sous vide results in great texture and tenderness. It is also juicier and more flavorful than many corned beefs. Sometimes the corned beef will turn out too salty. If that is the case, place it back in a Ziploc-brand bag, add some warm water to the bag, and place the bag back in the water bath. You can change the water in the bag every 10 to 15 minutes, testing the salt levels as over time the water in the bag will draw out the salt from the corned beef.

PREPARE THE CORNED BEEF

Preheat a water bath to 135°F (57.2°C).

Place the corned beef in a sous vide bag with any spices that were included in the package then seal the bag. Place the bag in the water bath and cook for 1 to 3 days.

TO ASSEMBLE

Heat a pan over medium-high heat.

Take the corned beef out of the sous vide bag and pat the meat dry. Quickly sear the meat in the pan until just browned, 1 to 2 minutes per side. Remove the meat from the heat and slice it into thin strips.

Brush one side of the bread slices with the oil and toast them. Place the cheese on the untoasted side of the bread slices and toast in a toaster oven or under a broiler until the cheese melts.

Spread the Thousand Island dressing on four of the bread slices and the Dijon on the other four. Pile the corned beef on the slices with the Dijon and top with the sauerkraut. Close the sandwiches and serve.

FOR THE CORNED BEEF

2 to 3 pounds cured, uncooked corned beef

TO ASSEMBLE

8 slices rye bread

Olive oil, for brushing

8 slices Swiss cheese

1 cup Thousand Island dressing

High-quality Dijon mustard

1 cup sauerkraut

RIBEYE SANDWICHES with BALSAMIC ONIONS

COOKS: **131°F (55°C) for 2 to 8 hours** · PREP: **15 minutes** · SERVES: **4**

FOR THE STEAK

1/2 teaspoon garlic powder

1/2 teaspoon onion powder

1/2 teaspoon ground coriander

1/2 teaspoon ancho chile powder

1 1/2 pounds ribeye, cut into bun-size portions

Salt and freshly ground black pepper

FOR THE ONIONS

Canola or olive oil

2 onions, thinly sliced

1 tablespoon minced garlic

2 tablespoons balsamic vinegar

TO ASSEMBLE

4 slices Provolone cheese

4 sandwich rolls or buns

Rich ribeye is wonderfully offset by sweet and tangy balsamic onions. Ribeye Sandwiches with Balsamic Onions is great with steak fries or macaroni and cheese. Cooking the steak sous vide ensures it is nice and tender, making it easy to bite through. I prefer Provolone cheese but my wife really likes them topped with melted blue cheese.

PREPARE THE STEAK

Preheat a water bath to 131°F (55°C).

In a small bowl, combine the spices. Season the steaks with salt and pepper then sprinkle them with the spice mixture. Place the steaks in a sous vide bag then seal the bag. Place the bag in the water bath and cook for 2 to 8 hours.

PREPARE THE ONIONS

Add some oil to a pan over medium heat and warm. Add the onions and season them with salt and pepper. Cook until they are soft, about 15 minutes. About 10 minutes into the cooking time add the garlic and balsamic vinegar and stir well.

TO ASSEMBLE

Take the steaks out of the sous vide bag and pat them dry. Sear the steaks over high heat. Flip the steaks and top with the cooked onions and the cheese. Cover the steaks and let cook for 1 to 2 minutes, or until the cheese has started to melt.

Place the steak on the buns and serve.

PORK CHOP SANDWICHES
with SPICY SLAW

COOKS: **140°F (60°C) for 2 to 3 hours** · PREP: **20 minutes** · SERVES: **4**

Pork Chop Sandwiches with Spicy Slaw makes a great lunchtime meal. It's hard to go wrong with flavorful pork chops kept moist from cooking sous vide then combined with a crunchy slaw on soft rolls with melted cheese! For sides, I like to serve these with macaroni and cheese or a cold pasta salad.

PREPARE THE PORK

Preheat a water bath to 140°F (60°C).

In a small bowl, combine the spices. Season the pork chops with salt and pepper then sprinkle them with the spice mixture. Place the chops in a sous vide bag then seal the bag. Place the bag in the water bath and cook for 2 to 3 hours.

PREPARE THE SLAW

In a large bowl whisk together the mustard and the vinegar. While whisking, slowly drizzle in the oil just until the mixture comes together. Add the cabbage, carrots, and red pepper flakes and stir to thoroughly combine.

TO ASSEMBLE

Take the pork chops out of the sous vide bag and pat them dry. Sear the pork chops until just browned, about 1 minute per side.

Preheat the broiler on the oven. Place the pork chops on a roasting sheet. Cover the top of the pork chops with the cheese. Cut the rolls in half and place on the sheet with the cut side up. Place the whole roasting sheet under the broiler until the cheese melts and the buns begin to brown.

Remove the sheet from the oven, place the pork chops on top of the buns, top with the coleslaw, garnish with pickles, and serve.

FOR THE PORK

$1/2$ teaspoon paprika

$1/2$ teaspoon garlic powder

$1/2$ teaspoon ground cumin

$1/2$ teaspoon ground coriander

$1/2$ teaspoon ancho chile powder or other chile powder

4 pork chops

Salt and freshly ground black pepper

FOR THE SLAW

1 tablespoon Dijon mustard

1 tablespoon apple cider vinegar

2 tablespoons olive oil

2 cups shredded cabbage

1 cup shredded carrots

$1/2$ teaspoon red pepper flakes

TO ASSEMBLE

4 slices Gruyère cheese

4 sandwich rolls

4 dill pickles, garnish

BBQ BACON CHICKEN SANDWICHES

COOKS: **141°F (60.5°C) for 2 to 4 hours** · PREP: **15 minutes** · SERVES: **4**

FOR THE CHICKEN

4 chicken breasts

$1/2$ teaspoon cayenne pepper

2 sprigs thyme

2 sprigs rosemary

Salt and freshly ground black pepper

TO ASSEMBLE

4 rolls, halved

Canola oil, for drizzling

BBQ sauce

4 slices extra sharp cheddar cheese

8 slices bacon, cooked

¼ red onion, thinly sliced

BBQ Bacon Chicken Sandwich has spicy chicken, crunchy onions, and smoky bacon, all combined with a sweet BBQ sauce on a crusty, grilled roll. It's great when served with corn on the cob, onion rings, or macaroni and cheese.

PREPARE THE CHICKEN

Preheat a water bath to 141°F (60.5°C).

Lightly season the chicken breasts with salt and pepper then sprinkle them with the cayenne. Place the chicken breasts in a sous vide bag with the thyme and rosemary then seal the bag. Place the bag in the water bath and cook for 2 to 4 hours.

TO ASSEMBLE

Drizzle the cut side of the rolls with the canola oil and then toast them just until browned; remove the rolls from the heat.

Take the chicken breasts out of the sous vide bag and pat them dry. Coat them with the BBQ sauce. Quickly sear the chicken breasts until the sauce begins to caramelize. Top with the cheese then remove from the heat.

Place the chicken on the rolls and top with the bacon and red onion and serve.

CHICKEN and MUSHROOM SANDWICHES

COOKS: **141°F (60.5°C) for 2 to 4 hours** · PREP: **20 minutes** · SERVES: **4**

Paprika adds some smokiness and depth of flavor to some-times bland chicken. Finishing the chicken breasts off on a hot grill adds even more smoky flavor, but you can always sear them in a pan, under the broiler, or even with a blow torch. These chicken sandwiches are great with steamed veggies or a side salad and a helping of kettle chips or fresh French fries.

PREPARE THE CHICKEN

Preheat a water bath to 141°F (60.5C).

In a small bowl, combine the spices. Season the chicken breasts with salt and pepper then sprinkle them with the spice mixture. Place the chicken breasts in a sous vide bag then seal the bag. Place the bag in the water bath and cook for 2 to 4 hours.

PREPARE THE ONIONS AND MUSHROOMS

In a skillet over medium heat, add some oil and heat until the oil is hot. Add the onions and mushrooms and cook, stirring occasionally, until they are soft, 10 to 20 minutes.

TO ASSEMBLE

Heat a grill to high heat.

Place the buns, cut side down, on the grill and let cook until they just begin to brown. Remove the buns from the heat.

Take the chicken breasts out of the sous vide bag and pat the breasts dry. Grill the chicken breasts for 1 minute over high heat then flip and top each with a slice of cheese. Close the lid of the grill and cook for another 2 minutes, or until the cheese just begins to melt.

Place the chicken on the buns, top with the onions and mushrooms, and serve with the dill pickles.

FOR THE CHICKEN

1 teaspoon paprika

$1/2$ teaspoon garlic powder

$1/2$ teaspoon ground cumin

4 chicken breasts

Salt and freshly ground black pepper

FOR THE ONIONS AND MUSHROOMS

Canola or olive oil

1 onion, thickly sliced

14 mushrooms, thickly sliced

TO ASSEMBLE

4 hamburger buns or rolls, halved

4 slices Swiss cheese

4 dill pickles

SHAVED CHICKEN REUBENS

COOKS: **141°F (60.5°C) for 2 to 4 hours** · PREP: **15 minutes** · SERVES: **4**

FOR THE CHICKEN

$1/2$ teaspoon garlic powder

$1/2$ teaspoon onion powder

$1/2$ teaspoon cayenne pepper

$1/2$ teaspoon dried thyme

4 chicken breasts

Salt and freshly ground black pepper

TO ASSEMBLE

4 sandwich rolls

4 slices Gruyère cheese

Thousand Island dressing

1 cup sauerkraut

Shaved chicken or turkey makes a great meat for a Rueben sandwich. The sandwiches come together pretty quickly, especially when you cook the meat sous vide, requiring very little hands-on time.

PREPARE THE CHICKEN

Preheat a water bath to 141°F (60.5°C).

In a small bowl, combine the spices. Season the chicken breasts with salt and pepper then sprinkle them with the spice mixture. Place the chicken breasts in a sous vide bag then seal the bag. Place the bag in the water bath and cook for 2 to 4 hours.

TO ASSEMBLE

Preheat the oven broiler.

Take the chicken breasts out of the sous vide bag and pat them dry. Slice the breasts as thinly as possible

Place four piles of the chicken, about the width of the rolls, onto a baking sheet and top them with the cheese. Place the rolls on the baking sheet with the cut side up. Place the baking sheet under a broiler until the cheese melts and the rolls begin to brown.

Remove the baking sheet from the oven. Spread the dressing on the rolls, add the sauerkraut, and place the chicken on top of the rolls and serve.

TURKEY BREAST SANDWICHES
with AVOCADO

COOKS: **141°F (60.5°C) for 2 to 4 hours** · PREP: **15 minutes** · SERVES: **4**

Avocado adds richness to these light sandwiches. The arugula adds some crispness and bite while the bacon contributes some great smokiness. The dried orange peel also lightens the flavor with a bright citrus taste. You can serve these sandwiches with a side salad, macaroni salad, or fresh potato chips.

PREPARE THE TURKEY

Preheat a water bath to 141°F (60.5°C).

In a small bowl, stir together the spices and dried orange peel. Season the turkey breast fillets with salt and pepper then sprinkle them with the spices. Place the fillets in a sous vide bag then seal the bag. Place the bag in the water bath and cook for 2 to 4 hours.

TO ASSEMBLE

Take the turkey breast fillets out of the sous vide bag and pat them dry. Sear the breasts over high heat, about 1 minute per side. Remove the breasts from the heat and top them with the cheese.

Place the turkey on the rolls, top with the avocado, bacon, and arugula and serve.

FOR THE TURKEY

1/2 teaspoon garlic powder

1/2 teaspoon onion powder

1 teaspoon dried orange peel

4 turkey breast fillets

Salt and freshly ground black pepper

TO ASSEMBLE

4 slices of Provolone cheese

4 sandwich rolls, halved

1 avocado, sliced

8 strips bacon, cooked

1 cup arugula

TURKEY and AVOCADO ROLLS

COOKS: **141°F (60.5°C) for 2 to 4 hours** · PREP: **10 minutes** · SERVES: **2**

FOR THE TURKEY

2 turkey breast fillets

Garam masala powder

Salt and freshly ground
   black pepper

TO ASSEMBLE

2 sandwich rolls, halved

1 avocado, sliced

1 red bell pepper, sliced

2 slices Provolone cheese

Dijon mustard

Mayonnaise

Turkey and avocado go great together because the avocado adds richness that turkey normally lacks. These are very simple sandwiches to put together but they have a great flavor. The garam masala adds depth of flavor to the turkey, the crunchy bell peppers add wonderful bursts of sweetness, and the Dijon lends great acidity and sharpness.

PREPARE THE TURKEY

Preheat a water bath to 141°F (60.5°C).

Season the turkey breast fillets with salt and pepper then sprinkle them with the garam masala. Place the fillets in a sous vide bag and seal the bag. Place the bag in the water bath and cook for 2 to 4 hours.

TO ASSEMBLE

Take the turkey breasts out of the sous vide bag and pat them dry. Sear the breasts on a very hot grill or in a hot pan, about 1 minute per side. Remove the breasts from the heat, assemble the sandwiches as desired, and serve.

CLASSIC HOT BUTTERED LOBSTER ROLLS

COOKS: **131°F (55°C) for 20 to 40 minutes** · PREP: **20 minutes** · SERVES: **4**

These classic lobster rolls are very simple to make and are deliciously rich. Just serve them with crispy potato chips, coleslaw, or French fries, and you're all set to close your eyes and pretend you're at the beach.

You can buy meat that has been removed from the shells, or you can quickly boil a lobster for 30 to 60 seconds–just until the lobster meat starts to firm up, making it easy to remove.

PREPARE THE LOBSTER

Preheat a water bath to 131°F (55°C).

Place the lobster meat, butter, and basil leaves in a sous vide bag. Season the lobster with salt and pepper then seal the bag. Place the bag in the water bath and cook for 20 to 40 minutes.

TO ASSEMBLE

Warm the buns in the oven. Take the lobster meat out of the sous vide bag and divide it among the buns. Spoon some of the liquid from the sous vide bag on top of the rolls. Top with the fresh tarragon and garnish with the lemon wedges.

FOR THE LOBSTER

Meat from 2 (1- to 1½-pound) lobsters

6 tablespoons salted butter

8 basil leaves

Salt and freshly ground black pepper

TO ASSEMBLE

4 New England–style hot dog buns, split at the top

1 teaspoon chopped fresh tarragon

4 lemon wedges

LOBSTER SALAD ROLLS

COOKS: **131°F (55°C) for 20 to 40 minutes** · PREP: **20 minutes** · SERVES: **4**

Lobster Salad Rolls is the other classic lobster roll preparation. The lobster is tossed in a light mayonnaise-based salad. Like the hot buttered rolls, just serve these with potato chips, coleslaw, or French fries for a great lunch.

You can buy meat that has been removed from the shells, or you can quickly boil a lobster for 30 to 60 seconds–just until the lobster meat starts to firm up, making it easy to remove.

PREPARE THE LOBSTER

Preheat a water bath to 131°F (55°C).

Place the lobster meat, butter, and thyme sprigs in a sous vide bag. Season the lobster with salt and pepper then seal the bag. Place the bag in the water bath and cook for 20 to 40 minutes.

PREPARE THE MAYONNAISE SALAD

In a large bowl, stir together the mayonnaise, celery, bell pepper, shallots, parsley, and chives until thoroughly combined.

Take the lobster meat out of the sous vide bag and place the meat in the bowl with the mayonnaise mixture. Stir together until the meat is thoroughly coated then refrigerate for 10 to 15 minutes to chill the lobster and let the flavors meld.

TO ASSEMBLE

When ready to serve, place the lobster mixture on the buns and garnish with a lemon wedge.

FOR THE LOBSTER

Meat from 2 (1- to 1 1/2-pound) lobsters

6 tablespoons salted butter

4 sprigs thyme

Salt and freshly ground black pepper

FOR THE MAYONNAISE SALAD

1/2 cup mayonnaise

1 celery stalk, diced

1/2 sweet red bell pepper, diced

2 tablespoons minced shallots

2 tablespoons fresh parsley, chopped

1 teaspoon fresh chives, finely chopped

TO ASSEMBLE

4 New England style hot dog buns, split at the top

4 lemon wedges

CLASSIC AMERICAN BURGERS

COOKS: **131°F (55°C) for 2 to 4 hours** · PREP: **10 minutes** · SERVES: **4**

FOR THE MEAT

4 hamburger patties, preferably at least 1 inch thick

Salt and freshly ground black pepper

TO ASSEMBLE

4 slices American cheese

4 high-quality hamburger buns

4 slices tomato

4 to 8 large lettuce leaves

8 pickle slices, such as "bread and butter" or dill

Mustard

Ketchup

This is the classic American burger. It's simple, but when cooked perfectly, it can be great. Using sous vide to precook the patties creates a super moist, medium-rare hamburger that is still safe to eat. If you prefer a more traditional level of doneness, you can cook the meat at 141°F (60.5°C) and the results will still be very good. Serving this with home-made French fries, sweet potato fries, or kettle chips is a terrific way to round out the meal.

PREPARE THE MEAT

Preheat a water bath to 131°F (55°C).

Season the patties with salt and pepper. Place the patties in a sous vide bag then seal the bag. Place the bag in the water bath and cook for 2 to 4 hours.

TO ASSEMBLE

Take the beef patties out of the sous vide bag and pat them dry. Quickly sear the patties over high heat for about 1 minute per side then top each with a slice of cheese. Cover the patties and let the cheese melt.

Remove the patties from the heat and place them on the buns. You can top them with the tomato, lettuce, and pickles or leave the additions on the side. Serve with the mustard and ketchup on the side.

BBQ BACON BURGERS

COOKS: **131°F (55°C) for 2 to 4 hours** · PREP: **15 minutes** · SERVES: **4**

BBQ bacon burgers are probably my favorite hamburger style. The addition of the paprika, chipotle, and liquid smoke, as well as the bacon, will result in a very smoky, flavorful burger. This is balanced by the sharp cheddar cheese, the tangy pickles, and the sweet BBQ sauce.

PREPARE THE MEAT

Preheat a water bath to 131°F (55°C).

Season the patties with salt and pepper then sprinkle them with the paprika and chile powder and place them in a sous vide bag. Add the liquid smoke then seal the bag. Place the bag in the water bath and cook for 2 to 4 hours.

TO ASSEMBLE

Place the bacon strips in a pan over medium heat and cook until the fat is rendered and the bacon is crispy. Set the bacon aside.

Take the beef patties out of the sous vide bag and pat them dry. Quickly sear the patties over high heat for about 1 minute per side then top each with a slice of cheese. Cover the patties and let the cheese melt.

Remove the burgers from the heat and place them on the buns. Top each with 2 bacon slices and the BBQ sauce and serve with the pickles on the side.

FOR THE MEAT

4 hamburger patties, preferably at least 1 inch thick

1 teaspoon paprika

$1/2$ teaspoon chipotle chile powder

1 teaspoon liquid smoke

Salt and freshly ground black pepper

TO ASSEMBLE

8 strips bacon

4 slices sharp cheddar cheese

4 high-quality hamburger buns, halved

BBQ sauce, preferably sweet

Several sweet pickles

MUSHROOM SWISS BURGERS with BACON

COOKS: **131°F (55°C) for 2 to 4 hours** · PREP: **10 minutes** · SERVES: **4**

FOR THE MEAT

4 hamburger patties, preferably at least 1 inch thick

Salt and freshly ground black pepper

FOR THE BACON AND MUSHROOMS

8 strips bacon

1 pint baby bella mushrooms

TO ASSEMBLE

4 high-quality hamburger buns, halved

Canola oil

4 slices Swiss cheese

My second favorite hamburger toppings are mushrooms, bacon, and Swiss cheese. Just before the hamburgers are ready, you sauté the bacon strips then cook the mushrooms in the rendered fat, resulting in a salty, bacon-flavored hamburger. The burgers are finished on the grill, but you can also use a hot pan or a blow torch to sear them.

PREPARE THE MEAT

Preheat a water bath to 131°F (55°C).

Season the patties with salt and pepper and place them in a sous vide bag. Place the bag in the water bath and cook for 2 to 4 hours.

PREPARE THE BACON AND MUSHROOMS

Place the bacon strips in a pan over medium heat and cook until the fat is rendered and the bacon is crispy. Set the bacon aside.

Pour out half the rendered fat. Add the mushrooms to the pan and cook, stirring occasionally, until they are soft, 10 to 20 minutes.

TO ASSEMBLE

Preheat a grill to very hot.

Take the beef patties out of the sous vide bag and pat them dry. Drizzle the cut side of the buns with canola oil and place them cut side down on the grill. Cook just until they start to brown then remove from the grill.

Quickly sear the burgers on the grill for 1 minute then flip them over and top each with a slice of cheese. Close the lid of the grill at let the cheese melt. Remove the burgers from the heat and place them on the buns. Top with bacon and mushrooms and serve.

CHICKEN BURGERS with ONIONS and PEPPERS

COOKS: **141°F (60.5°C) for 2 to 4 hours** · PREP: **15 minutes** · SERVES: **4**

I wasn't a big fan of chicken burgers until I made them myself using sous vide. Now I'll sometimes make them instead of hamburgers! The flavorful spices ensure a delicious patty while the sous vide process keeps them from overcooking. I like to cook the peppers and onions on the grill, but you can cook under the broiler or even in a hot pan. Make sure you have a few napkins on hand as these can get messy!

PREPARE THE CHICKEN

Preheat a water bath to 141°F (60.5°C).

In a small bowl, combine the spices. Season the chicken patties with salt and pepper then sprinkle them with the spice mixture. Place the patties in a sous vide bag then seal the bag. Place the bag in the water bath and cook for 2 to 4 hours.

PREPARE THE PEPPERS AND ONIONS

Peel the onions and then cut them into $1/2$- to $3/4$-inch-thick slices, keeping the rings of each slice together. You can also thread the onion slices onto a skewer.

Core and seed the bell peppers, leaving the sides in large pieces. Season the onions and peppers with salt and pepper then drizzle them with the canola oil.

Heat a grill to high heat. Add the onions and peppers and cook until they begin to brown and are fully cooked through.

TO ASSEMBLE

Take the chicken patties out of the sous vide bag and pat them dry. Grill the patties for about 1 minute per side over high heat then cover each with a slice of cheese. Close the lid and cook for another 2 minutes, or until the cheese just begins to melt. Place the chicken burgers on the buns, top with the cooked peppers and onions, and serve.

FOR THE CHICKEN PATTIES

$1/2$ teaspoon garlic powder

$1/2$ teaspoon onion powder

$1/2$ teaspoon paprika

4 ground-chicken patties

$1/2$ teaspoon dried basil

Salt and freshly ground
   black pepper

FOR THE PEPPERS
AND ONIONS

2 yellow or sweet onions

3 bell peppers, either red,
   yellow, or orange

2 tablespoons canola oil

TO ASSEMBLE

4 slices fresh mozzarella
   cheese

4 sandwich rolls or panini
   bread

SMOKY TURKEY BURGERS

COOKS: **141°F (60.5°C) for 2 to 4 hours** · PREP: **10 minutes** · SERVES: **4**

FOR THE TURKEY

4 ground-turkey patties

$1/2$ teaspoon paprika

$1/4$ teaspoon ground
  chipotle pepper

Salt and freshly ground
  black pepper

FOR THE ONIONS
AND MUSHROOMS

Canola oil, for frying

$1/2$ onion, thickly sliced

10 mushrooms, sliced

TO ASSEMBLE

4 slices smoked gouda or
  smoked provolone cheese

4 hamburger buns, halved

$1/2$ cup BBQ sauce

4 dill pickles

Turkey can sometimes be a little bland, so adding sautéed mushrooms and onions, as well as a flavorful BBQ sauce, adds some much needed sweetness and a little kick. I also like these turkey burgers when finished on the grill, since grilling adds even more wonderful smoky flavor to the meal. Use your favorite BBQ sauce, preferably one with a little spice to it.

PREPARE THE TURKEY

Preheat a water bath to 141°F (60.5°C).

Season the turkey patties with salt and pepper then sprinkle them with the paprika and chipotle pepper powder. Place the patties in a sous vide bag and seal the bag. Place the bag in the water bath and cook for 2 to 4 hours.

PREPARE THE ONIONS AND MUSHROOMS

Heat the oil in a skillet over medium to medium-high heat. Add the onions and mushrooms and cook, stirring occasionally, until they just begin to brown and are fully cooked. Remove them from the heat.

TO ASSEMBLE

Take the turkey patties out of the sous vide bag and pat them dry. Sear the patties for 1 minute per side over high heat then cover each with a slice of cheese. Cover the pan and cook just until the cheese just starts to melt.

Place the turkey patties on the buns, top with the BBQ sauce, sautéed mushrooms and onions, and serve with the dill pickles.

BBQ TURKEY BURGERS

COOKS: **141°F (60.5°C) for 2 to 4 hours** · PREP: **15 minutes** · SERVES: **4**

Sous vide turkey with paprika and chipotle chile powder adds a smoky undertone to the meat. The resulting turkey is a great base for the mushrooms and onions while the BBQ sauce adds some sweetness and a little kick. These turkey burgers are great with normal burger accompaniments such as chips or fries and potato salad.

PREPARE THE TURKEY

Preheat a water bath to 141°F (60.5°C).

Season the turkey breast fillets with salt and pepper then sprinkle them with the paprika and chile powder. Place the fillets in a sous vide bag then seal the bag. Place the bag in the water bath and cook for 2 to 4 hours.

PREPARE THE ONIONS AND MUSHROOMS

Heat the oil in a skillet over medium to medium-high heat. Add the onions and mushrooms and cook, stirring occasionally, until they just begin to brown and are fully cooked. Stir in the BBQ sauce and set aside.

TO ASSEMBLE

Preheat the oven broiler.

Take the turkey breasts out of the sous vide bag and pat them dry. Place the breasts on a baking sheet. Cover the breasts with the onions and mushrooms mixture and top each with a slice of cheese. Place the rolls on the sheet with the cut side up. Place the baking pan under the broiler until the cheese melts and the rolls begin to brown.

Remove the baking sheet from the oven and transfer the turkey to the sandwich rolls, spooning any extra mushrooms and onions on top. Cover with the tops of the rolls and serve with the dill pickles.

FOR THE TURKEY

4 turkey breast fillets

1/2 teaspoon paprika

1/4 teaspoon chipotle chile powder

Salt and freshly ground black pepper

FOR THE ONIONS AND MUSHROOMS

Canola or olive oil

1/2 onion, thickly sliced

10 mushrooms, thickly sliced

1/2 cup BBQ sauce

TO ASSEMBLE

4 slices smoked gouda or smoked Provolone cheese

4 sandwich rolls, halved

4 dill pickles

SMOKY HOT DOGS

COOKS: **141°F (60.5°C) for 2 to 3 hours** · PREP: **10 minutes** · SERVES: **4**

FOR THE HOT DOGS

4 high-quality hot dogs

4 tablespoons unsalted butter

1 teaspoon liquid smoke

TO ASSEMBLE

4 high-quality buns, split

Mustard, preferably coarse grained

Pickle relish

Smoky Hot Dogs adds some smokiness to the classic hot dog by sealing and cooking them with liquid smoke, which was inspired by chef Chuck Friedhoff. The secret to a great hot dog is using high-quality ingredients, so try to use the best hot dogs and the freshest buns. Although raw hot dogs are used here, using precooked hot dogs will result in a lot of flavor as well.

PREPARE THE HOT DOGS

Preheat a water bath to 141°F (60.5°C).

Place the hot dogs in a sous vide bag and add the butter and liquid smoke then seal the bag. Place the bag in the water bath and cook for 2 to 3 hours.

TO ASSEMBLE

Heat a grill to high heat.

Take the hot dogs out of the sous vide bag, reserving the juices in the bag, and pat them dry. Quickly sear the hot dogs on two sides over high heat, about 1 minute per side.

Smear the mustard on the inside of the buns then remove the hot dogs from the heat and place them in the buns. Drizzle some of the sous vide juices on each hot dog and serve with a spoonful of the relish on top.

BEER and BRATS

COOKS: **141°F (60.5°C) for 2 to 3 hours** · PREP: **10 minutes** · SERVES: **4**

Beer and Brats was inspired by the classic recipes where bratwurst is simmered in beer. I call for the beer to be a lager, but a dark beer can add even more complex flavors. Because this simple dish relies so heavily on the brats, you should use ones of only the highest quality.

Once cooked, you can eat the brats any way you choose. They are great on hoagie rolls with onions and bell peppers, as instructed below, or served with sauerkraut and potato salad.

PREPARE THE BRATWURST

Preheat a water bath to 141°F (60.5°C).

Place the bratwurst links in a sous vide bag and add the beer then seal the bag. Place the bag in the water bath and cook for 2 to 3 hours.

PREPARE THE ONIONS AND BELL PEPPERS

Heat a pan over medium heat.

Add the oil to the hot pan. When the oil is hot, add the onion, season with salt and pepper, and cook until they begin to soften, 10 to 15 minutes. Add the garlic and bell pepper and cook for another 5 minutes. Add the chicken stock and vinegar, and stir to thoroughly combine. Season with salt and pepper. Cook until the liquid begins to thicken; set aside.

TO ASSEMBLE

Heat a grill to high heat. Take the bratwurst out of the sous vide bag and pat dry. Quickly sear the bratwurst on two sides over high heat, 1 to 2 minutes per side.

Remove the bratwurst from the heat and place in the rolls. Top with the onions and bell peppers and serve.

FOR THE BRATWURST

8 bratwurst links

5 ounces beer, preferably a lager

FOR THE ONIONS
AND BELL PEPPERS

2 tablespoons canola or olive oil

1 onion, sliced into ¼-inch-thick strips

4 cloves garlic, minced

1 red bell pepper, sliced into ¼-inch-thick strips

½ cup chicken stock

2 tablespoons apple cider vinegar

Salt and freshly ground black pepper

TO ASSEMBLE

4 hoagie or sub rolls, split to hold the brats

BRATWURST GRINDERS

COOKS: **135°F (57.2°C) for 2 to 3 hours** · PREP: **21 minutes** · SERVES: **4**

FOR THE BRATWURST

4 large bratwurst links

TO ASSEMBLE

Olive oil

4 hoagie or sub rolls, split to hold the links

Any high-quality mustard

8 slices Provolone cheese

1/4 sweet onion, diced

Pickle relish

Bratwurst Grinders are a great meal to have during the week when you want something filling from the grill without spending too much time making it. You can even sous vide the bratwurst ahead of time and reheat it when searing. I've listed the toppings I prefer on my grinders, but you can substitute any toppings you like.

PREPARE THE BRATWURST

Preheat a water bath to 135°F (57.2°C).

Place the bratwurst links in a sous vide bag. Place the sous vide bag in the water bath and cook for 2 to 3 hours.

TO ASSEMBLE

Heat a grill to high heat.

Brush some oil on the inside of the hoagie rolls. Press the rolls cut side down on the grill and cook just until they start to brown. Remove from the heat, smear each cut side with some mustard, and place 2 slices of cheese on each roll.

Take the bratwurst out of the sous vide bag and pat dry. Sear the bratwurst on the grill, turning as the casing cooks, until nicely browned and heated through.

Remove the bratwurst from the heat and transfer them to the rolls. Top each with some diced onion and relish and serve.

CHICKEN GRINDERS
with CAPRESE SALSA

COOKS: **141°F (60.5°C) for 2 to 3 hours** · PREP: **15 minutes** · SERVES: **4**

Caprese salads are traditionally basil, tomatoes, and mozzarella, and they are a classic pairing. I like to turn a caprese salad into a salsa and use it to top chicken sausage that is cooked sous vide and then grilled. You can either serve this as a main dish or put it on a fresh hoagie roll as a great grinder, which is what I prefer.

PREPARE THE SAUSAGES

Preheat a water bath to 141°F (60.5°C).

Place the sausage and sage leaves in a sous vide bag then seal the bag. Place the sous vide bag in the water bath and cook for 2 to 3 hours.

PREPARE THE CAPRESE SALSA

In a small bowl, stir together the tomato, basil, balsamic vinegar, and oil until thoroughly combined. Season with salt and pepper.

TO ASSEMBLE

Lightly toast the cut sides of the hoagie rolls. Remove them from the heat and place 2 slices of the mozzarella on each.

Take the chicken sausages out of the sous vide bag and pat them dry. Sear the sausages over high heat, turning them as the casing cooks, until nicely browned. Remove the sausages from the heat and place them on the toasted rolls. Top with the salsa and serve.

FOR THE SAUSAGES

4 to 6 chicken sausages, about 1 inch in diameter

4 sage leaves

FOR THE CAPRESE SALSA

2 tomatoes, diced

1 bunch basil, chopped

1 tablespoon balsamic vinegar

1 tablespoon olive oil

Salt and freshly ground black pepper

TO ASSEMBLE

4 hoagie or sub rolls, split to hold the sausages

8 ($1/_8$-inch-thick) slices fresh mozzarella

TURKEY SAUSAGE GRINDERS

COOKS: **141°F (60.5°C) for 2 to 3 hours** · PREP: **10 minutes** · SERVES: **4**

FOR THE SAUSAGES

4 turkey sausages, about
   1 inch in diameter

2 sprigs thyme

1 teaspoon ancho chile
   powder

TO ASSEMBLE

6 hoagie or sub rolls, split
   to hold the sausages

4 slices provolone cheese

Honey mustard

Turkey Sausage Grinder takes turkey sausages and turns them into a more filling and flavorful meal. It's a very easy meal to make and will definitely impress your guests because the sous vide will ensure the sausages are juicy.

PREPARE THE SAUSAGES

Preheat a water bath to 141°F (60.5°C).

Place the sausages in a sous vide bag with the thyme and ancho pepper then seal the bag. Place the bag in the water bath and cook for 2 to 3 hours.

TO ASSEMBLE

Heat a grill to high heat.

Place the rolls on the grill, cut side down, and cook until they begin to char. Remove from the heat and place the cheese on them.

Take the sausages out of the sous vide bag and pat them dry. Quickly sear the sausages on two sides over high heat, about 1 minute per side.

Place a sausage on each roll and top with the honey mustard.

CHAPTER THREE

BEEF

FILET MIGNON with BLUE CHEESE SAUCE

COOKS: **131°F (55°C) for 2 to 4 hours** · PREP: **10 minutes** · SERVES: **4**

FOR THE STEAK

4 portions of filet mignon

4 sprigs thyme

2 sprigs rosemary

Salt and freshly ground black pepper

FOR THE BLUE CHEESE SAUCE

$1/4$ cup crumbled blue cheese

2 tablespoons heavy cream

1 tablespoon fresh lemon juice

4 tablespoons olive oil

Since filet mignon is normally a blander cut of meat, it can usually use a pick-me-up. Blue cheese is a classic pairing with a filet, and combining the cheese with heavy cream and lemon juice creates a flavorful sauce that helps add some richness to the otherwise lean filet. I like to serve this with a green bean casserole or loaded baked potato.

PREPARE THE STEAK

Preheat a water bath to 131°F (55°C).

Season the steaks with salt and pepper then place them in a sous vide bag. Add the thyme and rosemary sprigs then seal the bag. Place the bag in the water bath and cook for 2 to 4 hours.

PREPARE THE BLUE CHEESE SAUCE

Place all the ingredients in a bowl and whisk together with a fork. If the sauce is too thick you can add more oil or water to thin it out. It can also be made in a blender or food processor.

TO ASSEMBLE

Take the steaks out of the sous vide bag and pat them dry. Sear them until just browned, 1 to 2 minutes per side. Place the steaks on a plate and spoon the blue cheese sauce over the top and serve.

PEPPERED FILET MIGNON with GORGONZOLA CHEESE

COOKS: **131°F (55°C) for 2 to 3 hours** · PREP: **15 minutes** · SERVES: **4**

This is a quick and easy way to have a classic steakhouse meal. The Gorgonzola adds a nice richness to the steak without overwhelming the flavor of the meat, and the peppercorns provide a perfect peppery finish. This dish is great when served with thick steak fries or a loaded baked potato.

PREPARE THE STEAK

Preheat a water bath to 131°F (55°C).

Season the steaks with salt and pepper then place them in a sous vide bag. Add the thyme and rosemary sprigs then seal the bag. Place the bag in the water bath and cook for 2 to 3 hours.

TO ASSEMBLE

Preheat the oven broiler.

Take the steaks out of the sous vide bag and pat them dry. Season the steak with salt, grind some peppercorns on top, and sear until browned, 1 to 2 minutes per side. Remove the steaks from the heat and place them on a baking sheet.

Cover the steaks with the Gorgonzola. Place the steaks under the broiler and cook them until the cheese begins to bubble. Remove from the heat and serve.

FOR THE STEAK

4 portions of filet mignon

2 sprigs thyme

1 sprig rosemary

Salt and freshly ground black pepper

TO ASSEMBLE

Fresh peppercorns, coarsely ground

$1/2$ cup crumbled Gorgonzola cheese

FILET MIGNON with HERB BUTTER

COOKS. **131°F (55°C) for 2 to 4 hours** · PREP: **10 minutes** · SERVES: **4**

Since filet mignon can be a little on the dry side, I like to serve it with this flavorful herb butter. I call for parsley, basil, and tarragon, but you can use any combination of herbs that you like, or even add some roasted garlic or chile powder. Store any extra butter in the freezer and just cut off a slice whenever you need it. I usually pair this with a sautéed kale salad and some cherry tomatoes.

PREPARE THE STEAKS

Preheat a water bath to 131°F (55°C).

Season the steaks with salt and pepper then place them in a sous vide bag. Add the garlic powder then seal the bag. Place the bag in the water bath and cook for 2 to 4 hours.

PREPARE THE BUTTER

Place all the ingredients in a bowl and thoroughly mash them together using a fork.

TO ASSEMBLE

Take the steaks out of the sous vide bag and pat them dry. Sear the steaks over high heat until just browned, 1 to 2 minutes per side. Place the steaks on a plate and top with a dollop or two of the butter.

FOR THE STEAK

4 portions of filet mignon

1 teaspoon garlic powder

Salt and freshly ground black pepper

FOR THE BUTTER

4 tablespoons unsalted butter, room temperature

1 tablespoon finely chopped fresh parsley

1 tablespoon finely chopped fresh basil

1 tablespoon finely chopped fresh tarragon

1/8 teaspoon freshly ground black pepper

SPRING SALSA
on SIRLOIN STEAK

COOKS: **131°F (55°C) for 2 to 10 hours** · PREP: **10 minutes** · SERVES: **4**

FOR THE STEAK

1 teaspoon ground coriander

1 teaspoon fresh thyme leaves

$1/2$ teaspoon ground cumin

1 to 2 pounds sirloin steak

Salt and freshly ground black pepper

FOR THE SALSA

1 cup halved cherry tomatoes

1 cup diced zucchini

1 cup cooked corn kernels

$1/4$ red onion, diced

2 tablespoons coarsely chopped fresh basil

2 tablespoons coarsely chopped fresh oregano

1 tablespoon red wine vinegar

1 tablespoon olive oil

Sirloin steak is a favorite cut of mine to cook sous vide. I generally cook it a little bit longer, up to 10 hours, to fully tenderize it and it turns out great. Combining it with a simple spring salsa really adds some lightness and sweetness to the dish, which is great to make in late spring when cherry tomatoes are just starting to ripen.

PREPARE THE STEAK

Preheat a water bath to 131°F (55°C).

In a small bowl, combine the spices. Season the steaks with salt and pepper then sprinkle them with the spice mixture. Place the steaks in a sous vide bag then seal the bag. Place the bag in the water bath and cook for 2 to 10 hours.

PREPARE THE SALSA

In a large bowl, stir together all the ingredients until thoroughly combined. Season with salt and pepper.

TO ASSEMBLE

Take the steaks out of the sous vide bag and pat them dry. Sear the steaks until just browned, 1 to 2 minutes per side.

Place the steaks on a plate and top with a spoonful or two of the salsa and serve.

SIRLOIN in ORANGE SAUCE

COOKS: **131°F (55°C) for 2 to 10 hours** · PREP: **10 minutes** · SERVES: **4**

Sirloin in Orange Sauce is my take on the orange beef that can be found at many Chinese restaurants. The sauce is also very good with chicken, pork, or even swordfish steaks. .

FOR THE BEEF

1 teaspoon garlic powder

$\frac{1}{2}$ teaspoon ground ginger

$\frac{1}{2}$ teaspoon onion powder

2 pounds sirloin steak

Salt and freshly ground black pepper

FOR THE SAUCE

3 tablespoons sesame oil

3 scallions, thinly sliced

2 tablespoons minced garlic

1 tablespoon fresh minced ginger

$1\frac{1}{2}$ cups orange juice

2 tablespoons soy sauce

2 tablespoons honey

2 cups mandarin orange sections, divided

TO ASSEMBLE

4 tablespoons cornstarch

4 tablespoons cold water

4 cups cooked white rice

1 teaspoon orange zest

$\frac{1}{2}$ cup chopped fresh parsley

PREPARE THE BEEF

Preheat a water bath to 131°F (55°C).

In a small bowl, combine the spices. Season the steaks with salt and pepper then sprinkle them with the spice mixture. Place the steaks in a sous vide bag then seal the bag. Place the bag in the water bath and cook for 2 to 10 hours.

PREPARE THE SAUCE

In a pan over medium heat, heat the oil until hot. Add the scallions and cook for 1 to 2 minutes. Add the garlic and ginger and cook for 1 to 2 minutes. Add the orange juice, soy sauce, and honey. Season with salt and pepper and add one-fourth of the orange sections. Cook until the liquid thickens slightly, about 5 minutes. Remove from the heat and keep warm until ready to complete.

TO ASSEMBLE

Take the steaks out of the sous vide bag and pat them dry. Sear the steaks until browned, 1 to 2 minutes per side. Remove the steaks from the heat and cut into bite-size pieces.

Add some of the juices from the sous vide bag to the orange sauce and bring to a simmer. Stir together the cornstarch and cold water in a small bowl then gradually whisk the mixture into the sauce until it thickens to your desired consistency. Stir the steak pieces and remaining orange sections into the sauce and remove from the heat.

Put a large spoonful of white rice on a plate or in a bowl and top with the beef and orange mixture. Sprinkle with the orange zest and parsley and serve.

TUSCAN-STYLE BEEF TENDERLOIN

COOKS: **131°F (55°C) for 3 to 6 hours** · PREP. **20 minutes** · SERVES: **4 to 8**

Tuscan-Style Beef Tenderloin uses bold herbs to add a lot of flavor to a tenderloin that can otherwise be bland. You can use any spice rub you prefer, but I give my super-herby Tuscan-style version below. You can also use tougher cuts of meat such as top round or bottom round to save money but be sure to cook them longer.

PREPARE THE TUSCAN-STYLE RUB

Place all the ingredients in a food processor and process until thoroughly combined.

PREPARE THE STEAK

Preheat a water bath to 131°F (55°C).

Rub the tenderloin with some of the rub (reserve the remaining rub) then place the tenderloin in a sous vide bag and seal the bag. Place the bag in the water bath and cook for 3 to 6 hours.

TO ASSEMBLE

Take the tenderloin out of the sous vide bag and pat the tenderloin dry. Quickly sear the tenderloin until just browned, 1 to 2 minutes per side. Slice the tenderloin and serve with the remaining rub.

FOR THE TUSCAN-STYLE RUB

2 tablespoons chopped fresh rosemary leaves

2 tablespoons chopped fresh oregano

1 tablespoon chopped fresh parsley

2 teaspoons fresh thyme leaves

1/2 cup olive oil

FOR THE STEAK

3 pounds whole tenderloin or tenderloin roast

Salt and freshly ground black pepper

HORSERADISH-MUSTARD GLAZED RIBEYE

COOKS: **131°F (55°C) for 2 to 8 hours** · PREP: **15 minutes** · SERVES: **2**

FOR THE STEAK

1 teaspoon sweet paprika

1 teaspoon garlic powder

$^1/_2$ teaspoon chipotle chile powder

$^1/_2$ teaspoon ground thyme

1 to 1$^1/_2$ pounds ribeye steak

Salt and freshly ground black pepper

FOR THE GLAZE

4 tablespoons mustard, preferably Dijon

2 tablespoons bottled horseradish

6 mint leaves, coarsely chopped

3 tablespoons honey

Horseradish-Mustard Glazed Ribeye combines mustard and horseradish with mint to make a sweet glaze with some bite. The steaks also have chipotle chile powder and paprika on them for additional flavor. The result is a steak with a complex flavor that I just love. They are great when served with pureed sweet potatoes or sweet corn on the cob.

It's best to sear these steaks on a grill or under a broiler so the glaze can caramelize and stick to the meat.

PREPARE THE STEAK

Preheat a water bath to 131°F (55°C).

In a small bowl, combine the spices. Season the steaks with salt and pepper then sprinkle them with the spice mixture. Place the steaks in a sous vide bag then seal the bag. Place the bag in the water bath and cook for 2 to 8 hours.

PREPARE THE GLAZE

In a small bowl, whisk together all the ingredients and set aside.

TO ASSEMBLE

Take the steaks out of the sous vide bag and pat them dry. Coat the steaks with the glaze and sear 1 to 2 minutes per side, brushing on more glaze when you flip them. Remove the steaks from the heat and serve.

GRILLED STEAK KEBABS

COOKS: **131°F (55°C) for 2 to 8 hours** · PREP: **20 minutes** · SERVES: **4 to 8**

Kebabs are a great meal to serve in summer when vegetables are fresh from the garden. I'll usually just pick up whatever vegetables are currently in season and that look great, so feel free to substitute any you love. You can also use any type of meat you like, just adjust the cooking time accordingly. If you are having a party, it is easy to substitute chuck, top round, or another tough steak and tenderize it with sous vide over a few days before grilling it.

PREPARE THE STEAK

Preheat a water bath to 131°F (55°C).

In a small bowl, combine the thyme, rosemary, and chile powder to make a rub. Season the steak with salt and pepper then sprinkle it with the rub. Place the steaks in a sous vide bag and seal the bag. Place the bag in the water bath and cook for 2 to 8 hours.

TO ASSEMBLE

Heat a grill to high heat (you won't be cooking the meat long, so use the hottest setting).

Take the steak cubes out of the sous vide bag and pat them dry. Skewer the steak cubes, zucchini, bell pepper, onion, and tomatoes, alternating them.

Cook the kebabs on the grill until the zucchini begins to soften, turning at least once. Remove from the heat and serve.

FOR THE STEAK

$1/2$ teaspoon dried thyme

$1/2$ teaspoon dried rosemary

$1/2$ teaspoon ancho chile powder

2 pounds ribeye steak, cut into 1-inch cubes

Salt and freshly ground black pepper

TO ASSEMBLE

1 zucchini, cut into $1/2$-inch-thick slices

1 sweet red bell pepper, cut into 1 by 1-inch slices

1 sweet onion, cut into 1-inch wedges

1 pint cherry tomatoes

PORTERHOUSE with PICO DE GALLO

COOKS: **131°F (55°C) for 2 to 4 hours** · PREP: **15 minutes** · SERVES: **4**

FOR THE STEAK

1 tablespoon garlic powder

$\frac{1}{2}$ teaspoon allspice

$\frac{1}{4}$ teaspoon chipotle chile powder or chile powder of your choice

2 porterhouse steaks

Salt and freshly ground black pepper

FOR THE PICO DE GALLO

1 avocado, diced

1 clove garlic, minced

Juice from 1 lime

$\frac{1}{2}$ red onion, diced

2 jalapeño chiles, seeded and diced

2 medium tomatoes, diced

2 tablespoons olive oil

2 tablespoons chopped fresh cilantro

2 tablespoons chopped oregano

A porterhouse steak is the best of both worlds, containing both the tenderloin and the strip steak together. Porterhouse can be a heavy steak, so I like to use a fresh pico de gallo salsa to lighten it up. It is especially good in summer when the ingredients are fresh from the garden or a farmers market. If you have different vegetables or herbs on hand, feel free to substitute them.

PREPARE THE STEAK

Preheat a water bath to 131°F (55°C).

In a small bowl, combine the spices. Season the steaks with salt and pepper then sprinkle them with the spice mixture. Place the steaks in a sous vide bag then seal the bag. Place the bag in the water bath and cook for 2 to 4 hours.

PREPARE THE PICO DE GALLO

In a large bowl, stir together all the ingredients until thoroughly combined.

TO ASSEMBLE

Take the steaks out of the sous vide bag and pat them dry. Sear the steaks over high heat until browned, 1 to 2 minutes per side. Remove the steaks from the heat and serve with the pico de gallo on the side.

HANGER STEAK with RED WINE MUSHROOMS

COOKS: **131°F (55°C) for 2 to 3 hours** · PREP: **15 minutes** · SERVES: **4**

Cooking with hanger steak is becoming more and more common. It's a very tender but beefy cut that works great in many dishes. These red wine mushrooms pair great with it and add a lot to the overall flavor of the dish without taking a long time to prepare. If you can't find hanger steak you can substitute sirloin, strip steak, or filet.

PREPARE THE STEAK

Preheat a water bath to 131°F (55°C).

Season the steak with salt and pepper then sprinkle it with the garlic and thyme. Place the steak in a sous vide bag then seal the bag. Place the sous vide bag in the water bath and cook for 2 to 3 hours.

PREPARE THE RED WINE MUSHROOMS

Take the steaks out of the sous vide bag, reserving the juices, and pat them dry.

In a skillet, heat the oil over high heat until hot. Add the mushrooms and cook until tender, 5 to 7 minutes, stirring occasionally. Add the garlic and shallot and cook for 1 minute. Add the red wine and 1/2 cup of the reserved sous vide juices. Cook until thickened, about 5 minutes. Add the vinegar and Dijon and stir to thoroughly combine. Stir in the butter, thyme, and parsley then season with salt and pepper.

TO ASSEMBLE

Sear the steaks over high heat until browned, 1 to 2 minutes per side. Spoon the mushrooms and their sauce over the steaks and serve.

FOR THE STEAK

1 to 2 pounds hanger steak

1 teaspoon garlic powder

1 teaspoon dried thyme

Salt and freshly ground black pepper

FOR THE RED WINE MUSHROOMS

1 tablespoon olive oil

1 package baby bella mushrooms, sliced

3 cloves garlic, minced

1 shallot, minced

1/2 cup red wine

1 tablespoon balsamic vinegar

1/2 teaspoon Dijon mustard

2 tablespoons salted butter, cut into large pieces

1 teaspoon fresh thyme

1 tablespoon chopped fresh parsley

HERB-CRUSTED FLANK STEAK

COOKS: **131°F (55°C) for 2 to12 hours** · PREP: **10 minutes** · SERVES: **4**

The dried herbs in this rub help to add some depth of flavor to the steak, especially once it is seared. This steak pairs nicely with some sautéed asparagus and cherry tomatoes or even with a side of angel hair pasta with garlic and olive oil. The longer you sous vide the flank steak, the more tender it will be.

PREPARE THE STEAK

Preheat a water bath to 131°F (55°C).

In a small bowl, combine the spices. Season the steaks with salt and pepper then sprinkle them with the spice mixture. Place the steaks in a sous vide bag then seal the bag. Place the bag in the water bath and cook for 2 to 12 hours.

TO ASSEMBLE

Take the steaks out of the sous vide bag and pat them dry. Quickly sear the steaks until just browned, 1 to 2 minutes per side. Remove the steaks from the heat and serve.

FOR THE STEAK

2 tablespoons dried rosemary

2 teaspoons dried oregano

2 teaspoons dried basil

1 teaspoon dried parsley

1 teaspoon sage

1 teaspoon garlic powder

2 to 3 pounds flank steak

Salt and freshly ground black pepper

FLANK STEAK with TOMATILLO SALSA

COOKS: **131°F (55°C) for 2 to 12 hours** · PREP: **10 minutes** · SERVES: **4**

FOR THE STEAK

$1/2$ teaspoon garlic powder

$1/2$ teaspoon ground coriander

$1/4$ teaspoon ground cumin

$1/8$ teaspoon chipotle chile powder

1 to 2 pounds flank steak

Salt and freshly ground black pepper

FOR THE SALSA

4 to 8 tomatillos, diced (to make 1 to 2 cups)

1 cup cooked corn kernels

$1/4$ cup coarsely chopped cilantro

2 tablespoons coarsely chopped oregano

1 shallot, diced

1 tablespoon apple cider vinegar

1 tablespoon olive oil

This tangy tomatillo salsa perfectly offsets the beefiness of flank steak. The corn adds a sweet undertone and a little crunch that I love. I prefer my flank steak to have some bite to it, so I normally cook it for 2 to 12 hours, but some people prefer it to be meltingly tender and cook it for 1 to 2 days. Refried beans and yellow rice nicely complement this dish.

PREPARE THE STEAK

Preheat a water bath to 131°F (55°C).

In a small bowl, combine the spices. Season the steak with salt and pepper then sprinkle it with the spice mixture. Place the steak in a sous vide bag then seal the bag. Place the bag in the water bath and cook for 2 to 12 hours.

PREPARE THE SALSA

Place all the ingredients in a bowl and stir to thoroughly combine.

TO ASSEMBLE

Take the steaks out of the sous vide bag and pat them dry. Sear the steaks over high heat until just browned, 1 to 2 minutes per side. Cut the steak against the grain into $1/4$- to $1/2$-inch strips and place on a plate. Top with a spoonful or two of the salsa and serve.

FLANK STEAK FAJITAS

COOKS: **131°F (55°C) for 2 to 12 hours** · PREP: **20 minutes** · SERVES: **4**

Beef fajitas are a favorite dish of mine, and using a sous vided flank steak ensures a beefy, tender meat. When it comes to fajitas everyone has their own preference for what goes into them. I've listed some of the optional sides but feel free to serve your fajitas with whatever you like best.

PREPARE THE STEAK

Preheat a water bath to 131°F (55°C).

In a small bowl, combine the spices. Season the steaks with salt and pepper then sprinkle them with the spice mixture. Place the steaks in a sous vide bag then seal the bag. Place the bag in the water bath and cook for 2 to 12 hours.

PREPARE THE PEPPER AND ONION SIDES

In a pan over medium to medium-high heat, heat the oil until hot. Add the onions and the bell and poblano peppers and cook until they just begin to brown and are cooked through. Remove from the heat and set aside.

TO ASSEMBLE

Take the steaks out of the sous vide bag and pat them dry. Quickly sear the steaks over high heat until just browned, 1 to 2 minutes per side. Slice the steaks against the grain and serve with the onions and peppers, tortilla wrappers, and any of the other sides, as desired.

FOR THE STEAK

1 teaspoon ground coriander

1/2 teaspoon ground cumin

1/2 teaspoon garlic powder

1/4 teaspoon ancho chile powder

1 to 2 pounds flank steak

Salt and freshly ground black pepper

FOR THE PEPPER AND ONION SIDES

2 tablespoons canola oil

2 onions, preferably Vidalia or sweet, sliced

3 bell peppers (green and red), sliced

1 to 2 poblano peppers, sliced

TO ASSEMBLE

10 tortilla wrappers

6 cups sliced lettuce

4 tomatoes, diced

Refried beans

Mexican rice

Grated cheddar cheese

Sour cream

FLANK STEAK with SALSA VERDE

COOKS: **131°F (55°C) for 2 to 12 hours** · PREP: **15 minutes** · SERVES: **4 to 6**

FOR THE STEAK

2 pounds flank steak

1 teaspoon dried oregano

1 teaspoon ground cumin

Salt and freshly ground black pepper

FOR THE SALSA VERDE

8 to 10 tomatillos, coarsely chopped

$1/2$ cup fresh cilantro

1 shallot, coarsely chopped

3 cloves garlic, coarsely chopped

1 jalapeño chile, seeded and coarsely chopped

1 tablespoon fresh lime juice

1 tablespoon olive oil

The tang of salsa verde nicely complements the beefiness of flank steak. Salsa verde is very easy to prepare, and you can adjust the amount of jalapeño to tweak it to your preferred spice levels. Refried beans and yellow rice nicely complement this dish, as do fried plantains.

PREPARE THE STEAK

Preheat a water bath to 131°F (55°C).

Season the steaks with salt and pepper then sprinkle it with the oregano and cumin. Place the steaks in a sous vide bag then seal the bag. Place the bag in the water bath and cook for 2 to 12 hours.

PREPARE THE SALSA VERDE

Place all the ingredients in a food processor and process until thoroughly combined.

TO ASSEMBLE

Take the steaks out of the sous vide bag and pat them dry. Sear the steaks until just browned, 1 to 2 minutes per side. Cut the steaks into $1/4$-inch- to $1/2$-inch-thick strips and place on a plate. Top with a spoonful or two of the salsa verde and serve.

SKIRT STEAK with POBLANO-ONION SALSA

COOKS: **131°F (55°C) for 2 to 24 hours** · PREP: **15 minutes** · SERVES: **4**

The chicken stock helps add a depth of flavor to the poblano-onion salsa while the poblano peppers contribute a mild heat to the dish. Skirt steak can be cooked for as little as a few hours, or, for a more tender steak, up to 24 hours. I generally prefer around 8 to 12 hours.

PREPARE THE STEAK

Preheat a water bath to 131°F (55°C).

In a small bowl, combine the spices. Season the steaks with salt and pepper then sprinkle them with the spice mixture. Place the steaks in a sous vide bag then seal the bag. Place the bag in the water bath and cook for 2 to 24 hours.

PREPARE THE SALSA

In a pan over medium to medium-high heat, heat the oil until hot. Add the onions and cook until they just begin to brown. Add the poblano peppers and cook until they soften. Stir in the garlic and chicken stock; season with salt and pepper. Cook until the liquid is reduced, a few minutes. Stir in the cilantro and remove from the heat.

TO ASSEMBLE

Take the steaks out of the sous vide bag and pat them dry. Sear the steaks over high heat until browned, 1 to 2 minutes per side. Place the steaks on a plate and top with several spoonfuls of the salsa and serve.

FOR THE STEAK

1 teaspoon ground coriander

$1/2$ teaspoon ancho chile powder

1 teaspoon dried oregano

1 to 2 pounds skirt steak, cut into 4 portions

Salt and freshly ground black pepper

FOR THE SALSA

2 tablespoons canola oil

2 onions, diced

2 poblano peppers, diced

6 cloves garlic, minced

$1/2$ cup chicken stock

$1/4$ cup chopped cilantro

SKIRT STEAK QUESADILLAS

COOKS: **131°F (55°C)** for 2 to 24 hours · PREP: **15 minutes** · SERVES: **4**

FOR THE STEAK

1 teaspoon paprika

1/2 teaspoon garlic powder

1/2 teaspoon ground cumin

1/2 teaspoon coriander
    seeds

1/2 teaspoon dry mustard
    powder

1 pound skirt steak

Salt and freshly ground
    black pepper

TO ASSEMBLE

8 flour tortillas

Shredded cheddar cheese

Shredded Muenster cheese

1 poblano pepper, thinly
    sliced

1/2 cup chopped watercress

1 tomato, diced

1/4 cup cooked corn kernels

Canola or olive oil

Skirt steak is one of my favorite cuts of beef and quesa-dillas are a great way to put it to use. These quesadillas are very fast to put together and precooking the steak sous vide means it stays very moist. Feel free to substitute any cheeses you prefer and to have fun playing around with the ingredients inside the quesadillas. The longer you cook the skirt steak, the more tender it will be.

PREPARE THE STEAK

Preheat a water bath to 131°F (55°C).

In a small bowl, combine the spices. Season the steak with salt and pepper then sprinkle it with the spice mixture. Place the steak in a sous vide bag then seal the bag. Place the bag in the water bath and cook for 2 to 24 hours.

TO ASSEMBLE

Preheat a grill to high heat or a pan to medium-high heat.

Take the steaks out of the sous vide bag and pat them dry. Sear the steaks until just browned, 1 to 2 minutes per side. Cut the steak into 1/4- to 1/2-inch strips and place on a plate.

Lay out 4 tortillas and evenly divide the steak and the re-maining ingredients among them. Top each with one of the remaining tortillas.

Brush the top of the quesadilla with the oil and place it on the grill or in the pan. Cover the quesadilla while it is cook-ing. Once the bottom turns golden brown, flip the quesadilla over and continue cooking until the cheese is melted and the quesadilla is browned on both sides. Remove from the heat, cut into quarters, and serve.

IMPRESS the NEIGHBORS STEAK

COOKS: **131°F (55°C) for 36 to 60 hours** · PREP: **10 minutes** · SERVES: **4 to 8**

The best way to win over your neighbors? Serve them great steaks. They never have to know you used inexpensive meat instead of filet mignon! "Impress the Neighbors" Steak demonstrates a great way to take an inexpensive and tough cut of meat and turn it into tender steaks. I prefer to finish them on the grill, but you can pan sear them just as easily.

PREPARE THE STEAK

Preheat a water bath to 131°F (55°C).

Season the meat with salt and pepper then place it in a sous vide bag. Place the rosemary and thyme sprigs in the bag then seal the bag. Place the bag in the water bath and cook for 36 to 60 hours.

TO ASSEMBLE

Preheat a grill to very hot.

Take the meat out of the sous vide bag and pat the meat dry. Quickly sear the meat on the grill, 1 to 2 minutes per side. Brush both sides with the BBQ sauce and grill for 30 seconds on each side.

Take the beef off the grill and serve as you would a steak.

FOR THE STEAK

3 to 4 pounds chuck roast, cut into 1½-inch-thick slabs

4 sprigs rosemary

4 sprigs thyme

Salt and freshly ground black pepper

TO ASSEMBLE

BBQ Sauce

CUBAN SPICED CHUCK STEAK

COOKS: **131°F (55°C)** for **36 to 60 hours** · PREP: **30 minutes** · SERVES: **4**

This lightly spiced chuck roast goes great with the fresh and chunky salsa. The garlic, cumin, and oregano are classic Cuban spices and add some background flavors to the steak. The salsa is a combination of sweet and tart that adds bursts of flavor to the dish. Using chuck is also a terrific way to save money since it's normally about one-third the cost of "better" cuts of steak.

PREPARE THE BEEF

Preheat a water bath to 131°F (55°C).

In a small bowl, combine the spices. Season the chuck roast with salt and pepper then sprinkle it with the spice mixture. Place the roast in a sous vide bag with the bay leaf then seal the bag. Place the bag in the water bath and cook for 36 to 60 hours.

PREPARE THE SALSA

Place all the ingredients in a bowl and stir to thoroughly combine. Season with salt and pepper.

TO ASSEMBLE

Take the steaks out of the sous vide bag and pat them dry. Sear the steaks until just browned, 1 to 2 minutes per side. Remove the steaks from the heat and serve with a scoop or two of the salsa on top.

FOR THE BEEF

1 tablespoon garlic powder

2 teaspoons ground cumin

1 teaspoon dried oregano

1 bay leaf

2 pounds chuck roast or steak, cut into 1-inch- to 1$\frac{1}{2}$-inch-thick serving portions

Salt and freshly ground black pepper

FOR THE SALSA

3 tomatillos, diced

2 medium tomatoes, diced

$\frac{1}{2}$ red onion, diced

1 red pepper, diced

1 cup cooked corn kernels

2 tablespoons chopped fresh oregano

1 tablespoon orange juice

1 tablespoon fresh lime juice

2 tablespoons olive oil

CLASSIC POT ROAST with ROOT VEGETABLES

COOKS: **176°F (80°C) for 12 to 18 hours** · PREP: **10 minutes** · SERVES: **4 to 8**

FOR THE ROAST

3 pounds pot roast, or chuck steak

3 sprigs rosemary

4 sage leaves

Salt and freshly ground black pepper

FOR THE ROASTED VEGETABLES

10 large carrots

20 multi-colored baby potatoes

1 medium onion, chopped

1 red pepper, chopped

10 cloves garlic, roughly diced

4 tablespoons olive oil

2 tablespoons thyme leaves

FOR THE GRAVY

1 cup beef or chicken stock

2 tablespoons all-purpose flour

2 tablespoons cold water

4 tablespoons unsalted butter, cut into slices

When you are looking for a more traditional texture for a pot roast, there are several time and temperature combinations as options. The highest temperature at which I usually cook a pot roast sous vide is 176°F (80°C), which results in a much more traditional texture with fall-apart meat and a lot of breakdown in the collagen. I love to serve this pot roast with flavorful vegetables roasted in the oven.

PREPARE THE ROAST

Preheat a water bath to 176°F (80°C).

Season the roast with salt and pepper then place the roast in a sous vide bag. Add the rosemary sprigs and sage leaves then seal the bag. Place the bag in the water bath and cook for 12 to 18 hours.

PREPARE THE ROASTED VEGETABLES

Preheat an oven to 425°F (218°C).

Peel the carrots and cut them into ¾-inch pieces. Cut the baby potatoes into ¾-inch pieces. Toss all the vegetables together with the oil and thyme then season them with salt and pepper. Place the vegetables in a roasting pan or rimmed baking sheet in a single layer. Roast in the oven until they start to brown and the carrots and potatoes have softened and are cooked through, 30 to 45 minutes. Remove from the heat.

PREPARE THE GRAVY

Take the roast out of the sous vide bag, reserving the liquid, and pat the roast dry.

Place the reserved liquid into a pan with the stock and bring to a boil. Stir together the flour and cold water in a bowl

then whisk the mixture into the liquid in the pan to make a gravy. Bring to a boil then reduce the heat to medium low.

TO ASSEMBLE

Quickly sear the pot roast over high heat until browned, 1 to 2 minutes per side.

While the meat is cooking, stir the butter into the gravy 1 tablespoon at a time, stirring until incorporated between each addition.

Remove the meat from the heat, and slice it and place it on a plate with the root vegetables. Serve with the gravy poured over the top or in a bowl on the side.

PERFECT POT ROAST

COOKS: **156°F (68.8°C) for 18 to 24 hours** · PREP: **15 minutes** · SERVES: **4 to 8**

FOR THE ROAST

3 pounds pot roast, trimmed of excess fat and silver skin

1 tablespoon garlic powder

1 tablespoon paprika

3 sprigs rosemary

3 sprigs thyme

Salt and freshly ground black pepper

FOR THE GRAVY

1 cup beef or chicken stock

2 tablespoons all-purpose flour

2 tablespoons cold water

4 tablespoons unsalted butter, cut into slices

While higher temperatures result in a more traditional pot roast, my favorite way to cook pot roast is at 156°F (68.8°C). At this temperature, the roast comes out very tender but still with some bite and a lot more moisture than traditional pot roasts. The roast is best when served with roasted vegetables or Brussels sprouts and cherry tomatoes.

PREPARE THE ROAST

Preheat a water bath to 156°F (68.8°C).

Season the roast with salt and pepper then sprinkle it with the garlic and paprika. Place the roast in a sous vide bag with the rosemary and thyme sprigs then seal the bag. Place the bag in the water bath and cook for 18 to 24 hours.

TO ASSEMBLE

Take the roast out of the sous vide bag and pat the roast dry. Quickly sear the roast over high heat until just browned, 1 to 2 minutes per side.

Take the pot roast off the heat and serve it with your sides.

ACHIOTE CHUCK ROAST with JALAPEÑO POLENTA

COOKS: **165°F (73.9°C) for 18 to 24 hours** · PREP: **15 minutes** · SERVES: **4 to 6**

FOR THE ROAST

2 pounds chuck roast

3 tablespoons achiote paste

Salt and freshly ground
    black pepper

FOR THE POLENTA

2 tablespoons unsalted
    butter

2 jalapeño chiles, seeded
    and diced

1/4 cup milk

2 cups chicken stock

Water, as needed

1 1/3 cups quick-cooking
    polenta

TO ASSEMBLE

2 tablespoons chopped
    fresh cilantro

Achiote is a richly flavored paste from Central and South America made from annatto seeds mixed with other spices, such as coriander, oregano, cumin, and garlic. You can find it in the international aisle of many grocery stores. I like to pair it with a creamy polenta with jalapeño.

I like the beef to have a shreddable texture, but if you prefer it more like steak you can decrease the temperature to 131°F (55°C) and increase the cooking time to 36 to 60 hours.

PREPARE THE ROAST

Preheat a water bath to 165°F (73.9°C).

Coat the roast evenly with the achiote paste then season it with salt and pepper. Place the roast in a sous vide bag then seal the bag. Place the bag in the water bath and cook for 18 to 24 hours.

PREPARE THE POLENTA

In a pot over medium-high heat, melt the butter. Add the jalapeño and cook until softened, 2 to 3 minutes. Add the milk, chicken stock, and enough water to bring the volume of liquid to the amount called for in the directions on the polenta package. Bring the liquid to a boil then whisk in the polenta and cook, stirring, until thickened. Remove from the heat.

TO ASSEMBLE

Take the roast out of the sous vide bag and pat the roast dry. Quickly sear the roast until just browned, 1 to 2 minutes per side, then remove it from the heat and lightly shred or break it into serving-size pieces.

Spoon some polenta into a bowl and top with some of the beef. Sprinkle the cilantro on top and serve.

CITRUS SHORT RIBS

COOKS: **131°F (55°C) for 2 to 3 days** · PREP. **15 minutes** · SERVES: **4**

These short ribs have a tasty sauce that is inspired by Asian flavors. I season the ribs with Chinese five-spice powder before sous viding them and then make a simple sauce to pour over them. I usually serve these with some white rice to soak up the sauce.

This time and temperature combination results in a steak-like texture for the ribs. If you want a texture more similar to what you get from braising, you can increase the temperature up to 156°F (68.8°C) for 1 to 2 days, or even 176°F (80°C) for only 12 to 24 hours.

PREPARE THE RIBS

Preheat your sous vide water bath to 131°F (55°C).

Season the ribs with salt and pepper then sprinkle them with the Chinese five-spice powder. Place the ribs in a sous vide bag then seal the bag. Place the bag in the water bath and cook for 2 to 3 days.

PREPARE THE SAUCE

Whisk together all the ingredients until thoroughly combined.

TO ASSEMBLE

Take the short ribs out of the sous vide bag and pat them dry. Quickly sear the ribs until just browned, 1 to 2 minutes per side.

Place the ribs on individual plates, spoon the sauce over them, sprinkle with the scallions and orange zest, and serve.

FOR THE RIBS

3 to 4 pounds short ribs, trimmed of excess fat and silverskin

2 tablespoons Chinese five-spice powder

Salt and freshly ground black pepper

FOR THE SAUCE

1 tablespoon rice wine vinegar

2 tablespoons orange juice

1 tablespoon peanut or olive oil

2 tablespoons oyster sauce

1 tablespoon packed brown sugar

$1/2$ teaspoon chipotle chile powder or chile powder of your choice

TO ASSEMBLE

2 scallions, sliced

2 tablespoons orange zest

BEEF CHILI

COOKS: **156°F (68.8°C) for 18 to 24 hours** · PREP: **15 minutes** · SERVES: **8**

FOR THE MEAT

1 teaspoon garlic powder

1 teaspoon ancho powder
or chile powder of your
choice

$1/2$ teaspoon ground cumin

$1/2$ teaspoon ground
coriander

$1/4$ teaspoon chipotle
powder or chile powder of
your choice

2 pounds stew meat or
chuck roast cut into
$1/2$-inch-thick pieces

Salt and freshly ground
black pepper

FOR THE CHILI BASE

Oil, for frying

1 onion, diced

1 red bell pepper, diced

1 large carrot, diced

6 cloves garlic, diced

2 teaspoons paprika

1 teaspoon cayenne pepper

1 teaspoon chipotle pepper

2 bay leaves

I love a flavorful beef chili but sometimes the meat dries out while cooking. Cooking the meat sous vide ensures it will stay moist and tender.

Some people prefer their chili meat very tender, but I prefer it cooked at a slightly lower temperature so it has more bite to it. For really tender meat, you can cook it up to 176°F (80°C) for 12 to 18 hours, or, for steak-like meat, as low as 131°F (55°C) for 36 to 60 hours.

PREPARE THE MEAT

Preheat a water bath to 156°F (68.8°C).

In a small bowl, combine the spices. Season the meat with salt and pepper then sprinkle it with the spice mixture. Place the meat in a sous vide bag then seal the bag. Place the bag in the water bath and cook for 18 to 24 hours.

PREPARE THE CHILI BASE

Heat up some oil in a deep pot over medium-high heat.

Add the onion to the pot and cook for several minutes, just until translucent. Add the bell pepper and carrot and cook for another 5 minutes.

Add the remaining ingredients to the pot and stir to thoroughly combine. Cook until the mixture begins to thicken, 20 to 30 minutes. Let simmer for up to an hour, if desired, to intensify the flavor and to thicken it more.

TO ASSEMBLE

Remove the meat from the sous vide bag and add it to the pot along with the liquid in the bag; stir well to combine. Remove the bay leaves and ladle the chili into bowls and top with the cilantro, cheese, and a dollop of sour cream and serve.

28 ounces canned diced
   tomatoes

14 ounces canned crushed
   tomatoes

$1/2$ cup tomato paste

1 can black beans

1 cup chicken stock

TO ASSEMBLE

2 tablespoons chopped
   fresh cilantro

$1/4$ cup shredded cheddar
   cheese

Sour cream

SHORT RIBS with BASIL–BALSAMIC SAUCE

COOKS: **156°F (58.3°C) for 1 to 2 days** · PREP: **20 minutes** · SERVES: **4**

Short ribs are full of fatty flavor, and the balsamic–basil sauce cuts through the fattiness nicely. Cooking the short ribs at a higher temperature, but still lower on the braising side, allows them to break down even more while ensuring they do not overcook. The ribs go well with a side of mashed potatoes or roasted vegetables.

PREPARE THE RIBS

Preheat a water bath to 156°F (58.3°C).

In a small bowl, combine the spices. Season the ribs with salt and pepper then sprinkle them with the spice mixture. Place the ribs in a sous vide bag with the thyme and rosemary sprigs then seal the bag. Place the bag in the water bath and cook for 1 to 2 days.

PREPARE THE SAUCE

Place all the ingredients in a blender or food processor and process until thoroughly combined.

TO ASSEMBLE

Take the short ribs out of the sous vide bag and pat them dry. Quickly sear the ribs until just browned, 1 to 2 minutes per side.

Place the ribs on individual plates, spoon the sauce over them, sprinkle with the basil, and serve.

FOR THE RIBS

2 teaspoons garlic powder

1 teaspoon onion powder

1 teaspoon ground cumin

3 to 4 pounds short ribs

4 sprigs thyme

4 sprigs rosemary

Salt and freshly ground black pepper

FOR THE SAUCE

3 tablespoons balsamic vinegar

1 teaspoon coarsely chopped garlic

1/3 cup coarsely chopped fresh basil leaves

1/2 cup olive oil

TO ASSEMBLE

2 tablespoons coarsely chopped fresh basil leaves

BEEF RIBS with CHILE SAUCE

COOKS: **131°F (55°C) for 1 to 2 days** · PREP: **15 minutes** · SERVES: **4**

FOR THE RIBS

3 to 4 pounds of beef ribs

1 teaspoons garlic powder

1 teaspoon paprika

$1/4$ teaspoon cayenne pepper

Salt and freshly ground black pepper

FOR THE CHILE SAUCE

4 to 7 dried chiles

Olive oil

3 ounces tomato paste

$1/4$ cup dark rum

3 tablespoons balsamic vinegar

2 tablespoons honey

2 tablespoons packed brown sugar

1 tablespoon Worcestershire sauce

1 tablespoon minced garlic

I love rich beef ribs served with this flavorful chile sauce. The ribs are cooked for a long time which results in super-tender meat, but you can also cook them for a shorter period of time if you prefer more chew to them, or increase the temperature for a more fall-apart texture. I like to serve the ribs with traditional BBQ sides such as macaroni and cheese or collard greens.

PREPARE THE RIBS

Preheat a water bath to 131°F (55°C).

Season the ribs with salt and pepper then sprinkle them with the garlic powder, paprika, and cayenne. Place the ribs in a sous vide bag then seal the bag. Place the bag in the water bath and cook for 1 to 2 days.

PREPARE THE CHILE SAUCE

Soak the chiles in water for 30 minutes. Remove the stems and seeds.

Heat the oil in a pan over medium heat until hot, add the tomato paste then cook until just starting to darken. Add the soaked chiles, the remaining ingredients, and $1/2$ cup of water and bring to a simmer. Let cook for at least 5 minutes for the flavors to meld, or up to 30 minutes for a thicker sauce.

2 teaspoons ground cumin

2 teaspoons ground
coriander

2 teaspoons garlic powder

2 teaspoons onion powder

1 teaspoon paprika

TO ASSEMBLE

2 tablespoons coarsely
chopped fresh basil

TO ASSEMBLE

Take the ribs out of the sous vide bag and pat them dry.
Quickly sear the ribs over high heat until just browned, 1 to
2 minutes per side.

Place the ribs on individual plates, spoon the sauce over
them, sprinkle with the basil, and serve.

SMOKY BEEF RIBS with TROPICAL SALSA

COOKS: **156°F (58.3°C) for 18 to 36 hours** · PREP: **15 minutes** · SERVES: **4**

FOR THE RIBS

2 tablespoons paprika

1 tablespoon onion powder

1/2 tablespoon ground coriander

1/2 tablespoon chipotle chile powder or chile powder of your choice

2 to 3 pounds beef ribs

1 to 2 tablespoons liquid smoke

Salt and freshly ground black pepper

FOR THE SALSA

1 avocado, diced

1 cup diced pineapple

1/2 cup cooked corn kernels

1 tablespoon fresh lime juice

2 tablespoons olive oil

3 tablespoons chopped fresh cilantro

These ribs are very easy to make and come out very flavorful and tender. For even more flavor, you can serve them with your favorite BBQ sauce. The salsa is an easy way to add flavors to the meal while still letting the ribs shine.

PREPARE THE RIBS

Preheat a water bath to 156°F (58.3°C).

In a small bowl, combine the spices. Season the ribs with salt and pepper then sprinkle them with the spice mixture. Place the ribs in a sous vide bag with the liquid smoke then seal the bag. Place the bag in the water bath and cook for 18 to 36 hours.

PREPARE THE SALSA

Preheat a grill to high heat or a pan to medium-high heat.

In a small bowl, stir together all the ingredients until thoroughly combined and set aside.

TO ASSEMBLE

Take the ribs out of the sous vide bag and pat them dry. Quickly sear the ribs on the grill or pan until just browned, 1 to 2 minutes per side. Remove the ribs from the heat and serve with a spoonful or two of the salsa.

NOT-SMOKED BEEF BRISKET

COOKS: **165°F (73.9°C) for 1 to 2 days** · PREP: **15 minutes** · SERVES: **4 to 8**

During the work week, it's hard to find the extra time to smoke foods, so using liquid smoke helps to impart smoky flavor without all the hard work. I often serve this brisket with corn bread and macaroni and cheese. You can also add your favorite BBQ sauce to it at the end for even more flavor. This time and temperature will result in a more traditional texture of brisket, but if you prefer a more steak-like texture, you can cook it at 131°F (55°C) for 2 to 3 days.

PREPARE THE RUB

In a small bowl, stir all the spices together until thoroughly combined and set aside.

PREPARE THE BEEF

Preheat a water bath to 165°F (73.9°C).

Season the brisket with salt and pepper then coat it with the rub. Place the brisket in a sous vide bag with the liquid smoke then seal the bag. Place the bag in the water bath and cook for 1 to 2 days.

TO ASSEMBLE

Take the brisket out of the sous vide bag and pat the brisket dry. Quickly sear the brisket until just browned, 1 to 2 minutes per side.

Take the brisket off the heat, slice 1/8- to 1/4-inch thick, and serve.

FOR THE RUB

2 tablespoons paprika

1 tablespoon garlic powder

1 tablespoon ground cumin

1 tablespoon ground coriander

1 teaspoon ground cinnamon

1 teaspoon dried oregano

1/2 teaspoon chipotle powder

FOR THE BEEF

3 to 4 pounds brisket

1 tablespoon liquid smoke

Salt and freshly ground black pepper

SAVORY and SWEET BEEF ROAST

COOKS: **131°F (55°C) for 2 to 3 days** · PREP: **20 minutes** · SERVES: **4 to 6**

FOR THE RUB

4 tablespoons packed brown sugar

1 tablespoon dried thyme

1 tablespoon onion powder

1 tablespoon garlic powder

1 tablespoon ground coriander

$1/2$ teaspoon mustard powder

$1/2$ teaspoon cayenne pepper or chile powder of your choice

$1/2$ teaspoon celery seeds

FOR THE ROAST

2 to 3 pounds bottom round roast, trimmed of excess fat and silverskin

Salt and freshly ground black pepper

This sweet and savory rub comes together quickly and works well on most kinds of beef. It's also good on chicken and pork. I like to serve this roast with sautéed green beans, onions and mushrooms, or thinly sliced and piled onto a roll for a French dip sandwich.

A great time saving tip is to make more beef than you need for one meal then chill the extra. Once it's cold you can thinly slice it and use it as lunch meat for the week. Or dice it and use it in stir fries or chili.

PREPARE THE RUB

In a small bowl, stir all the ingredients together until thoroughly combined and set aside.

PREPARE THE ROAST

Preheat a water bath to 131°F (55°C).

Season the roast with salt and pepper then coat it with the rub (any extra rub can be kept in a sealed container in a cabinet for several months). Place the roast in a sous vide bag then seal the bag. Place the bag in the water bath and cook for 2 to 3 days.

TO ASSEMBLE

Take the roast out of the sous vide bag and pat the roast dry. Quickly sear the roast until just browned, 1 to 2 minutes per side.

Slice the roast and serve. You can serve the juices from the bag on the side as au jus, if desired.

GARLIC CRUSTED TOP ROUND ROAST

COOKS: **131°F (55°C) for 1 to 3 days** · PREP: **15 minutes** · SERVES: **4 to 6**

FOR THE ROAST

1 tablespoon garlic powder

1 tablespoon onion powder

1 tablespoon paprika

2 teaspoons mustard powder

1 teaspoon ancho chile powder or chile powder of your choice

3 to 4 pounds top round roast

4 sprigs thyme

4 sprigs rosemary

Salt and freshly ground black pepper

FOR THE CRUST

8 cloves garlic, peeled

2 to 4 tablespoons olive oil

4 sprigs thyme

4 sprigs rosemary

2 to 4 tablespoons sweet marjoram

I find top round roasts to be a little drier and less flavorful than other roasts. However, they are usually pretty inexpensive. Cooking them sous vide helps to remedy some of the dryness and applying a flavorful garlic-and-herb crust helps to fix the blandness.

This is a meal with bold flavors that traditionally would take hours in the kitchen to prepare, but by using sous vide, you can reduce the actual work time to a few minutes. Roasting the garlic takes longer than the other steps, but it can be done a day or two ahead of time and stored in the refrigerator.

PREPARE THE ROAST

Preheat a water bath to 131°F (55°C).

In a small bowl, combine the spices. Season the roast with salt and pepper then sprinkle it with the spice mixture. Place the roast in a sous vide bag with the thyme and rosemary sprigs then seal the bag. Place the bag in the water bath and cook for 1 to 3 days.

PREPARE THE CRUST

Forty to 60 minutes before the roast is done, wrap the garlic cloves in foil with the oil, season with salt, and place in a 400°F (204°C) oven or toaster oven for 30 to 45 minutes, or until soft. Remove and set aside to cool.

Preheat the oven broiler.

Just before the sous vide roast is done, make the herb paste for the crust. Combine the roasted garlic, thyme, rosemary, and marjoram in a food processor and process until it forms a thick paste.

TO ASSEMBLE

Take the roast out of the sous vide bag and pat the roast dry. Place the roast in a roasting pan. Smear the sides and top of the roast with the paste. Place the roast in the oven until the crust begins to brown, about 5 minutes.

Thinly slice the roast (I prefer very thin or as much as $1/2$ inch thick) and serve. You can also serve the juices from the pouch as au jus.

BEEF GOULASH

COOKS: **131°F (55°C) for 1 to 2 days** · PREP: **10 minutes** · SERVES: **4**

FOR THE BEEF

2 pounds top round or
    stew meat cut into 1-inch
    pieces

2 teaspoons paprika

$1/2$ teaspoon garlic powder

Salt and freshly ground
    black pepper

FOR THE GOULASH

2-4 tablespoons olive or
    canola oil, divided

1 large onion, diced

4 cloves garlic, diced

2 green bell peppers, diced

2 tablespoons paprika

1 package baby bella or
    button mushrooms, diced

2 (14-ounce) cans diced
    tomatoes

1 cup beef stock

4 tablespoons cold water

2 tablespoons all-purpose
    flour

TO ASSEMBLE

2 tablespoons chopped
    fresh parsley

Goulash is a great wintertime dish and is really hearty, especially when served with a good sticky rice or mashed potatoes. The beef is cooked sous vide and only added to the goulash near the end, so the meat is not overcooked. I like to use top round because it's mild and is a less expensive cut.

PREPARE THE BEEF

Preheat a water bath to 131°F (55°C).

Season the meat with salt and pepper then sprinkle it with the paprika and garlic powder. Place the meat in a sous vide bag then seal the bag. Place the bag in the water bath and cook for 1 to 2 days.

PREPARE THE GOULASH

Make the goulash 30 to 45 minutes before serving. In a deep-frying pan or pot, heat 1 to 2 tablespoons of oil until hot. Add the onion and garlic and sauté for several minutes, until the onions begin to turn translucent. Add the bell peppers and paprika and sauté for another 5 minutes.

Remove the onions and pepper mixture from the pan and add the remaining 1 to 2 tablespoons of oil and the mushrooms. Cook until the mushrooms begin to brown and release their liquid. Add the onion and pepper mixture back to the pan with the mushrooms, and add the tomatoes and stock. Stir to combine and let simmer for 10 to 15 minutes to thicken the sauce.

In a small bowl, stir together the cold water and the flour. Gradually add the flour mixture to the simmering goulash, stirring thoroughly, until it reaches a desired consistency.

TO ASSEMBLE

Remove the meat from sous vide bag and add it to the goulash, along with the liquids from the bag. Add the parsley to the goulash, stir well, and serve.

SPAGHETTI and MEATBALLS

COOKS: **131°F (55°C) for 2 to 4 hours** · PREP: **45 minutes** · SERVES: **4**

Using sous vide to precook meatballs ensures they are fully cooked through and safe to eat. Combining several types of meat adds a lot of flavor and depth, but you can go with 100 percent ground beef, if you prefer. To save more time, you can use store-bought meatballs. You can also use your favorite packaged pasta sauce.

PREPARE THE MEATBALLS

Preheat a water bath to 131°F (55°C).

In a large bowl, use your hands to gently mix all the meatball ingredients until combined. Form into 2-inch balls and place them into a sous vide bag. Gently seal the bag, being careful not to crush the meatballs. Place the sous vide bag in the water bath and cook for 2 to 4 hours.

PREPARE THE MARINARA SAUCE

In a large pot, heat the oil until hot. Add the garlic and cook the garlic for 1 minute then add the onion and cook until the onion begins to soften and turn translucent. Add the bell pepper and cook for 2 to 3 minutes. Add the tomato paste and cook, stirring, for 2 minutes. Add the crushed tomatoes and balsamic vinegar and let simmer for several minutes until thickened and to allow the flavors to come together.

TO ASSEMBLE

Take the meatballs out of the sous vide bag and pat them dry. Sear the meatballs until browned on all sides, 1 to 2 minutes per side. Remove the meatballs from the heat and set aside under foil.

Place the spaghetti into bowls and top with a spoonful or two of the marinara sauce. Add the meatballs to each bowl, grate the Parmesan on top, sprinkle on the herbs, and serve.

FOR THE MEATBALLS

$2/3$ pound ground beef

$2/3$ pound ground pork

4 cloves garlic, minced

1 large egg

$1/4$ cup grated Parmesan cheese

1 slice bread, diced

Salt and freshly ground black pepper

FOR THE MARINARA SAUCE

2 tablespoons olive oil

4 cloves garlic, minced

$1/2$ yellow onion, diced

1 red bell pepper, diced

2 tablespoons tomato paste

1 (28-ounce) can crushed tomatoes

2 tablespoons balsamic vinegar

TO ASSEMBLE

Cooked spaghetti

Parmesan cheese

2 tablespoons chopped fresh basil

1 tablespoon chopped fresh oregano

KEFTA KEBABS

COOKS: **131°F (55°C) for 2 to 4 hours** · PREP: **20 minutes** · SERVES: **4 to 8**

FOR THE BEEF

2 pounds ground beef

5 cloves garlic, minced

1 medium onion, finely minced

2 teaspoons ground cumin

2 teaspoons turmeric

$1/4$ cup chopped fresh parsley

$1/4$ cup chopped fresh cilantro

1 teaspoon ground cinnamon

1 teaspoon chipotle chile powder

$1/2$ teaspoon ground black pepper

1 teaspoon salt, or to taste

Kefta are Moroccan beef kebabs and are a spicy and smoky treat. They are made of ground beef here but ground lamb can also be used, or a combination of the two. Cooking them sous vide ensures they are perfectly cooked and need only a quick sear at the end. I prefer them finished on the grill, but you can sear them any way you like. You can use more or less chile powder, depending on your preference for spiciness.

PREPARE THE BEEF

Preheat a water bath to 131°F (55°C).

In a large bowl combine all the ingredients. Form elongated meatballs about 1 inch in diameter and 3 to 5 inches long; they will have a similar shape to a hot dog or sausage link. Place them in a sous vide bag and lightly seal the bag so as not to flatten their shape. Place in the water bath and cook for 2 to 4 hours.

TO ASSEMBLE

Preheat a grill to very hot.

Take the meatballs out of the sous vide bag and pat them dry. Place the meatballs onto a skewer and cook them on the grill until lightly browned, turning at least once. Remove the meatballs from the heat and serve.

CHAPTER FOUR

LAMB

MUSTARD and ROSEMARY LAMB CHOPS

COOKS: **131°F (55°C) for 2 to 4 hours** · PREP: **20 minutes** · SERVES: **4**

FOR THE RUB

1 tablespoon whole yellow mustard seeds

2 tablespoons garlic powder

Leaves from 4 sprigs rosemary, chopped

1 tablespoon Worcestershire sauce

1 tablespoon olive oil

1 tablespoon packed dark brown sugar

2 teaspoons mustard powder

FOR THE LAMB

8 to 10 lamb chops

Salt and freshly ground black pepper

A bold rub, such as one with mustard and rosemary, helps bring out the natural flavors of lamb. I prefer my lamb cooked medium rare so I've gone with 131°F (55°C) as my temperature, but you can adjust that up or down to meet your preference.

PREPARE THE RUB

Grind the mustard seeds in a spice grinder or place them in a Ziploc bag and crack them by rolling over them with a rolling pin. Place the mustard seeds and remaining ingredients into a bowl and stir to combine.

PREPARE THE LAMB

Preheat a water bath to 131°F (55°C).

Season the lamb chops with salt and pepper then rub the rosemary-mustard rub all over them. Place the lamb chops in a sous vide bag and seal the bag (any excess rub can be refrigerated for about a week). Place the bag in the water bath and cook for 2 to 4 hours.

TO ASSEMBLE

Take the lamb chops out of the sous vide bag and pat them dry. Sear the lamb chops over high heat until browned, 1 to 2 minutes per side. Remove the lamb chops from the heat and serve.

LAMB CHOPS with MELON RELISH

COOKS: **131°F (55°C) for 2 to 4 hours** · PREP: **10 minutes** · SERVES: **4**

Lamb can be a little on the rich side, so sometimes I like to pair it with a relish featuring pieces of melon and cucumber, which help bring out the sweetness in the lamb. I also like to add jalapeños for a little heat and added bite.

PREPARE THE LAMB

Preheat a water bath to 131°F (55°C).

In a small bowl, combine the spices. Season the lamb chops with salt and pepper then sprinkle them with the spice mixture. Place the lamb chops in a sous vide bag then seal the bag. Place the bag in the water bath and cook for 2 to 4 hours.

PREPARE THE MELON RELISH

Whisk the lime juice, brown sugar, ginger, and cinnamon together in a bowl until the sugar is dissolved. Add the remaining ingredients and toss to coat.

TO ASSEMBLE

Take the lamb chops out of the sous vide bag and pat them dry. Sear the lamb chops over high heat until just browned, 1 to 2 minutes per side.

Serve the lamb chops with a spoonful or two of the relish on top.

FOR THE LAMB

1 teaspoon fresh thyme leaves

1 teaspoon garlic powder

$1/2$ teaspoon ground cumin

8 lamb chops

Salt and freshly ground black pepper

FOR THE MELON RELISH

$1/4$ cup fresh lime juice

2 tablespoons packed brown sugar

1 tablespoon minced fresh ginger

$1/2$ teaspoon ground cinnamon

2 cups diced watermelon

2 cups diced cantaloupe or honeydew

1 cucumber, peeled, seeded, and diced

$1/2$ cup diced red onion

1 to 3 jalapeño chiles, seeded and diced

$1/4$ cup chopped fresh mint

BRAZILIAN LAMB CHOPS

COOKS: **131°F (55°C) for 2 to 4 hours** · PREP: **15 minutes** · SERVES: **4**

I love the bright and acidic flavors of my Brazilian sauce, especially when paired with lamb chops. These lamb chops make for a memorable meal when served with sautéed vegetables and farro in a grain bowl.

PREPARE THE LAMB

Preheat a water bath to 131°F (55°C).

Season the lamb chops with salt and pepper then sprinkle them with the paprika and fennel seeds. Place the lamb chops in a sous vide bag then seal the bag. Place the bag in the water bath and cook for 2 to 4 hours.

PREPARE THE BRAZILIAN SAUCE

Place all the ingredients in a blender or food processor and pulse several times until thoroughly combined.

TO ASSEMBLE

Take the lamb chops out of the sous vide bag and pat them dry. Sear the lamb chops over high heat until just browned, 1 to 2 minutes per side. Remove from the heat, spoon the sauce over top, and serve.

FOR THE LAMB

10 to 12 lamb chops

1 teaspoon paprika

1/2 teaspoon fennel seeds

Salt and freshly ground black pepper

FOR THE BRAZILIAN SAUCE

6 cloves garlic, coarsely chopped

2 teaspoons salt

1/4 cup fresh lime juice

1/4 cup white wine

1 tablespoon red wine vinegar

2 teaspoons hot sauce

3 tablespoons coarsely chopped fresh parsley

1 tablespoon coarsely chopped fresh rosemary

1 tablespoon coarsely chopped fresh mint

LAMB CHOPS with HARISSA

COOKS: **131°F (55°C) for 2 to 4 hours** · PREP: **10 minutes** · SERVES: **4**

FOR THE LAMB

10 to 12 lamb chops

1 teaspoon ground cumin

1 teaspoon ground coriander

Salt and freshly ground black pepper

FOR THE HARISSA

1 teaspoon ground cumin

1 teaspoon caraway seeds

1 large roasted red bell pepper, coarsely chopped

3 cloves garlic, coarsely chopped

1 to 2 small hot red chiles, coarsely chopped

1 teaspoon kosher salt

3 tablespoons olive oil

1/4 cup chopped cilantro

Juice of 1 lemon

4 tablespoons olive oil

Sometimes it's fun to enhance traditional lamb chops with a little extra twist. Using harissa is a great way to do that, adding bold flavors to the lamb. Harissa is a hot chile sauce often eaten in North Africa and widely used in Middle Eastern cooking, and my version is easy to make at home using common ingredients. If you don't feel like making your own harissa, you can sometimes find it in the international aisle of grocery stores.

PREPARE THE LAMB

Preheat a water bath to 131°F (55°C).

Sprinkle the lamb chops with the cumin and coriander then season them with salt and pepper. Place the lamb chops in a sous vide bag then seal the bag. Place the bag in the water bath and cook for 2 to 4 hours.

PREPARE THE HARISSA

Place all the ingredients in a blender or food processor and puree until smooth; the harissa can be stored in the refrigerator for several weeks.

TO ASSEMBLE

Take the lamb chops out of the sous vide bag and pat them dry. Sear the lamb chops over high heat until just browned, 1 to 2 minutes per side.

Serve the lamb chops with the harissa sauce spooned on top or in small bowls on the side.

HERBY RACK of LAMB

COOKS: **131°F (55°C) for 2 to 4 hours** · PREP: **15 minutes** · SERVES: **4**

Rack of lamb is a classic, family-style preparation that traditionally is roasted. Using sous vide allows you to cook the lamb evenly to the exact desired temperature. Herby Rack of Lamb is very rustic and simple, with only a few herbs for flavoring and a rich gravy to finish it off. It's great when served with home-style mashed potatoes and roasted vegetables.

PREPARE THE LAMB

Preheat a water bath to 131°F (55°C).

Season the lamb with salt and pepper. Place the lamb in a sous vide bag and add the thyme and rosemary sprigs then seal the bag. Place the bag in the water bath and cook for 2 to 4 hours.

TO ASSEMBLE

Take the lamb out of the sous vide bag, reserving the liquid from the bag, and pat the lamb dry.

Pour the reserved juices from the bag into a cold pan on the stove and add the stock. In a small bowl, whisk together the cold water and the flour then whisk the mixture into the pan. Turn the heat up and bring to a simmer, stirring regularly, until thickened.

Sear the lamb over high heat until just browned, 1 to 2 minutes per side. Remove the lamb from the heat and cut it into serving-size pieces.

Serve the lamb with the gravy spooned on top or in a small dish on the side.

FOR THE LAMB

2 (1-pound) racks of lamb, frenched

4 sprigs thyme

4 sprigs rosemary

Salt and freshly ground black pepper

TO ASSEMBLE

1 cup veal or chicken stock

2 tablespoons cold water

2 tablespoons all-purpose flour

RACK of LAMB with SPICY MINT RELISH

COOKS: **131°F (55°C) for 2 to 4 hours** · PREP: **10 minutes** · SERVES: **4**

FOR THE LAMB

1 teaspoon dried thyme

1 teaspoon garlic powder

2 (1-pound) racks of lamb, frenched

Salt and freshly ground black pepper

FOR THE RELISH

3 tablespoons fresh lime juice

1 cucumber, peeled, seeded, and diced

$1/2$ cup diced red onion

1 to 3 jalapeño chiles, seeded and diced

$1/3$ cup chopped fresh mint

Rack of lamb pairs well with a spicy, minty relish. My relish is very simple to prepare and also goes well with chicken or turkey.

PREPARE THE LAMB

Preheat a water bath to 131°F (55°C).

In a small bowl, combine the spices. Season the lamb with salt and pepper then sprinkle it with the spice mixture. Place the lamb in a sous vide bag then seal the bag. Place the bag in the water bath and cook for 2 to 4 hours.

PREPARE THE RELISH

In a large bowl, stir together all the ingredients until thoroughly combined.

TO ASSEMBLE

Take the lamb chops out of the sous vide bag and pat them dry. Sear the lamb chops over high heat until just browned, 1 to 2 minutes per side. Remove from the heat and cut into serving portions.

Serve the lamb chops with a spoonful or two of the relish on top.

BROWN SUGAR-GLAZED
LEG of LAMB

COOKS: **131°F (55°C) for 2 to 6 hours** · PREP: **15 minutes** · SERVES: **4**

Leg of lamb can benefit a lot from sous vide. It's an easy way to maintain an even temperature through the whole leg. Leg of lamb is a pretty tasty cut on its own, but sometimes I like to add a glaze to it at the end to wrap it in additional flavor. A brown sugar glaze also works great with pork loin.

PREPARE THE LAMB

Preheat a water bath to 131°F (55°C).

In a small bowl, combine the spices. Season the lamb with salt and pepper then sprinkle it with the spice mixture. Place the lamb in a sous vide bag with the thyme and rosemary sprigs then seal the bag. Place the bag in the water bath and cook for 2 to 6 hours.

PREPARE THE GLAZE

In a small bowl, stir together all the ingredients until thoroughly combined.

TO ASSEMBLE

Preheat a grill to high heat or use the oven broiler.

Take the lamb out of the sous vide bag and pat the lamb dry. Sear the lamb over high heat until just browned, 1 to 2 minutes per side. Brush the lamb with the glaze and cook for another 1 minute per side. Brush on more glaze once or twice more while the lamb is searing. Remove the lamb from the heat, slice it, and serve with some glaze drizzled on top.

FOR THE LAMB

1 teaspoon garlic powder

1 teaspoon onion powder

1 teaspoon ground coriander

2 pounds boneless leg of lamb

2 sprigs thyme

2 sprigs rosemary

Salt and freshly ground black pepper

FOR THE GLAZE

$1/2$ cup firmly packed brown sugar

3 tablespoons orange juice

2 tablespoons prepared mustard

2 tablespoons apple cider vinegar

LEG of LAMB CURRY

COOKS: **131°F (55°C) for 2 to 4 hours** · PREP: **15 minutes** · SERVES: **4**

FOR THE LAMB

2 pounds boneless leg of lamb

1 teaspoon garam masala

Salt and freshly ground black pepper

FOR THE CURRY

3 onions, chopped and divided

5 cloves garlic

1 (1$^1/_2$-inch) piece fresh ginger, peeled and coarsely chopped

3 tablespoons canola oil

2 medium carrots, peeled and diced

1 red bell pepper, diced

2 teaspoons ground coriander

$^1/_4$ to 1 teaspoon cayenne pepper

2 teaspoons garam masala

$^1/_2$ teaspoon ground cloves

$^1/_2$ cup plain yogurt,

TO ASSEMBLE

$^1/_4$ cup heavy cream

$^1/_4$ cup chopped fresh parsley

This is a classic curry featuring leg of lamb. You can easily control the spice level by adding more or less cayenne. I like to serve this with rice and bread to soak up the sauce, and maybe a crisp salad to offset the richness of the curry.

PREPARE THE LAMB

Preheat a water bath to 131°F (55°C).

Cut the lamb into 1- to 2-inch pieces and season them with the garam masala and salt and pepper. Place the lamb pieces in a sous vide bag then seal the bag. Place the bag in the water bath and cook for 2 to 4 hours.

PREPARE THE CURRY

Thirty to 45 minutes before the lamb has finished cooking, begin the curry.

Place half the onion and all the garlic and ginger in a food processor and process to a paste. In a pan over medium-high heat, heat the canola oil until hot. Add the remaining onion and cook until it begins to soften, about 5 minutes. Add the carrots and cook for another 5 minutes. Add the bell pepper and cook for another 5 minutes.

Add the pureed onion mixture, coriander, cayenne, garam masala, and cloves to the pan. Season with salt and pepper. Cook for about 10 minutes, stirring occasionally. Add the yogurt and 1$^1/_2$ cup of water and bring to a simmer.

TO ASSEMBLE

Take the lamb out of the sous vide bag and add the lamb to the pan along with some of the juices from the bag. Stir in the cream and parsley and serve, preferably over rice or with crusty bread.

SPICED LAMB KEBABS

COOKS: **131°F (55°C) for 2 to 4 hours** · PREP: **20 minutes** · SERVES: **4**

If you like lamb then these kebabs are for you. Cooking the lamb leg sous vide ensures it is cooked through, then all the kebabs need are a quick sear on the grill to finish them off and to cook the vegetables. Adding saffron rice, tzatziki sauce, and a simple side salad will finish the meal off nicely.

PREPARE THE LAMB

Preheat a water bath to 131°F (55°C).

In a small bowl, combine the spices. Season the lamb with salt and pepper then sprinkle it with the spice mixture. Place the lamb in a sous vide bag then seal the bag. Place the bag in the water bath and cook for 2 to 4 hours.

TO ASSEMBLE

Heat a grill to high heat (you won't be cooking the meat long, just searing it, so use the hottest setting).

Take the lamb out of the sous vide bag and pat the lamb dry. Skewer the lamb and vegetables, alternating them.

Cook the kebabs on the grill until the tomatoes begin to burst, turning once or twice. Remove from the heat and serve.

FOR THE LAMB

1 teaspoon dried parsley

1 teaspoon ground coriander

$1/2$ teaspoon garlic powder

$1/2$ teaspoon paprika

$1/4$ teaspoon ground cinnamon

$1/4$ teaspoon dried chipotle chile

1 to 2 pounds leg of lamb, cut into 1-inch cubes

Salt and freshly ground black pepper

TO ASSEMBLE

1 pint cherry tomatoes

1 pint pearl onions

1 pint baby bella mushrooms, stemmed

ROGAN JOSH SPICED LAMB LOIN

COOKS: **131°F (55°C) for 2 to 4 hours** · PREP: **15 minutes** · SERVES: **4**

FOR THE LAMB

1 teaspoon garlic powder

1 teaspoon paprika

1 teaspoon ground coriander

$1/2$ teaspoon ground cloves

$1/2$ teaspoon ground cinnamon

$1/4$ teaspoon ancho chile powder or chile powder of your choice

$1/4$ teaspoon cayenne pepper or chile powder of your choice

2 to 3 pounds lamb loin

1 bay leaf

Salt and freshly ground black pepper

TO ASSEMBLE

$1/2$ cup chopped fresh mint

$1/4$ cup chopped fresh dill

1 cup arugula

1 cup frisée lettuce, coarsely chopped

2 tablespoons olive oil

1 lemon

Rogan Josh is a classic lamb dish from Kashmir, India. I take the spices normally used in it to create a rub for the lamb loin. I then combine it with an herbal salad which adds brightness to counteract the richness and flavor of the Rogan Josh spiced loin.

PREPARE THE LAMB

Preheat a water bath to 131°F (55°C).

In a small bowl, combine the spices. Season the lamb with salt and pepper then sprinkle it with the spice mixture. Place the lamb in a sous vide bag with the bay leaf then seal the bag. Place the bag in the water bath and cook for 2 to 4 hours.

TO ASSEMBLE

Take the lamb out of the sous vide bag and pat the lamb dry. Sear the lamb over high heat just until browned, 1 to 2 minutes per side. Remove the lamb from the heat and cut into $1/4$-inch- to $1/2$-inch-thick slices.

Place the slices of lamb on plates and top with the herbs, arugula, and frisée. Season with salt and pepper. Drizzle the oil over top and add an equal squeeze of lemon over each portion.

TURKISH MARINATED LOIN ROAST

COOKS: **131°F (55°C) for 2 to 4 hours** · PREP: **20 minutes** · SERVES: **4**

The lamb in Turkish Marinated Loin Roast needs to be marinated for several hours, but the extra time is worth it. The marinade adds a lot of flavor to the lamb loin. The yogurt also slightly changes the meat, making it even more tender. The lamb is very good when served with some creamy polenta or rustic mashed potatoes.

PREPARE THE MARINADE

Place the yogurt in a bowl and stir in the remaining marinade ingredients until combined.

Cover the lamb loin with the marinade and refrigerate for 6 to 12 hours.

PREPARE THE LAMB

Preheat a water bath to 131°F (55°C).

Remove the lamb from the marinade and place it in a sous vide bag then seal the bag. Place the bag in the water bath and cook for 2 to 4 hours.

TO ASSEMBLE

Take the lamb loin out of the sous vide bag and pat the lamb dry. Sear the lamb over high heat until just browned, 1 to 2 minutes per side. Remove the lamb from the heat, slice it into serving-size pieces, and serve.

FOR THE MARINADE

2 cups plain whole-milk yogurt

1/2 cup olive oil

3 tablespoons fresh lemon juice

1 onion, chopped

3 cloves garlic, minced

1 teaspoon salt

1/2 teaspoon ground black pepper

1/2 teaspoon red pepper flakes

FOR THE LAMB

2 to 3 pounds lamb loin

APRICOT LAMB SHOULDER TAJINE

COOKS: **156°F (68.8°C) for 18 to 24 hours** · PREP: **20 minutes** · SERVES: **2**

FOR THE LAMB

2 teaspoons sweet paprika

1/2 teaspoon saffron
threads

2 to 3 pounds lamb
shoulder

1 bay leaf

Salt and freshly ground
black pepper

FOR THE SAUCE

Olive or canola oil

2 white onions, sliced

¾ tablespoon chopped
ginger

1 tablespoon sweet paprika

1/2 teaspoon saffron
threads

1 bay leaf

Juice of 2 oranges

1/2 cup honey

1 tablespoon ground
cinnamon

Salt and freshly ground
black pepper

Apricot Lamb Shoulder Tajine is an exotic dish that really brings out the flavor of the lamb. I like to have a more traditional texture to the shoulder, but for a steak-like texture you can drop the temperature to 131°F (55°C) and cook it for 1 to 2 days. It's best when served with rice or crusty bread to soak up all the sauce.

PREPARE THE LAMB

Preheat a water bath to 156°F (68.8°C).

In a small bowl, combine the paprika and saffron. Season the lamb with salt and pepper then sprinkle it with the spices. Place the lamb in a sous vide bag with the bay leaf then seal the bag. Place the bag in the water bath and cook for 18 to 24 hours.

PREPARE THE SAUCE

In a pan over medium heat, heat the oil until hot. Add the onions and cook until they begin to soften, about 15 minutes. Add the ginger and cook for 2 minutes. Add the remaining ingredients and 2 cups of water, season with salt and pepper, then simmer for 15 minutes.

For added flavor, you can stir in some of the juices from the sous vide bag when you take the lamb out for browning.

TO ASSEMBLE

8 dried apricots, cut into
1-inch pieces

½ cup roasted almonds

TO ASSEMBLE

Take the lamb out of the sous vide bag and pat the lamb dry. Quickly sear the lamb over high heat until just browned, 1 to 2 minutes per side. Remove the lamb from the heat and cut it into serving-size pieces.

Place the lamb in a shallow bowl and pour the sauce over the top. Top with the apricots and almonds and serve with a warm, crusty loaf of bread.

LAMB SHANK with ROASTED TOMATOES

COOKS: **156°F (68.8°C) for 18 to 24 hours** · PREP: **10 minutes** · SERVES: **4**

FOR THE LAMB

4 lamb shanks, 2 to 3 pounds total

2 sprigs thyme

2 sprigs rosemary

Salt and freshly ground black pepper

FOR THE TOMATOES

1 pint cherry tomatoes

1 tablespoon fresh thyme leaves

2 tablespoons chopped fresh rosemary

2 tablespoons olive oil

FOR THE DRESSING

1 cup plain whole yogurt

$1/4$ cup finely chopped mint leaves

$1^1/_2$ tablespoons fresh lemon juice

TO ASSEMBLE

Fresh mint, coarsely chopped

I love to combine lamb with roasted tomatoes and a mint-yogurt sauce. Besides the sous viding time, this is a quick recipe that is full of flavor and easy to make. I like a lamb shank with a more traditional braise-like texture that still has a lot of firmness, but if you want a real fall-apart texture, you can increase the temperature up to 176°F (80°C) and cook it for 12 to 18 hours.

PREPARE THE LAMB

Preheat a water bath to 156°F (68.8°C).

Season the shanks with salt and pepper and place them in a sous vide bag. Add the thyme and rosemary sprigs then seal the bag. Place the bag in the water bath and cook for 18 to 24 hours.

PREPARE THE TOMATOES

Preheat the oven to 400°F (204°C).

Toss the tomatoes with the herbs and oil then season them with salt and pepper. Place the tomatoes on a rimmed baking sheet and bake until the tomatoes burst, 10 to 25 minutes.

PREPARE THE DRESSING

Place all the ingredients in a bowl and stir to combine.

TO ASSEMBLE

Take the shanks out of the sous vide bag and pat them dry. Sear the shanks over high heat until just browned, 1 to 2 minutes per side. Remove the shanks from the heat and place them on individual plates. Drizzle the shanks with the dressing and top with the roasted tomatoes. Sprinkle with the fresh mint and serve.

MINT-FENNEL LAMB SHANK

COOKS: **131°F (55°C) for 1 to 2 days** · PREP: **15 minutes** · SERVES: **4 to 6**

The rich and heavy lamb shank is brightened up by the mint and fennel in the butter. A side of braised or roasted fennel complements this dish perfectly, as does a cucumber salad. By keeping the temperature low, the shank will turn out almost chop-like. For a more fall-apart texture, you can cook the shank between 156°F (68.8°C) and 176°F (80°C) and reduce the cook time to 12 to 24 hours.

PREPARE THE LAMB SHANKS

Preheat a water bath to 131°F (55°C).

Season the shanks with salt and pepper then sprinkle them with the garam masala. Place the shanks in a sous vide bag then seal the bag. Place the bag in the water bath and cook for 1 to 2 days.

PREPARE THE BUTTER

Place all the ingredients in a bowl and mash them together thoroughly using a fork.

TO ASSEMBLE

Take the shanks out of the sous vide bag and pat them dry. Sear the shanks over high heat until just browned, 1 to 2 minutes per side.

Place the lamb shanks on a plate, put a dollop or two of the butter on top, and serve.

FOR THE LAMB SHANKS

4 lamb shanks, 2 to 3 pounds total

2 teaspoons garam masala

Salt and freshly ground black pepper

FOR THE BUTTER

4 tablespoons unsalted butter, softened

1 tablespoon finely chopped fresh mint

$1/2$ teaspoon fennel seeds

$1/4$ teaspoon grated lemon zest

$1/8$ teaspoon freshly ground black pepper

LAMB SAUSAGE PITA

COOKS: **135°F (57.2°C) for 2 to 3 hours** · PREP: **10 minutes** · SERVES: **4**

FOR THE SAUSAGES

4 to 6 lamb sausages, about 1 inch in diameter

1 teaspoon paprika

$1/2$ teaspoon cayenne pepper

TO ASSEMBLE

$1/2$ cup tzatziki sauce

4 pitas

1 fennel bulb, sliced

1 red onion, thinly sliced

$1/2$ cup coarsely chopped cilantro

Lamb sausage is less common than other types of sausage, but it can be a great addition to your cooking repertoire. I love it served in a warm pita with fennel, red onion, and tzatziki sauce. Lamb sausage is also great as a topping for a salad or in pasta.

PREPARE THE SAUSAGE

Preheat a water bath to 135°F (57.2°C).

Place the sausages in a sous vide bag, and sprinkle in the paprika and cayenne, then seal the bag. Place the bag in the water bath and cook for 2 to 3 hours.

TO ASSEMBLE

Take the sausages out of the sous vide bag and pat them dry. Quickly sear the sausages over high heat, 1 to 2 minutes per side.

Smear the tzatziki sauce in the pitas. Place one sausage in each pita and top with the fennel, red onion, and cilantro, and serve.

CHAPTER FIVE

PORK

APPLE CIDER PORK CHOPS

COOKS: **140°F (60°C) for 2 to 5 hours** · PREP: **10 minutes** · SERVES: **4**

FOR THE PORK CHOPS

4 thick pork chops

4 sprigs thyme

Salt and freshly ground black pepper

FOR THE SAUCE

2 apples, sliced

1 tablespoon salted butter

$1/2$ teaspoon ground cinnamon

$1/4$ teaspoon ground cloves

2 cloves garlic, diced

1 teaspoon granulated sugar

$2/3$ cup hard apple cider

1 teaspoon apple cider vinegar

1 tablespoon whole-grain mustard

Sweet apples meld perfectly with cider and mustard to bring out the flavors of pork chops. Using sous vide to cook the pork chops ensures they'll be perfectly cooked and tender. Mashed potatoes, cabbage, or even Brussels sprouts and bacon make perfect accompaniments.

Most tender pork cooked between 135°F to 145°F (57.2°C to 62.8°C). My favorite temperature is 140°F (60°C) because it is still super tender but loses most of the pink coloring. I will sometimes go lower when I want a better sear since I wouldn't have to worry about heating up the middle during this step.

PREPARE THE PORK CHOPS

Preheat a water bath to 140°F (60°C).

Lightly season the pork chops with salt and pepper. Place the pork chops in a sous vide bag with the thyme sprigs. Place the bag in the water bath and cook for 2 to 5 hours.

PREPARE THE SAUCE

About 20 minutes before serving, begin the sauce. In a pan over medium-high heat, cook the apples with the butter, cinnamon, cloves, and garlic until the juices begin to brown and the apples are beginning to soften. Add the sugar, apple cider, vinegar, and mustard and bring to a simmer. Season with salt and pepper then remove from the heat.

TO ASSEMBLE

Take the pork chops out of the sous vide bag, reserving the liquid. Add about $1/2$ cup of the juices from the pork chops to the pan with the apples and stir to thoroughly combine.

Pat the pork chops dry. Quickly sear both sides of the pork chops on a grill or in a pan over high heat, 1 to 2 minutes per side. Serve the pork chops with the sauce on top.

PORK CHOPS with PEPPERS and BROCCOLI

COOKS: **140°F (60°C) for 2 to 3 hours** · PREP: **15 minutes** · SERVES: **4**

It is possible to cook a perfect pork chop using traditional methods, but when it is cooked sous vide it takes all the guesswork out of preparing it perfectly. I like my pork cooked at 140°F (60°C) for 2 to 3 hours, but feel free to raise or lower the temperature as you see fit. I prefer to pasteurize my pork, but some people are fine cooking it for shorter periods of time.

PREPARE THE PORK CHOPS

Preheat a water bath to 140°F (60°C).

In a small bowl, combine the spices. Lightly season the pork chops with salt and pepper then sprinkle them with the spice mixture. Place the pork chops in a single layer in a sous vide bag then seal the bag. Place in the water bath and cook for 2 to 3 hours, or until heated through or pasteurized.

PREPARE THE BROCCOLI

In a pan over medium heat, heat the oil until hot. Add the garlic and broccoli and cook until tender, stirring regularly.

PREPARE THE ROASTED PEPPERS

Cut the sides off the bell peppers and discard the stem and seeds. Toss the peppers in the oil then season them with salt and pepper. Cook under a broiler or in a hot pan until they have taken on color and become tender.

TO ASSEMBLE

Take the pork chops out of the sous vide bag and pat them dry. Quickly sear the pork chops on both sides on a grill or in a pan over high heat, 1 to 2 minutes per side. Place the pork chops on a plate and surround them with the bell peppers. Top with the broccoli, add a drizzle of the oil and a sprinkle of salt, and serve.

FOR THE PORK CHOPS

1 teaspoon garlic powder

1 teaspoon onion powder

1/2 teaspoon ground coriander

1/2 teaspoon ground cumin

4 pork chops, preferably thick cut

Salt and freshly ground black pepper

FOR THE BROCCOLI

Olive oil

2 teaspoons diced garlic

2 medium heads broccoli, cut into florets

FOR THE ROASTED PEPPERS

2 red bell peppers

2 yellow bell peppers

Olive oil

TO ASSEMBLE

Olive oil

Salt

PORK CHOPS with MOJO SAUCE

COOKS: **140°F (60°C) for 2 to 5 hours** · PREP: **10 minutes** · SERVES: **4**

FOR THE PORK CHOPS

4 pork chops

1 tablespoon garlic powder

1 bay leaf

Salt and freshly ground
    black pepper

FOR THE MOJO SAUCE

3 tablespoons olive oil

9 cloves garlic, minced

$1/3$ cup orange juice

$1/3$ cup fresh lime juice

1 teaspoon ground cumin

1 tablespoon chopped fresh
    oregano

Mojo sauce is a traditional Cuban sauce often used for marinating pork. It customarily uses sour orange juice, but I substitute equal parts lime juice and regular orange juice. It is a really simple sauce to make and adds wonderfully bright notes to the pork chops. I often serve these with black beans and rice on the side, and maybe a few slices of avocado.

PREPARE THE PORK CHOPS

Preheat a water bath to 140°F (60°C).

Lightly season the pork chops with salt and pepper then sprinkle them with the garlic powder. Place the pork chops in a sous vide bag with the bay leaf then seal the bag. Place the bag in the water bath and cook for 2 to 5 hours.

PREPARE THE MOJO SAUCE

In a pan over medium-high heat, heat the oil until hot. Add the garlic and cook until the garlic begins to soften; add the orange juice, lime juice, and cumin. Season with salt and pepper. Bring to a simmer then stir in the oregano and remove from the heat.

TO ASSEMBLE

Take the pork chops out of the sous vide bag and pat them dry. Sear them over high heat until just browned, 1 to 2 minutes per side. Remove the pork chops from the heat and serve them with the mojo sauce spooned on top.

HOISIN-GLAZED PORK CHOPS

COOKS: **135°F (57.2°C) for 2 to 5 hours** · PREP: **15 minutes** · SERVES: **4**

These hoisin pork chops have a sweet and salty Asian-inspired glaze on them that really ups the flavor. I recommend cooking them on the grill, but you can also cook them under the broiler in your oven. Because the glazing process takes a few extra minutes, you can sous vide the pork chops at a lower temperature than you normally would, so a little increase in temperature won't hurt them at all. I often serve them with steamed baby bok choy and white rice.

PREPARE THE PORK CHOPS

Preheat a water bath to 135°F (57.2°C).

Season the pork chops with salt and pepper then sprinkle them with the Chinese five-spice powder. Place the pork chops in a sous vide bag then seal the bag. Place the sous vide bag in the water bath and cook for 2 to 5 hours.

PREPARE THE GLAZE

In a large bowl, stir together all the glaze ingredients until thoroughly combined.

TO ASSEMBLE

Preheat a grill to high heat.

Take the pork chops out of the sous vide bag and pat them dry. Sear the pork chops on the grill until grill marks form, about 2 minutes per side. Once browned, brush the glaze on each and turn the pork chops as soon as the sauce begins to caramelize, 30 to 45 seconds. Repeat several times until they are coated with the glaze.

Remove the pork chops from the heat and serve with the cilantro and sesame seeds on top.

FOR THE PORK CHOPS

4 pork chops

1 teaspoon Chinese five-spice powder

Salt and freshly ground black pepper

FOR THE GLAZE

1/2 cup hoisin sauce

1/4 cup rice vinegar

1/4 cup soy sauce

2 tablespoons honey

1 tablespoon fresh lime juice

2 teaspoons minced ginger

2 cloves garlic, minced

TO ASSEMBLE

1/4 cup chopped fresh cilantro

1 teaspoon sesame seeds

JERK PORK CHOPS

COOKS: **140°F (60°C) for 2 to 5 hours** · PREP: **20 minutes** · SERVES: **4**

FOR THE PORK CHOPS

$^1/_3$ cup packed dark brown sugar

$^1/_4$ cup salt

1 tablespoon black pepper

1 tablespoon garlic powder

1 tablespoon onion powder

1 to 3 teaspoons scotch bonnet or habanero chile powder

2 teaspoons dried thyme

1 teaspoon ground coriander

1 teaspoon ground allspice

1 teaspoon ground cumin

$^1/_2$ teaspoon ground ginger

$^1/_2$ teaspoon ground cinnamon

$^1/_4$ teaspoon ground cloves

$^1/_4$ teaspoon ground nutmeg

4 pork chops

Jerk Pork Chops makes a well-rounded meal when served with traditional Jamaican side dishes, such as mashed or fried plantains and rice and peas. The heat from the rub elevates the flavor of pork chops and other cuts of meat, like chicken breast or pork tenderloin, that can otherwise be bland. Leftover rub can be stored in an air-tight container for several weeks.

PREPARE THE PORK CHOPS

Preheat a water bath to 140°F (60°C).

Make the Jamaican rub by combining all the spice ingredients in a bowl and stirring to thoroughly combine. Sprinkle the rub over the pork chops and place them in a sous vide bag then seal the bag. Place the bag in the water bath and cook for 2 to 5 hours.

TO ASSEMBLE

Take the pork chops out of the sous vide bag and pat them dry. Quickly sear the pork chops over high heat until just browned, 1 to 2 minutes per side. Remove the pork chops from the heat and serve.

COCOA-CRUSTED PORK LOIN

COOKS: **140°F (60°C) for 3 to 6 hours** · PREP: **15 minutes** · SERVES: **4**

FOR THE PORK

1 tablespoon ground coriander

1 teaspoon ground cinnamon

$^1/_2$ teaspoon ground nutmeg

$^1/_2$ teaspoon ground cloves

2 pounds pork loin roast

Salt and freshly ground black pepper

FOR THE COCOA SPICE RUB

2 tablespoons unsweetened cocoa powder

2 teaspoons ground cinnamon

$^1/_2$ teaspoon chipotle chile powder or chile powder of your choice

TO ASSEMBLE

Olive oil

Most people think cocoa, cinnamon, and nutmeg can only be used in desserts, but these ingredients are also great with savory foods. Here I add them to a pork loin roast for an unusual flavor that will have your family wanting more. This pork loin goes great with sautéed green beans or Brussels sprouts.

PREPARE THE PORK

Preheat a water bath to 140°F (60°C).

In a small bowl, combine the spices. Lightly season the pork with salt and pepper then sprinkle it with the spice mixture. Place the pork in a sous vide bag then seal the bag. Place the bag in the water bath and cook for 3 to 6 hours.

PREPARE THE COCOA SPICE RUB

Combine the cocoa, cinnamon, and chile powder in a bowl; set aside.

TO ASSEMBLE

Take the pork out of the sous vide bag and pat the pork dry. Lightly coat the pork with the cocoa spice rub. Brush the pork with the oil to facilitate browning. Sear the pork until it begins to brown, 1 to 2 minutes per side.

Remove the pork from the heat, slice into serving-size pieces, drizzle with more oil, and serve.

RED PORK CURRY

COOKS: **140°F (60°C) for 2 to 5 hours** · PREP: **15 minutes** · SERVES: **4**

This is a classic red curry featuring the pork, but it is also great on chicken or lamb. Red curry paste can be found in many supermarkets or ordered online; it is also possible to make your own. Use more or less of it depending on how spicy you want your curry. I usually serve this curry alongside white or fried rice and some crusty bread or naan for soaking up the sauce.

PREPARE THE PORK

Preheat a water bath to 140°F (60°C).

Sprinkle the pork with the cumin then season with salt and pepper. Place the pork in a sous vide bag and add the brown sugar then seal the bag. Place the bag in the water bath and cook for 2 to 5 hours.

PREPARE THE RED CURRY

In a pan over medium heat, heat the oil until hot. Add the onion, garlic, and curry paste and stir constantly for about 1 minute. Add the coconut milk and 1 cup of water and bring to a boil. Turn down the heat and simmer, uncovered, for 10 to 15 minutes. Add the corn and peas and cook for 4 to 6 minutes.

Just before serving, stir in the fish sauce, lime juice, and honey.

TO ASSEMBLE

Take the pork out of the sous vide bag and place it in a serving dish. Pour the curry on top and garnish with the basil leaves.

FOR THE PORK

1 pound pork chop, cut into ¾-inch-thick pieces

1/2 tablespoon ground cumin

1 tablespoon packed brown sugar

Salt and freshly ground black pepper

FOR THE RED CURRY

2 tablespoons oil

1 onion, diced

3 cloves garlic, diced

2 tablespoons red curry paste

1 1/2 cups coconut milk

1 cup corn kernels

1 cup green peas

1 tablespoon fish sauce

1 tablespoon fresh lime juice

1 tablespoon honey

TO ASSEMBLE

1/2 cup chopped Thai or Italian basil

BOURBON-GLAZED TENDERLOIN

COOKS: **140°F (60°C) for 2 to 5 hours** · PREP: **15 minutes** · SERVES: **4**

FOR THE PORK

1 teaspoon dried sage

1 teaspoon allspice

1/2 teaspoon ginger

1 to 2 pounds pork tenderloin

Salt and freshly ground black pepper

FOR THE GLAZE

1 cup bourbon whiskey

1/2 cup packed brown sugar

1/2 cup ketchup

2 teaspoons Worcestershire sauce

1 teaspoon liquid smoke

1/4 cup apple juice

1 tablespoon fresh lemon juice

1 teaspoon minced garlic

1/2 teaspoon cayenne pepper

1/4 teaspoon mustard powder

This glaze appeared in my first cookbook, and it is still a favorite of my readers. There are a lot of ingredients, but it comes together pretty quickly and packs a huge flavor punch. The glaze takes a sometimes-bland pork tenderloin and adds layers of flavor. To save time, you can skip the step of reducing the sauce and use it just after you combine all the ingredients, but the flavors will not be as strong.

PREPARE THE PORK

Preheat a water bath to 140°F (60°C).

In a small bowl, combine the spices. Season the tenderloin with salt and pepper then sprinkle it with the spice mixture. Place the tenderloin in a sous vide bag then seal the bag. Place the bag in the water bath and cook for 2 to 5 hours.

PREPARE THE GLAZE

In a pot over medium-high heat, stir together all the ingredients and bring to a simmer, stirring occasionally. Cook for about 30 minutes, until slightly thickened.

TO ASSEMBLE

Preheat a grill to high heat or use the oven broiler.

Take the tenderloin out of the bag and pat the tenderloin dry. Sear the tenderloin on the grill until grill marks form on the first side, about 2 minutes. Brush the glaze on the side facing up and turn the tenderloin. Repeat several times until it is coated with the glaze, cooking 30 to 60 seconds per turn.

Remove the tenderloin from the heat, brush once more with the glaze, slice into 1/2-inch-thick rounds and serve with the remaining glaze.

PORK LOIN with OLIVE TAPENADE

COOKS: **140°F (60°C) for 3 to 6 hours** · PREP: **10 minutes** · SERVES: **4**

Olive tapenade is a salty, flavorful condiment that adds a ton of depth to the flavor of pork loin. The saltiness of the olives and anchovies brings out the flavor of the pork while the vinegar and pepper flakes add bright and spicy notes. This dish is great when served with roasted tomatoes or vegetables, or even a crisp salad. This tapenade is also very good with steak or lamb.

PREPARE THE PORK

Preheat a water bath to 140°F (60°C).

In a small bowl, combine the garlic powder, paprika, and cumin. Season the pork with salt and pepper then sprinkle it with the spice mixture. Add the pork to a sous vide bag then seal the bag. Place the bag in the water bath and cook for 3 to 6 hours.

PREPARE THE OLIVE TAPENADE

Place all the ingredients in a food processor and pulse several times until it forms a coarse puree. Season with salt and pepper.

TO ASSEMBLE

Take the pork out of the sous vide bag and pat the pork dry. Sear the pork over high heat until just browned, 1 to 2 minutes per side. Remove the pork from the heat and place it on a plate. Spoon the tapenade across the top and serve.

FOR THE PORK

1 teaspoon garlic powder

1 teaspoon paprika

1/2 teaspoon ground cumin

2 pounds pork loin roast

Salt and freshly ground black pepper

FOR THE OLIVE TAPENADE

1 cup pitted Kalamata olives

2 anchovy fillets, or 1 tablespoon capers

3 cloves garlic

1/4 teaspoon red pepper flakes

2 tablespoons chopped fresh parsley

2 tablespoons balsamic or red wine vinegar

3 tablespoons olive oil

PORK with ROSEMARY CARAMEL SAUCE

COOKS: **140°F (60°C) for 2 to 4 hours** · PREP: **15 minutes** · SERVES: **7 large to 15 small**

FOR THE PORK

2 pounds pork loin roast

1 teaspoon paprika

1 teaspoon onion powder

1/2 teaspoon mustard powder

2 sprigs rosemary

Salt and freshly ground black pepper

FOR THE ROSEMARY CARAMEL SAUCE

1 1/2 cups heavy cream

4 sprigs rosemary

1 cup granulated sugar

TO ASSEMBLE

Apple, cut into small cubes

Basil leaves

Rosemary is a go-to flavor when preparing pork, but rosemary caramel sauce is something else entirely. I really enjoy how the sweetness of caramel complements the meat. If you don't have rosemary on hand or want to try something different, you can use other herbs and spices for a wide variety of caramel flavors.

Melted sugar is very hot and can cause burns. Be sure to use a large enough pot because the cream will boil and expand when it is added to the heated sugar. The caramel sauce can be made several hours in advance as long as it's reheated before using it.

PREPARE THE PORK

Preheat a water bath to 140°F (60°C).

Cut the pork loin roast in slabs about 1 inch thick. In a small bowl, combine all the spices. Season the pork with salt and pepper then coat it with the spice mixture. Place the pork in a sous vide bag with the rosemary sprigs then seal the bag. Place the bag in the water bath and cook for 2 to 4 hours.

PREPARE THE ROSEMARY CARAMEL SAUCE

Place the cream in a pot. Remove the leaves from the rosemary sprigs and add them to the cream. Gently bring the cream to a simmer then remove from the heat and let steep for 15 minutes. Blend the heavy cream and rosemary together using a blender then strain the cream.

Combine the sugar and 2 tablespoons of water together in a large pot (the mixture should resemble wet sand). Heat the sugar over medium heat, without stirring, until it melts and bubbles. Once it starts to brown, stir it gently until

it turns a light amber color. If lumps form, continue cooking until the lumps melt; almost all lumps should eventually melt.

Once the sugar is an amber color, 10 to 20 minutes, pour in the rosemary cream while stirring, being sure not to burn yourself on the hot steam that will be released. Stir well to fully incorporate the cream into the sugar and cook for 2 minutes.

Remove from the heat and let the caramel sauce cool slightly.

TO ASSEMBLE

Take the pork out of the sous vide bag and pat the pork dry. Quickly sear each slab over high heat until just browned, 1 to 2 minutes per side. Remove from the heat and cut into serving-size pieces.

Place a piece of pork on a plate and drizzle it with the rosemary caramel sauce. Top with the apple cubes and basil leaves and serve.

MEMPHIS-STYLE RIBS

COOKS: **156°F (68.8°C) for 18 to 24 hours** · PREP: **15 minutes** · SERVES: **2 to 4**

FOR THE DRY RUB

2 teaspoons packed brown sugar

2 teaspoons paprika

2 teaspoons garlic powder

1/2 teaspoon onion powder

1/2 teaspoon dried thyme

1/4 teaspoon mustard powder

1/2 teaspoon chipotle chile powder or chile powder of your choice

1/2 teaspoon celery seeds

FOR THE RIBS

2 pounds baby back or back ribs, trimmed of excess fat and silverskin

Salt and freshly ground black pepper

These ribs use a pretty typical Memphis-style dry rub. I like to add half the rub before cooking so the ribs become infused with the flavor, then apply the other half after sous viding so you get more of the typical type of crust. Try this rub with any kind of pork ribs.

The ribs are cooked at 156°F (68.8°C) and have a texture closer to traditional ribs but with more bite. You can increase the temperature to 176°F (80°C) for an even more traditional texture.

PREPARE THE DRY RUB

In a small bowl, stir together all the ingredients until thoroughly combined.

PREPARE THE RIBS

Preheat a water bath to 156°F (68.8°C).

Cut the ribs into pieces that will easily fit into a sous vide bag. Season the ribs with salt and pepper then lightly coat them with half the rub.

Place the ribs into a sous vide bag then seal the bag (be sure the bag isn't sealed too tightly or the bones may pierce it). Place the bag in the water bath and cook for 18 to 24 hours.

TO ASSEMBLE

Preheat a grill to high heat or a pan to medium-high heat.

Take the ribs out of the sous vide bag and pat them dry. Sprinkle the meaty side of the ribs with the remaining spice rub.

Quickly grill the ribs just until the meat is seared, 1 to 2 minutes per side. Remove the ribs from the heat and serve.

ST. LOUIS–STYLE RIBS

COOKS: **135°F (57.2°C) for 1 to 2 days** · PREP: **15 minutes** · SERVES: **2 to 4**

Sous vide ribs are an easy weekday meal. After a few days in the water bath, they become very tender and are quick to finish cooking on a grill or under a broiler. It's also quite satisfying to dig into a big plate of them after a hard day of work. I use St. Louis-style ribs, but baby back ribs will also work well.

These ribs come out with an almost chop-like texture. For a more fall-apart texture, you can cook them between 156°F (68.8°C) and 176°F (80°C) for 12 to 24 hours.

PREPARE THE RIBS

Preheat a water bath to 135°F (57.2°C).

Combine the cumin, garlic, and lemon peel, if using, in a bowl. Cut the ribs into pieces that will easily fit into a sous vide bag. Season the ribs with salt and pepper then coat them with the spice mixture. Place the ribs into the sous vide bag, add the bay leaves, then seal the bag (be sure the bag isn't sealed too tightly or the bones may pierce it). Place the bag in the water bath and cook for 1 to 2 days.

TO ASSEMBLE

Preheat a grill to high heat.

Take the ribs out of the sous vide bag and pat them dry. Coat them with the BBQ sauce.

Quickly grill the ribs just until the BBQ sauce begins to caramelize, 30 to 45 seconds per side. Repeat a few times, remove the ribs from the heat, and serve.

FOR THE RIBS

1 teaspoon ground cumin

1 teaspoon garlic powder

1 teaspoon dried lemon peel (optional)

2 pounds St. Louis-style ribs, trimmed of excess fat and silverskin

2 dried bay leaves

Salt and freshly ground black pepper

TO ASSEMBLE

1/2 cup your favorite BBQ sauce

TERIYAKI-GLAZED SPARE RIBS

COOKS: **135°F (57.2°C) for 1 to 2 days** · PREP: **10 minutes** · SERVES: **2 to 4**

FOR THE SPARE RIBS

2 tablespoons Chinese five-spice powder

1 tablespoon ground ginger

2 to 3 pounds of pork spare ribs

Salt and freshly ground black pepper

FOR THE TERIYAKI SAUCE

$1/3$ cup soy sauce

$1/4$ cup hoisin sauce

$1/4$ cup packed brown sugar

$1/2$ cup diced pineapple

1 fresh red chile, diced

2 cloves garlic, diced

1 tablespoon grated ginger

3 tablespoons rice vinegar

Teriyaki is one of my favorite sauces. Much like BBQ sauce there are so many variations of it and no "right" one. Here is the combo that I enjoy and, as a bonus, it is easy to prepare. To save time, you can always use a bottle of your favorite teriyaki sauce, or make extra sauce and save it in the refrigerator or freezer for later use. These ribs will be tender with almost a pork chop–like texture to them.

PREPARE THE SPARE RIBS

Preheat a water bath to 135°F (57.2°C).

In a small bowl, combine the spices. Cut the ribs into pieces that will easily fit into a sous vide bag. Season the ribs with salt and pepper then sprinkle them with the spice mixture. Place the ribs in a sous vide bag and seal the bag (be sure the bag isn't sealed too tightly or the bones may pierce it). Place the bag in the water bath and cook for 1 to 2 days.

PREPARE THE TERIYAKI SAUCE

In a medium saucepan, combine all the ingredients and bring to a simmer. Gently simmer for 5 to 10 minutes then remove from the heat.

TO ASSEMBLE

Take the ribs out of the sous vide bag and pat them dry. Sear the ribs until just browned, 1 to 2 minutes per side. Brush with the sauce and cook for another 1 minute per side; add the glaze once or twice more while searing. Remove the ribs from the heat and serve with the teriyaki sauce on top.

SWEET APPLES and COUNTRY-STYLE RIBS

COOKS: **140°F (60°C) for 18 to 36 hours** · PREP: **10 minutes** · SERVES: **4**

Pork and apples are a classic food pairing, and here I create this with country-style ribs and a sweet apple topping. The ribs are cooked for 18 to 36 hours until they are meltingly tender, then the apples are cooked with butter and sugar until they begin to soften. Some mint and lemon juice pull the flavors together.

PREPARE THE RIBS

Preheat a water bath to 140°F (60°C).

In a small bowl, combine the spices. Cut the ribs into pieces that will easily fit into a sous vide bag. Season the ribs with salt and pepper then sprinkle them with the spice mixture.

Place the ribs in a sous vide bag then seal the bag (be sure the bag isn't sealed too tightly or the bones may pierce it). Place the bag in the water bath and cook for 18 to 36 hours.

PREPARE THE APPLES

Preheat a pan to medium-high heat.

Melt the butter in the pan. Add the apples and cook until they turn tender. Sprinkle the apples with the brown sugar and lemon juice and stir to combine. Remove from the heat and top with the chopped mint.

TO ASSEMBLE

Take the ribs out of the sous vide bag and pat them dry. Sear the ribs over high heat until just browned, 1 to 2 minutes per side. Remove the ribs from the heat, top with the apples, and serve.

FOR THE RIBS

1 teaspoon garlic powder

1/2 teaspoon ground cinnamon

1/2 teaspoon ground nutmeg

1/2 teaspoon ancho chile powder or chile powder of your choice

4 pounds country style ribs

Salt and freshly ground black pepper

FOR THE APPLES

3 tablespoons salted butter

3 to 4 red apples, cored and sliced

3 tablespoons packed brown sugar

1 1/2 tablespoons fresh lemon juice

2 tablespoons chopped mint

VINEGAR-SAUCED PULLED PORK

COOKS: **176°F (80°C) for 12 to 18 hours** · PREP: **20 minutes** · SERVES: **5 to 10**

FOR THE PULLED PORK

2 teaspoons ancho chile powder

2 teaspoons paprika

2 teaspoons ground coriander

4 to 5 pounds pork shoulder, trimmed of excess fat, sliced into 2-inch slabs

1 tablespoon Worcestershire sauce

1 tablespoon liquid smoke

Salt and freshly ground black pepper

FOR THE VINEGAR SAUCE

1 cup apple cider vinegar

3 tablespoons granulated sugar

1 tablespoon red pepper flakes

2 shallots, diced

2 tablespoons salt

1 teaspoon pepper

Sous vide pulled pork at 176°F (80°C) comes out very close in texture to the traditional style. There will be less smoke flavor, but the texture will be similar and the meat will actually be moister. This pulled pork can be eaten plain and also makes excellent sandwiches. You can also replace the vinegar sauce with your favorite BBQ sauce for a sweeter meal. I normally serve it with a side of cornbread, coleslaw, and some mac and cheese.

PREPARE THE PULLED PORK

Preheat a water bath to 176°F (80°C).

In a small bowl, combine the spices. Season the pork with salt and pepper then sprinkle it with the spice mixture. Place the pork in a sous vide bag with the Worcestershire sauce and liquid smoke then seal the bag. Place the bag in the water bath and cook for 12 to 18 hours.

PREPARE THE VINEGAR SAUCE

In a small bowl, whisk together all the ingredients and ¾ cup of water until thoroughly combined.

TO ASSEMBLE

Take the pork out of the sous vide bag and pat the pork dry. Quickly sear the pork on all sides in a pan over high heat or on a grill, 1 to 2 minutes per side. Remove the pork from the heat and shred it into pieces.

Serve with a spoonful of the vinegar sauce over top.

PORK CARNITAS

COOKS: **165°F (73.9°C) for 18 to 24 hours** · PREP: **15 minutes** · SERVES: **4 to 6**

Pork Carnitas are a tender and moist Mexican dish.
Traditionally you slow cook the pork butt in lard then shred it. Here, we cook it sous vide, which eliminates a lot of the fat content and also removes some of the cooking steps. I usually opt for a middle braise-like temperature of 165°F (73.9°C) so that it's easy to shred the meat at the end. This meat is also fantastic in burritos, on nachos, in tacos, or on pizza.

PREPARE THE PORK ROAST

Preheat a water bath to 165°F (73.9°C).

In a small bowl, combine the spices. Season the roast with salt and pepper then sprinkle it with the spice mixture. Place the roast in a bag with the thyme sprigs, liquid smoke, and butter then seal the bag. Place the bag in the water bath and cook for 18 to 24 hours.

TO ASSEMBLE

Take the pork out of the sous vide bag, reserving the juices, and pat the pork dry. Quickly sear the pork over high heat until just browned, 1 to 2 minutes per side. Remove from the heat.

Shred or roughly chop the pork and place it in a bowl. Add some of the juices from the sous vide bag until it is moist but not soupy.

Serve the pork with the warm corn tortillas and the remaining garnishes.

FOR THE PORK ROAST

2 pounds pork butt or picnic roast, sliced into 2-inch slabs

2 teaspoons garlic powder

1 teaspoon onion powder

1 teaspoon paprika

1 teaspoon dried oregano

1/2 teaspoon ancho chile powder or chile powder of your choice

1/4 teaspoon chipotle chile powder or chile powder of your choice

5 sprigs thyme

1 teaspoon liquid smoke

3 tablespoons salted butter

Salt and freshly ground black pepper

TO ASSEMBLE

Warm corn tortillas

1 lime, cut into 8 wedges

Shredded lettuce

Guacamole

Sour cream

Queso fresco or feta cheese

CHOPPED PORK with BOURBON BBQ SAUCE

COOKS: **156°F (68.8°C) for 18 to 24 hours** · PREP: **15 minutes** · SERVES: **5 to 10**

FOR THE PORK

1 teaspoon garlic powder

1 teaspoon ground cumin

1 teaspoon ground coriander

1/4 teaspoon cayenne pepper

4 to 5 pounds pork shoulder, trimmed of excess fat, sliced into 2-inch slabs

1 tablespoon Worcestershire sauce

1 tablespoon liquid smoke

Salt and freshly ground black pepper

FOR THE BBQ SAUCE

2 cups ketchup

1 cup Bourbon whiskey

1/2 cup packed brown sugar

1/4 cup balsamic vinegar

Chopped pork is very easy to make sous vide, and at 156°F (68.8°C) it will have a firm but very tender texture. Once done, you can roughly shred and chop it.

I also include a very flavorful BBQ sauce that I love, but you can save time by using your favorite store brand. I'll usually make extra sauce and keep it in the fridge to use throughout the week.

PREPARE THE PORK

Preheat a water bath to 156°F (68.8°C).

In a small bowl, combine the spices. Season the pork with salt and pepper then sprinkle it with the spice mixture. Place the pork in a sous vide bag with the Worcestershire sauce and the liquid smoke then seal the bag. Place the bag in the water bath and cook for 18 to 24 hours.

PREPARE THE BBQ SAUCE

In a saucepan over medium-high heat, whisk together all the ingredients and 1/2 cup of water and bring to a simmer. Gently simmer for 5 to 10 minutes then remove from the heat.

TO ASSEMBLE

Take the pork out of the sous vide bag and pat the pork dry. Quickly sear the pork over high heat until just browned, 1 to 2 minutes per side. Remove the pork from the heat and chop it into small pieces.

Serve with a spoonful of the BBQ sauce over top.

3 tablespoons chopped
   garlic

1 tablespoon ancho chile
   powder or chile powder of
   your choice

2 tablespoons liquid smoke

2 tablespoons
   Worcestershire sauce

$1/2$ tablespoon chipotle chile
   powder or chile powder of
   your choice

1 tablespoon molasses

2 tablespoons whole-grain
   mustard

SAUSAGE and SUMMER SQUASH PASTA

COOKS: **140°F (60°C) for 2 to 3 hours** · PREP: **10 minutes** · SERVES: **4**

FOR THE SAUSAGE

1 pound sweet Italian
　sausage links

2 sprigs rosemary

TO ASSEMBLE

1 yellow onion, cut into
　$1/4$-inch slices

1 zucchini, cut into $1/2$-inch-
　wide half moons

1 yellow squash, cut into
　$1/2$-inch-wide half moons

4 cloves garlic, diced

$1/2$ cup chicken stock

1 tablespoon fresh lemon
　juice

12 ounces farfalle pasta
　or pasta or your choice,
　cooked

2 tablespoons chopped
　fresh basil

Sweet Italian sausage over pasta is a favorite meal of mine. Sausage and Summer Squash Pasta incorporates flavorful summer squash and a light sauce made with chicken stock and lemon juice to round out the flavors. The sausage is first sous vided to ensure it is perfectly cooked, then it is quickly browned in the same pan you'll use for the pasta sauce. It's a meal that is both quick to assemble and very satisfying.

PREPARE THE SAUSAGE

Preheat a water bath to 140°F (60°C).

Add the sausage and rosemary to a sous vide bag then seal the bag. Place the sous vide bag in the water bath and cook for 2 to 3 hours.

TO ASSEMBLE

Preheat a pan to medium-high heat. Take the sausages out of the sous vide bag and pat them dry. Sear the sausages in the pan until browned on all sides, 1 to 2 minutes per side. Remove the sausages from the heat and slice them into $1/2$-inch rounds.

Add the onion to the pan and cook until it begins to turn translucent, 5 to 10 minutes. Add the zucchini, yellow squash, and garlic and cook until the squash begins to soften. Add the chicken stock, lemon juice, and pasta and cook until the sauce reduces slightly and coats the vegetables. Remove from the heat, top with the sausage rounds and the basil, and serve.

CHAPTER SIX

CHICKEN

MOLE CHICKEN

COOKS: 141°F (60.6°C) for 2 to 4 hours · PREP: **20 minutes** · SERVES: **8**

FOR THE CHICKEN

8 chicken breasts

Salt and freshly ground black pepper

FOR THE MOLE

8 assorted medium-heat dried chiles such as ancho, mulato, and pasilla

1 to 2 dried chipotle chiles

4 plum or Roma tomatoes

1 onion, coarsely chopped

5 cloves garlic, coarsely chopped

3 tablespoons slivered almonds

2 tablespoons sesame seeds

$1/2$ teaspoon cracked black peppercorns

1 teaspoon coriander seeds

1 cinnamon stick

2 whole cloves

$1/2$ teaspoon aniseed or fennel seed

$1/4$ cup chopped fresh cilantro

$1/4$ cup golden raisins

Mole is one of my favorite sauces, especially when done right. This is a more traditional preparation than the more mild and sweet versions found at chain restaurants. It takes advantage of the varied tastes and aromas of different types of chiles, making it bold and full of flavor. It also works well with chicken thighs or even pork. You can also make the mole ahead of time and refrigerate it until you need it.

PREPARE THE CHICKEN

Preheat a water bath to 141°F (60.6°C).

Season the chicken breasts with salt and pepper then place them in sous vide bags. Place the bags in the water bath and cook for 2 to 4 hours

PREPARE THE MOLE

You can make the mole while the chicken is cooking or make it up to a week ahead of time and refrigerate it.

Roast the chiles for 2 minutes per side in a dry pan over medium-high heat until fragrant. Set aside to cool.

On a rimmed baking sheet, roast the tomatoes, onion, and garlic in an oven at 400°F (204°C) until the onion softens, 15 to 30 minutes. Set aside to cool.

Add the almonds, sesame seeds, peppercorns, coriander, cinnamon, cloves, and aniseed to a pan, and toast them over medium heat until fragrant and just starting to brown, about 2 minutes. Set aside to cool. Once cool, place the toasted spices in a spice grinder or food processor and process to a fine powder.

Cut the roasted chiles in half and remove the seeds and stems. Put the chiles in enough hot water to cover them.

1/4 cup olive oil

2 cups chicken stock

2 ounces dark or
unsweetened chocolate

1 tablespoon honey

2 tablespoons apple cider
vinegar

After 30 minutes drain them.

In a food processor, place the tomatoes, onion, garlic, chiles, ground spices, cilantro, and raisins. Process to a smooth paste, adding water if the mixture is too thick.

In a pot or large saucepan with high sides over medium heat, heat the oil until hot. Add the puree from the food processor and cook for at least 5 minutes, stirring constantly, or until thickened.

Reduce the heat to medium low and add the chicken stock, chocolate, honey, and vinegar and stir to combine. Simmer the sauce for 10 minutes, stirring occasionally, or until it becomes thick but still pourable. Season with salt and pepper then remove from the heat.

TO ASSEMBLE

Take the chicken breasts out of the sous vide bags and add them to the pan with the mole. Toss to coat well.

Place one chicken breast on a plate and spoon the mole on top. The chicken and mole are best when served over rice or with tortilla shells.

MARSALA CHICKEN

COOKS: **141°F (60.6°C) for 2 to 4 hours** · PREP: **15 minutes** · SERVES: **4**

FOR THE CHICKEN

4 chicken breasts

1 teaspoon garlic powder

3 sprigs thyme

1 sprig rosemary

Salt and freshly ground black pepper

TO ASSEMBLE

Oil

1 cup all-purpose flour

3 tablespoons unsalted butter

3 cups sliced mushrooms such as baby bella, crimini, oyster, or porcini

¾ cup Marsala wine

¾ cup chicken stock

4 tablespoons chopped Italian parsley

Chicken Marsala is one of my favorite Italian dishes to make. Traditionally, the only tricky part is trying to make sure the chicken breasts are cooked through without turning them soggy. Using sous vide to precook the chicken breasts eliminates this issue and also allows you to use thicker chicken breasts. This dish goes well with some angel hair pasta to soak up all the flavorful sauce.

PREPARE THE CHICKEN

Preheat a water bath to 141°F (60.6°C).

Season the chicken breasts with salt and pepper then with the garlic powder. Place the chicken breasts in a sous vide bag with the thyme and rosemary sprigs then seal the bag. Place the bag in the water bath and cook for 2 to 4 hours.

TO ASSEMBLE

Heat oil in a sauté pan over medium-high heat until hot.

Take the chicken breasts out of the sous vide bag and pat them dry. Dredge the breasts in the flour then quickly sear them just until the coating has developed some color, 1 to 2 minutes per side. Remove the chicken breasts from the heat and set them aside in a warm spot.

Add 1 tablespoon of the butter to the pan and melt it. Add the mushrooms and cook until they begin to brown and release their liquid. Lower the heat to medium and add the Marsala wine. Simmer for about 1 minute to cook out the alcohol, scraping up the browned bits. Add the stock to the pan. Let simmer for 5 to 10 minutes to reduce the sauce to your desired thickness.

Stir 2 tablespoons of butter into the sauce. plate the chicken and top it with the sauce. Finish with parsley and serve.

HAWAIIAN KEBABS

COOKS: **141°F (60.5°C) for 2 to 4 hours** · PREP: **15 minutes** · SERVES: **4 to 8**

Hawaiian Kebabs is a twist on the classic Hawaiian pizza combination of ham and pineapple. I used orange peel and mace to season the chicken to give it a little citrus flavor but you can use any seasonings you want. You can also introduce some interesting flavor by adding teriyaki sauce before grilling. These kebabs make a great meal when served with rice or a vegetable stir fry.

PREPARE THE CHICKEN

Preheat a water bath to 141°F (60.5°C).

Season the chicken with salt and pepper then season it the orange peel and mace. Place the chicken in a sous vide bag and seal the bag. Place the bag in the water bath and cook for 2 to 4 hours.

TO ASSEMBLE

Preheat a grill to very hot.

Take the chicken out of the sous vide bag and pat the chicken dry. Skewer the chicken, pineapple, and ham, alternating them.

Cook the kebabs on the grill until the meat just begins to brown and the pineapple is warmed through, turning at least once. Remove the kebabs from the heat and serve.

FOR THE CHICKEN

2 pounds chicken, cut into 1-inch cubes

1 teaspoon dried orange peel

$1/2$ teaspoon ground mace

Salt and freshly ground black pepper

TO ASSEMBLE

2 cups pineapple, cut into 1-inch cubes

2 cups cooked ham, cut into $1/2$-inch cubes

CHICKEN and PESTO PASTA

COOKS: **141°F (60.5°C) for 2 to 4 hours** · PREP: **15 minutes** · SERVES: **4**

FOR THE CHICKEN

1 teaspoon garlic powder

$1/2$ teaspoon onion powder

$1/2$ teaspoon dried oregano

3 to 4 chicken breasts

Salt and freshly ground
    black pepper

FOR THE PESTO

$1^1/2$ cups fresh basil, packed

¾ cup fresh parsley, packed

$1/4$ cup pine nuts

$1/4$ cup fresh Parmesan
    cheese

2 tablespoons fresh lemon
    juice

5 cloves garlic, minced

$1/2$ cup olive oil

TO ASSEMBLE

Cooked fusilli pasta or
    pasta of your choice

1 red bell pepper, cut into
    $1/4$-inch slices

Fresh Parmesan cheese

Pesto is such a flavorful ingredient, and it's very easy to make. Here I pair it with some pasta, chicken, and red bell pepper to make a satisfying dinner. You can also use pesto on a variety of meats or even as a rub before grilling. The pesto will last in the refrigerator for a few days.

PREPARE THE CHICKEN

Preheat a water bath to 141°F (60.5°C).

In a small bowl, combine the spices. Season the chicken breasts with salt and pepper then sprinkle them with the spice mixture. Place the chicken breasts in a sous vide bag then seal the bag. Place the bag in the water bath and cook for 2 to 4 hours.

PREPARE THE PESTO

Place all the ingredients in a blender or food processor and process them to a smooth paste. Season with salt and pepper.

TO ASSEMBLE

Take the chicken breasts out of the sous vide bag and pat them dry. Sear the chicken breasts until just browned, 1 to 2 minutes per side. Remove the chicken breasts from the heat and cut into $1/2$-inch-thick slices.

Place the cooked pasta in a bowl, add the pesto, and stir to thoroughly coat the pasta. Top with the bell pepper and the chicken. Grate some fresh Parmesan on top and serve.

CHICKEN PARMESAN

COOKS: **141°F (60.5°C) for 2 to 4 hours** · PREP: **15 minutes** · SERVES: **4**

Chicken Parmesan is one of my favorite comfort foods. Here is a simple version that you can make at home where sous viding it cooks the chicken perfectly so you can focus on getting the crust nice and crispy. You can leave the chicken breasts whole or cut them widthwise in half for a higher "crust-to-chicken" ratio.

PREPARE THE CHICKEN

Preheat a water bath to 141°F (60.5°C).

Season the chicken breasts with salt and pepper then sprinkle them with the garlic and onion powders. Place the chicken breasts in a sous vide bag with the thyme and rosemary sprigs then seal the bag. Place the bag in the water bath and cook for 2 to 4 hours.

PREPARE THE COATING STATIONS

Combine the flour, salt, and pepper on one plate. In a separate bowl, lightly beat the two eggs. On another plate, combine the bread crumbs, Parmesan, and parsley.

TO ASSEMBLE

Preheat a frying pan to medium-high heat. Preheat the oven broiler.

Take the chicken breasts out of the sous vide bag and pat them dry. Dredge the chicken breasts first in the flour mixture, then in the eggs, then in the bread crumbs mixture.

Add about $1/2$ inch of oil to the pan and heat to 350°F to 375°F (176°C to 190°C). Fry the chicken on each side until golden brown.

On a sheet pan, top each fried chicken breast with basil and cover them with the mozzarella and Parmesan. Broil in the oven until the cheese is browned and bubbly. Remove from the heat and serve.

FOR THE CHICKEN

4 chicken breasts

$1/2$ teaspoon garlic powder

$1/2$ teaspoon onion powder

2 sprigs thyme

2 sprigs rosemary

Salt and freshly ground black pepper

FOR THE COATING STATIONS

$3/4$ cup all-purpose flour

2 teaspoons salt

$1/2$ teaspoon ground black pepper

2 eggs

$3/4$ cup dried Italian bread crumbs

$1/4$ cup grated Parmesan cheese

2 tablespoons chopped parsley

TO ASSEMBLE

Oil, for frying

$1/2$ cup chopped fresh basil

8 to 10 ($1/4$-inch) slices fresh mozzarella, or 1 cup shredded

4 tablespoons grated Parmesan cheese

CHICKEN FINGERS

COOKS: **141°F (60.5°C) for 2 to 4 hours** · PREP: **15 minutes** · SERVES: **4**

FOR THE CHICKEN

1 teaspoon garlic powder

$1/2$ teaspoon ground cumin

$1/2$ teaspoon ground coriander

4 chicken breasts, cut into 1-inch strips

4 sage leaves

Salt and freshly ground black pepper

FOR THE COATING STATIONS

¾ cup all-purpose flour

2 teaspoons salt

1 teaspoon ground black pepper

2 eggs

TO ASSEMBLE

Oil, for frying

BBQ Sauce

Honey Mustard

Ranch Dressing

Chicken tenders are a versatilely served finger food that both kids and adults love. Since the chicken is cooked sous vide it remains moist, so you only have to focus on browning the coating when you finish cooking it. Serve it with a variety of dipping sauces so everyone can enjoy their favorite combinations.

PREPARE THE CHICKEN

Preheat a water bath to 141°F (60.5°C).

In a small bowl, combine the spices. Season the chicken strips with salt and pepper then sprinkle them with the spice mixture. Place the chicken strips in a sous vide bag with the sage leaves then seal the bag. Place the bag in the water bath and cook for 2 to 4 hours.

PREPARE THE COATING STATIONS

Combine the flour, salt, and pepper on one plate. Place the eggs in a wide-mouth bowl and beat them lightly with a fork.

TO ASSEMBLE

Preheat a frying pan to medium-high heat.

Take the chicken strips out of the sous vide bag and pat them dry. Dredge the chicken strips first in the flour mixture, then in the eggs, then again in the flour mixture.

Add about $1/2$ inch of oil to the pan and fry the dredged chicken strips until the bottoms become golden brown then turn them and cook until golden brown on the other side. Remove the chicken strips from the heat and serve with the BBQ, honey mustard, and ranch dipping sauces.

CHICKEN PASTA with WALNUT SAUCE

COOKS: **141°F (60.5°C) for 2 to 4 hours** · PREP: **15 minutes** · SERVES: **6**

FOR THE CHICKEN

1 teaspoon garlic powder

$1/2$ teaspoon ground ginger

4 chicken breasts

Salt and freshly ground
   black pepper

FOR THE WALNUT SAUCE

1 cup walnuts

1 slice bread, coarsely
   chopped

$1/3$ cup whole milk

2 tablespoons heavy cream

3 cloves garlic, coarsely
   chopped

3 tablespoons olive oil

TO ASSEMBLE

Cooked whole wheat
   spaghetti or pasta of your
   choice

2 tablespoons chopped
   fresh parsley

2 tablespoons chopped
   fresh basil

2 tablespoons chopped
   walnuts

Parmesan cheese

This satisfyingly flavorful walnut sauce isn't found too often but is a memorable treat for those who have tried it before. Even though walnuts are mild tasting, they carry just a hint of tangy, sharp notes. For richer depth of flavor, you can toast the walnuts in a dry pan before you add them to the food processor.

PREPARE THE CHICKEN

Preheat a water bath to 141°F (60.5°C).

In a small bowl, combine the spices. Season the chicken breasts with salt and pepper then sprinkle them with the spice mixture. Place the chicken breasts in a sous vide bag then seal the bag. Place the bag in the water bath and cook for 2 to 4 hours.

PREPARE THE WALNUT SAUCE

Place all the ingredients in a blender or food processor and process to a smooth, thick sauce, adding more milk if the mixture is too thick.

TO ASSEMBLE

Take the chicken breasts out of the sous vide bag and pat them dry. Sear the chicken breasts over high heat until just browned, 1 to 2 minutes per side. Remove the chicken breasts from the heat and cut into $1/2$-inch-thick slices.

Place the cooked pasta in a bowl with the walnut sauce and stir to thoroughly combine. Top with the fresh herbs, walnuts, and chicken. Grate some fresh Parmesan on top and serve.

CHICKEN SOFT TACOS

COOKS: **141°F (60.5°C) for 2 to 4 hours** · PREP: **15 minutes** · SERVES: **4**

Chicken soft tacos are a great midweek meal because they come together so fast. You can always sear the chicken for more flavor, but I've found the unseared breasts work just fine. You can serve these with any accompaniments you like. Often I'll serve the sides in small bowls so guests can make their own tacos the way they like them.

PREPARE THE CHICKEN

Preheat a water bath to 141°F (60.5°C).

In a small bowl, combine the spices. Season the chicken breasts with salt and pepper then sprinkle them with the spice mixture. Place the chicken breasts in a sous vide bag then seal the bag. Place the bag in the water bath and cook for 2 to 4 hours.

TO ASSEMBLE

Take the chicken breasts out of the bag and cut them into ¹/₂-inch-thick strips.

Lay out the tortillas and top each one with the chicken, lettuce, tomato, cheese, and sour cream. Squeeze some lime juice over the top and serve.

FOR THE CHICKEN

1 teaspoon paprika

¹/₂ teaspoon ground cumin

1 teaspoon chipotle chile powder or your chile powder of choice

3 to 4 chicken breasts

Salt and freshly ground black pepper

TO ASSEMBLE

8 (6-inch) flour tortillas

1 cup shredded lettuce

1 tomato, diced

¹/₂ cup shredded cheddar cheese

Sour cream

1 lime, quartered

TIKKA MASALA CHICKEN

COOKS: **141°F (60.5°C) for 2 to 4 hours** · PREP: **15 minutes** · SERVES: **4**

FOR THE CHICKEN

1 teaspoon garlic powder

$1/2$ teaspoon onion powder

$1/2$ teaspoon ground coriander

$1/2$ teaspoon ground cumin

$1/4$ teaspoon cayenne pepper or your chile powder of choice

1 pound chicken breasts

Salt and freshly ground black pepper

FOR THE MASALA SAUCE

Olive or canola oil

1 onion, diced

4 cloves garlic, diced

3 teaspoons grated fresh ginger

1 jalapeño chile, seeded and diced

2 tablespoons tomato paste

2 tablespoons garam masala

1 (28-ounce) can crushed tomatoes

1 tablespoon honey

Tikka Masala Chicken is an Indian-inspired British dish served at curry houses. This is a simple sous vide take on the dish that brings out the flavors without taking too long to prepare. For an even quicker version, you can take the chicken out of the sous vide bag and place it directly into the sauce without grilling it.

PREPARE THE CHICKEN

Preheat a water bath to 141°F (60.5°C).

In a small bowl, combine the spices. Season the chicken breasts with salt and pepper then sprinkle them with the spice mixture. Place the chicken breasts in a sous vide bag then seal the bag. Place the bag in the water bath and cook for 2 to 4 hours.

PREPARE THE MASALA SAUCE

In a pan over medium to medium-high heat, heat the oil until hot. Add the onion and cook until translucent, 5 to 10 minutes. Add the garlic, ginger, and jalapeño and cook for another 5 minutes.

Add the tomato paste and garam masala and cook, stirring regularly, for 5 minutes. Add the crushed tomatoes and honey and simmer for about 15 minutes. Season with salt and pepper then remove from the heat.

TO ASSEMBLE

1 cup plain yogurt

1 cup heavy cream

$^1/_4$ cup chopped fresh cilantro leaves

TO ASSEMBLE

Preheat a grill to high heat.

Take the chicken breasts out of the sous vide bag and coat them in the yogurt. Place the chicken breasts on the grill and cook for 1 to 2 minutes per side then remove from the heat and cut into 1-inch pieces.

Add the chicken, cream, and cilantro to the sauce and stir to thoroughly combine. Season with salt and pepper. Remove from the heat and serve in bowls.

CHICKEN VERDE ENCHILADAS

COOKS: **141°F (60.5°C) for 2 to 4 hours** · PREP: **15 minutes** · SERVES: **4**

FOR THE CHICKEN

$1/2$ teaspoon onion powder

$1/4$ teaspoon chipotle chile powder or chile powder of your choice

1 pound chicken breasts

Salt and freshly ground black pepper

FOR THE SALSA VERDE

4 cloves garlic, halved

$1/2$ onion, roughly chopped

1 poblano pepper, stemmed and seeded

1 jalapeño chile, stemmed and seeded

9 tomatillos, stemmed, husks removed, and rinsed

Oil

1 tablespoon honey

$1/4$ cup coarsely chopped fresh cilantro

TO ASSEMBLE

12 small corn tortillas

1 (12-ounce) can black beans

Chicken Verde Enchiladas is a great way to utilize chicken breasts cooked sous vide. The roasting of the salsa ingredients adds a richness and depth of flavor to the dish. You can add anything to the enchiladas that you want and use more or less cheese and spices, depending on your preferences. You can even use leftover chicken in this dish, and it will reheat as the dish bakes. The salsa verde can be made a few days ahead of time or even stored in the freezer for later.

PREPARE THE CHICKEN

Preheat a water bath to 141°F (60.5°C).

In a small bowl, combine the spices. Season the chicken breasts with salt and pepper then sprinkle them with the spice mixture. Place the chicken breasts in a sous vide bag then seal the bag. Place the bag in the water bath and cook for 2 to 4 hours.

PREPARE THE SALSA VERDE

Preheat the oven broiler.

Place the garlic, onion, poblano, jalapeño, and tomatillos on a rimmed baking sheet. Season them with salt and pepper then drizzle them with the oil. Cook until the vegetables begin to soften and brown, 15 to 30 minutes. Remove the baking sheet from the oven and scrape the roasted veggies and their juices into a blender or food processor. Add the honey and cilantro and process to the consistency you prefer. Season with salt and pepper.

TO ASSEMBLE

Preheat the oven to 450°F (232°C).

1 cup cooked corn kernels

1/2 cup shredded mild
   cheddar cheese

1 1/2 cups shredded
   Monterey Jack cheese

2 cups diced tomatoes

Remove the chicken breasts from the sous vide bag and cut them into 1/2 inch thick strips. Cover the bottom of a baking dish with some of the salsa verde.

Lay out the tortillas and top each one with the chicken, black beans, corn, and cheddar. Roll up the tortillas and place them in the baking dish side by side. Top with the remaining salsa verde and the Monterey Jack. Place in the oven and bake until bubbly and the cheese is melted, 10 to 15 minutes. Remove from the oven, top with the diced tomatoes, and serve.

FRIED CHICKEN

COOKS: **141°F (60.5°C) for 2 to 4 hours** · PREP: **10 minutes** · SERVES: **4**

FOR THE CHICKEN

4 chicken breasts

4 sage leaves

4 lemon slices

Salt and freshly ground black pepper

FOR THE BATTER STATIONS

3 cups all-purpose flour

2 tablespoons garlic powder

2 tablespoons paprika

1 teaspoon chipotle chile powder or cayenne pepper

3 cups buttermilk

Canola oil, for frying

One of the biggest challenges with making fried chicken is ensuring the chicken is cooked through at the same time the crust is done. Using sous vide to cook the chicken ahead of time allows you to focus solely on the crust. These fried chicken breasts are great with fresh corn, mashed potatoes, or even macaroni and cheese.

PREPARE THE CHICKEN

Preheat a water bath to 141°F (60.5°C).

Season the chicken breasts with salt and pepper then place each one in a separate sous vide bag with a sage leaf and a lemon slice. Seal the bags, place them in the water bath, and cook for 2 to 4 hours.

PREPARE THE BATTER STATIONS

Combine the flour, garlic powder, paprika, and chipotle chile powder in a shallow dish and stir to thoroughly combine. Pour the buttermilk into a separate shallow dish. Fill a deep pot with canola oil to a depth of around 3 inches and heat to 365°F to 375°F (185°C to 195°C), or use a deep fryer if you have one. Be sure the oil fills the pot less than halfway since the oil will expand when the chicken breasts are added.

Take the chicken breasts out of the sous vide bags. Dredge each breast one at a time in the flour mixture, then in the buttermilk, and finally again in the flour mixture.

Add one chicken breast at a time slowly into the hot oil and cook it just until the coating is browned and very crunchy. Remove the finished breast from the oil, season it with salt and pepper, and place it on a wire rack to drain. Repeat with the remaining chicken breasts.

TO ASSEMBLE

Serve it with your favorite fried chicken sides.

CHICKEN SATAY

COOKS: **141°F (60.5°C) for 2 to 4 hours** · PREP: **20 minutes** · SERVES: **4**

Chicken Satay is a popular Thai appetizer incorporating a buttery peanut background with some aromatic punch from the chipotle. They are commonly served as an appetizer with a peanut sauce for dipping, but I also like to pair them with a vegetable stir fry and serve them as the main part of a meal.

PREPARE THE CHICKEN

Preheat a water bath to 141°F (60.5°C).

Place all the ingredients, except for the chicken, in a bowl and stir to thoroughly combine. Add the chicken and toss to thoroughly coat. Place the chicken in a sous vide bag then seal the bag. Place the bag in the water bath and cook for 2 to 4 hours.

PREPARE THE PEANUT SAUCE

Whisk together all the peanut sauce ingredients in a bowl until thoroughly combined.

TO ASSEMBLE

Take the chicken breasts out of the sous vide bag and pat them dry. Sear the chicken breasts over high heat until just browned, 1 to 2 minutes per side. Remove the chicken breasts from the heat and serve with the peanut sauce.

FOR THE CHICKEN

1/4 cup soy sauce

1/4 cup fresh lemon juice

2 teaspoons sesame oil

2 tablespoons packed brown sugar

2 cloves garlic, diced

1/2 teaspoon chipotle chile powder

4 chicken breasts, cut into 1-inch slices

FOR THE PEANUT SAUCE

1/4 cup chunky peanut butter

1/2 cup coconut milk

1 tablespoon fish sauce

1 tablespoon packed light-brown sugar

1 tablespoon fresh lime juice

3 teaspoons sriracha or other chile sauce

CAJUN-STYLE CHICKEN

COOKS: **141°F (60.5°C) for 2 to 4 hours** · PREP: **20 minutes** · SERVES: **4**

FOR THE CHICKEN

1 tablespoon paprika

2 teaspoons garlic powder

1½ teaspoons onion powder

1 teaspoon dried thyme

½ teaspoon cayenne pepper, or to taste

½ teaspoon ground bay leaf

¼ teaspoon freshly ground white pepper

4 chicken breasts

Salt and freshly ground black pepper

This is a traditional blackening rub that adds a spicy and flavorful kick to sometimes bland chicken breasts. It is very good when served with traditional sides, such as collard greens, coleslaw, and macaroni salad. Any leftover rub can be stored in a jar or lidded plastic bowl in a cabinet for several months.

PREPARE THE CHICKEN

Preheat a water bath to 141°F (60.5°C).

In a small bowl, combine all the spices. Season the chicken breasts with salt and pepper then coat both sides with the spice mixture. Place the chicken breasts in a sous vide bag then seal the bag. Place the bag into the water bath and cook for 2 to 4 hours.

TO ASSEMBLE

Take the chicken breasts out of the sous vide bag and pat them dry. Sear the chicken breasts over high heat until just browned, 1 to 2 minutes per side. Remove the chicken breasts from the heat and serve.

GREEN CURRY CHICKEN THIGHS

COOKS: **148°F (64.4°C) for 2 to 5 hours** · PREP: **20 minutes** · SERVES: **4**

FOR THE CHICKEN

1 pound chicken thighs, cut
into bite-size pieces

1/2 teaspoon garlic powder

1/2 teaspoon ground cumin

Salt and freshly ground
black pepper

FOR THE GREEN CURRY

1 tablespoon oil

1 onion, chopped

4 cloves garlic, minced

1 teaspoon ground cumin

2 tablespoons green curry
paste

1 1/2 cups coconut milk

2 tablespoons packed
brown sugar

2 carrots, peeled and cut
into 1/2-inch-thick rounds

2 medium potatoes, cubed

1 green bell pepper, diced

1/2 cup cooked corn kernels

1 tablespoon fish sauce

1 tablespoon fresh lime juice

TO ASSEMBLE

1/4 cup coarsely chopped
fresh basil leaves

This green curry has a balance of heat from the curry paste and sweetness from the vegetables, brown sugar, and coconut milk. You can add more or less curry paste to adjust the spicy zip to your personal preferences. I normally serve this with a pile of white rice on the side to absorb a lot of the sauce.

PREPARE THE CHICKEN

Preheat a water bath to 148°F (64.4°C).

Lightly season the chicken thighs with salt and pepper then dust them with the garlic powder and ground cumin. Place the chicken thighs in a sous vide bag then seal the bag. Place the bag in the water bath and cook for 2 to 5 hours.

PREPARE THE GREEN CURRY

In a pan over medium heat, heat the oil until hot. Add the onion, garlic, ground cumin, and curry paste and stir constantly for about 1 minute. Add the coconut milk and brown sugar and gently bring to a simmer. Add the carrots and potatoes and cook until tender. Add the bell pepper and corn then turn down the heat and simmer for 5 minutes. Just before serving, stir in the fish sauce and lime juice.

TO ASSEMBLE

Take the chicken thighs out of the sous vide bag and place the thighs in a serving dish. Pour the curry over the top, garnish with the basil, and serve.

CHICKEN THIGHS with JERK PASTE

COOKS: **148°F (64.4°C) for 2 to 5 hours** · PREP: **30 minutes** · SERVES: **4**

Chicken thighs stand up great to this traditional Jamaican jerk flavoring, but the paste can also be used on breasts or even pork chops or pork shoulder. A side of rice and beans or mashed plantains is a great complement to this dish. Any leftover paste can be stored in the refrigerator for about a week.

PREPARE THE JERK PASTE

Place all the dry ingredients (the first twelve) in a food processor and process to a coarse paste. Add the remaining liquid ingredients and process until the paste becomes spreadable.

PREPARE THE CHICKEN THIGHS

Preheat a water bath to 148°F (64.4°C).

Smear the thighs all over with the jerk paste. Add the thighs to a sous vide bag then seal the bag. Place the bag in the water bath and cook for 2 to 5 hours.

TO ASSEMBLE

Take the thighs out of the sous vide bag and pat them dry. Cook the thighs over high heat until just browned, 1 to 2 minutes per side. Remove the thighs from the heat and serve.

FOR THE JERK PASTE

1 to 3 habanero chiles, stemmed and halved

1 onion, coarsely chopped

4 scallions, trimmed and coarsely chopped

2 cloves garlic, coarsely chopped

1/4 cup coarsely chopped fresh parsley

1/4 cup coarsely chopped fresh cilantro

2 tablespoons packed brown sugar

1 tablespoon fresh thyme

2 teaspoons ground allspice

1 teaspoon coarsely chopped fresh ginger

1/2 teaspoon ground cinnamon

1/2 teaspoon freshly grated nutmeg

2 tablespoons lime juice

2 tablespoons olive oil

2 tablespoons cold water

1 tablespoon soy sauce

FOR THE CHICKEN THIGHS

2 to 3 pounds chicken thigh

ORANGE and MINT CHICKEN LEGS

COOKS: **148°F (64.5°C) for 2 to 5 hours** · PREP: **15 minutes** · SERVES: **4**

These chicken legs have an encompassing combination of sweet, spicy, and minty flavors. The sauce is very easy to make and is poured directly over the chicken thighs before serving. To help the sauce thicken more quickly, you can also add a mixture of equal quantities of cold water and cornstarch to it while it is cooking.

PREPARE THE CHICKEN

Preheat a water bath to 148°F (64.5°C).

In a small bowl, combine the spices. Season the chicken legs with salt and pepper then sprinkle them with the spice mixture. Place the chicken legs in a sous vide bag then seal the bag. Place the bag in the water bath and cook for 2 to 5 hours.

PREPARE THE ORANGE SAUCE

Add the oil and garlic to a pan and heat over medium to medium-high heat. Once it begins to sizzle, add the chipotle powder and orange juice and cook until slightly thickened, 10 to 15 minutes.

TO ASSEMBLE

Take the chicken legs out of the sous vide bag and pat them dry. Sear the chicken legs over high heat until they begin to brown, 1 to 2 minutes per side. Remove from the heat.

To serve, place the chicken legs on plates. Pour on the sauce and top with the chopped mint and basil and serve.

FOR THE CHICKEN

1 teaspoon garlic powder

1 teaspoon ground coriander

1 teaspoon ancho chile powder or your chile powder of choice

1 pound bone-in chicken legs

Salt and freshly ground black pepper

FOR THE ORANGE SAUCE

1 tablespoon olive oil

6 cloves garlic, diced

$1/4$ teaspoon chipotle chile powder or chile powder of your choice

$1^1/_2$ cups orange juice

TO ASSEMBLE

$1/4$ cup chopped fresh mint

$1/4$ cup chopped fresh basil

CHICKEN THIGHS with CURRY-LIME BUTTER

COOKS: **148°F (64.4°C) for 2 to 5 hours** · PREP: **10 minutes** · SERVES: **4**

FOR THE CHICKEN THIGHS

4 to 6 chicken thighs

Salt and freshly ground black pepper

FOR THE CURRY-LIME BUTTER

$1/2$ cup unsalted butter, softened

Zest and juice of 1 lime

1 tablespoon honey

1 tablespoon red curry paste

$1/2$ teaspoon rice wine or apple cider vinegar

$1/2$ teaspoon soy sauce

TO ASSEMBLE

$1/4$ cup chopped fresh cilantro, for garnish

The curry-lime butter adds a rich, complex flavor to the moist and tender chicken thighs. The curry adds some fiery spice while the lime contributes a wonderful brightness that comes through in the final dish. The butter can be made ahead of time and stored in the refrigerator for a few days or in the freezer for a month or two.

PREPARE THE CHICKEN THIGHS

Preheat a water bath to 148°F (64.4°C).

Season the chicken thighs with salt and pepper. Place the thighs in a sous vide bag then seal the bag. Place the bag in the water bath and cook for 2 to 5 hours.

PREPARE THE CURRY-LIME BUTTER

In a large bowl, thoroughly combine the butter, lime zest and juice, honey, red curry paste, vinegar, and soy sauce.

TO ASSEMBLE

Take the thighs out of the sous vide bag and pat them dry. Sear the thighs over high heat until just browned, 1 to 2 minutes per side.

Place a chicken thigh on a plate and place a spoonful of the curry-lime butter on top. Garnish with the cilantro and serve.

ROASTED TOMATO CHICKEN THIGHS

COOKS: **148°F (64.4°C) for 2 to 5 hours** · PREP: **15 minutes** · SERVES: **4**

Salsas are a refreshing, fun way to introduce more flavor to dishes, and roasting the vegetables first adds even more nuances to the salsa. I really like to serve these chicken thighs with sautéed green beans or roasted root vegetables.

PREPARE THE CHICKEN

Preheat a water bath to 148°F (64.4°C).

In a small bowl, combine the spices. Season the chicken thighs with salt and pepper then sprinkle them with the spice mixture. Place the chicken thighs in a sous vide bag then seal the bag. Place the bag in the water bath and cook for 2 to 5 hours.

PREPARE THE ROASTED TOMATO SALSA

Preheat the oven to 400°F (204°C).

Add the onion and tomatoes to a rimmed baking sheet then sprinkle with the thyme and garlic. Cook in the oven until they are softened and begin to brown, 15 to 20 minutes. Remove the baking sheet from the oven and transfer the onion and tomatoes to a bowl with the remaining ingredients. Stir well to combine.

TO ASSEMBLE

Take the thighs out of the sous vide bag and pat them dry. Sear the thighs over high heat until just browned, 1 to 2 minutes per side. Remove the thighs from the heat and serve with the roasted tomato salsa on top.

FOR THE CHICKEN

1 tablespoon garlic powder

1 teaspoon ancho chile powder or chile powder of your choice

6 chicken thighs

Salt and freshly ground black pepper

FOR THE ROASTED TOMATO SALSA

1 yellow onion, diced

5 large tomatoes, roughly chopped

1 tablespoon fresh thyme

5 cloves garlic, diced

2 tablespoons apple cider vinegar

2 tablespoons packed brown sugar

$1/2$ teaspoon chipotle chile powder

DOUBLE-COOKED CHICKEN WINGS

COOKS: **150°F (65.5°C) for 2 to 5 hours** · PREP: **10 minutes** · SERVES: **4 as appetizer**

FOR THE CHICKEN

2 pounds chicken wings

Salt and freshly ground
black pepper

TO ASSEMBLE

Peanut or canola oil, for
deep frying

Your favorite sauces or
coatings

Cooking your chicken wings sous vide helps eliminate most of the guesswork, always resulting in perfectly prepared chicken. The other benefit to having precooked wings is that the frying process is only used to crisp the skin, so frying can be done at a hotter temperature, resulting in a crispier wing.

Here, the wings are cooked at 150°F (65.5°C) for 2 to 5 hours, but anything between 148°F to 156°F (64.4°C to 68.8°C) will result in very tender chicken. For dryer, but even more tender, wings you can cook them at 160°F to 170°F (71°C to 76.6°C) for 4 to 12 hours. After the sous vide process is done you can also chill the wings in an ice bath and store them in the refrigerator or freezer. This allows you to fry the wings just before you need them.

PREPARE THE CHICKEN

Preheat a water bath to 150°F (65.5°C).

If using whole wings, cut them into drumettes and wing flats, discarding the tips. Season the chicken pieces with salt and pepper then place them in a sous vide bag then seal the bag. Place the bag in the water bath and cook for 2 to 5 hours.

Take the wings out of the sous vide bag and pat them dry. Let rest at least one hour.

TO ASSEMBLE

In heavy frying pan, heat the oil to 400°F (204°C). Set up a drying station with a wire rack set over a rimmed baking sheet.

Add the chicken to the oil in batches, being sure not to overcrowd the pan. Cook just until the skin is golden brown and crispy, turning if needed. Remove from the heat and transfer the wings to the rack to drain. Toss with any sauce or coating you are using and serve.

CHICKEN SAUSAGE with TOMATO-BASIL SALSA

COOKS: **141°F (60.5°C) for 2 to 3 hours** · PREP: **10 minutes** · SERVES: **4**

FOR THE SAUSAGE

4 to 6 chicken sausages, about 1 inch in diameter

4 sprigs thyme

FOR THE TOMATO-BASIL SALSA

3 large tomatoes, diced

12 basil leaves, coarsely chopped

1 tablespoon balsamic vinegar

2 tablespoons olive oil

Salt and freshly ground black pepper

Basil, tomato, and chicken are a classic pairing that I like to turn into a hearty meal. The tomato-basil salsa is very quick to prepare but it works best when plump, fresh tomatoes are used, so don't skimp. Since this is such an easy dish, I'll often use other fresh vegetables in the salsa including corn, red onion, and shallots to mix it up. I love these sausages served with some rich polenta or an herby risotto.

PREPARE THE SAUSAGE

Preheat a water bath to 141°F (60.5°C).

Place the sausages in a sous vide bag with the thyme sprigs then seal the bag. Place the bag in the water bath and cook for 2 to 3 hours.

PREPARE THE SALSA

Stir together the tomato, basil, balsamic vinegar, and oil in a bowl. Season with salt and pepper.

TO ASSEMBLE

Take the sausages out of the sous vide bag and pat them dry. Quickly sear the sausages over high heat, 1 to 2 minutes per side.

Serve the chicken sausages whole with the salsa spooned over top.

CHAPTER SEVEN

TURKEY

TURKEY WITH MINT
and PEA PESTO

COOKS: **141°F (60.5°C) for 2 to 4 hours** · PREP: **15 minutes** · SERVES: **4**

FOR THE TURKEY

1/2 teaspoon garlic powder

1/2 teaspoon paprika

1 to 2 pounds turkey breast

Salt and freshly ground
   black pepper

FOR THE PEA PESTO

2 cups frozen peas, thawed

1 cup fresh spinach, packed

1/2 cup pecans

3 cloves garlic, roughly
   chopped

10 mint leaves

1/2 cup olive oil

3 tablespoons grated
   Parmesan cheese

Turkey is often bland and overcooked. Using sous vide keeps it warm and this unusual mint and pea pesto adds just the right amount of flavor to it. Mint and peas go together very well and the turkey is a great way to showcase them. I'll often serve this with a side of roasted potatoes or a vegetable stir fry.

PREPARE THE TURKEY

Preheat a water bath to 141°F (60.5°C).

In a small bowl, combine the spices. Season the turkey with salt and pepper then sprinkle it with the spice mixture. Place the turkey in a sous vide bag then seal the bag. Place the bag in the water bath and cook for 2 to 4 hours.

PREPARE THE PEA PESTO

Place the peas, spinach, pecans, garlic, mint, and 1/4 cup water in a food processor and process until thoroughly combined. Add the oil and process until fully incorporated. Stir in the Parmesan then season with salt and pepper.

TO ASSEMBLE

Take the turkey breast out of the sous vide bag and pat them dry. Sear the turkey breasts over high heat until just browned, 1 to 2 minutes per side.

Serve the turkey with a dollop of pesto on top.

TURKEY with MANGO-JALAPEÑO SLAW

COOKS: **141°F (60.5°C) for 2 to 4 hours** · PREP: **15 minutes** · SERVES: **4**

One great way to pump up the taste of turkey breasts is with flavorful sides. This crunchy coleslaw is a mixture of sweet mango and spicy jalapeño, which adds an often-needed flavor enhancement to the mild turkey, as well as wonderful textures. You can incorporate more or less jalapeño depending on how spicy you like your food.

PREPARE THE TURKEY

Preheat a water bath to 141°F (60.5°C).

In a small bowl, combine the spices. Season the turkey breast with salt and pepper then sprinkle it with the spice mixture. Place the turkey breast in a sous vide bag then seal the bag. Place the bag in the water bath and cook for 2 to 4 hours.

PREPARE THE COLESLAW

Place all the coleslaw ingredients in a bowl and stir well to combine.

TO ASSEMBLE

Take the turkey breast out of the sous vide bag and pat the turkey breast dry. Sear the turkey breast over high heat until just browned, 1 to 2 minutes per side. Remove the turkey breast from the heat and serve with the spicy mango coleslaw.

FOR THE TURKEY

1 teaspoon dried oregano

1 teaspoon ground cumin

1/4 teaspoon chipotle chile powder

1 to 2 pounds turkey breast

Salt and freshly ground black pepper

FOR THE COLESLAW

2 tablespoons olive oil

Juice of 1 lime

1 jalapeño chile, seeded and diced

1/4 red onion, diced

1 cup shredded red cabbage

1 cup shredded green cabbage

1 large mango, peeled and diced

2 tablespoons chopped fresh mint

1 teaspoon ground cinnamon

CREAMY PESTO TURKEY

COOKS: **141°F (60.5°C) for 2 to 4 hours** · PREP: **15 minutes** · SERVES: **4**

FOR THE TURKEY

$1/2$ teaspoon garlic powder

$1/2$ teaspoon dried basil

$1/2$ teaspoon dried oregano

1 to 2 pounds turkey breast

Salt and freshly ground
black pepper

TO ASSEMBLE

5 bacon strips, cut
lengthwise $1/2$ inch wide

$1/4$ cup mayonnaise

$1/4$ cup pesto

$1/2$ pint cherry tomatoes,
halved

This flavorful meal gets a lot of complex flavors from the pesto. It's hearty enough to be served as a main course, especially if you add some romaine or bibb lettuce to bulk it out. The turkey always turns out really moist and the bacon gives it a kick of smoky flavor.

PREPARE THE TURKEY

Preheat a water bath to 141°F (60.5°C).

In a small bowl, combine the spices. Season the turkey breast with salt and pepper then sprinkle it with the spice mixture. Place the turkey breast in a sous vide bag then seal the bag. Place the bag in the water bath and cook for 2 to 4 hours.

TO ASSEMBLE

In a skillet over medium heat, fry the bacon until the fat is rendered and the bacon turns crisp. Transfer the bacon to drain on paper towels.

Whisk together the mayonnaise and pesto in a bowl.

Take the turkey breast out of the sous vide bag and pat the turkey breast dry. Sear the turkey breast over high heat until just browned, 1 to 2 minutes per side. Remove the turkey breast from the heat and cut it into strips.

Place the turkey breast strips on individual serving plates. Divide the mayonnaise mixture evenly among the plates on top of the turkey. Top with the tomatoes and bacon strips and serve.

GREEN TURKEY CURRY

COOKS: 141°F (60.5°C) for 2 to 4 hours · PREP: **15 minutes** · SERVES: **4**

FOR THE TURKEY

$1/2$ teaspoon garlic powder

$1/2$ teaspoon ground cumin

$1/2$ teaspoon ground ginger

1 to 2 pounds turkey breast

Salt and freshly ground black pepper

FOR THE CURRY

1 tablespoon oil

1 onion, chopped

2 carrots, peeled and cut into $1/4$-inch-thick rounds

2 cloves garlic, minced

1 teaspoon ground cumin

2 tablespoons green curry paste

$1^1/2$ cups coconut milk

$1/2$ cup green beans, cut into short pieces

1 tablespoon fish sauce

$1^1/2$ tablespoons fresh lime juice

1 tablespoon honey

TO ASSEMBLE

$1/4$ cup fresh cilantro leaves

I always enjoy the flavor of green curry and making Green Turkey Curry is a very easy way to enjoy it at home. You can always add more curry paste if you want a spicier curry, or even a diced jalapeño. I usually serve this with rice or bread to soak up all the liquid.

PREPARE THE TURKEY

Preheat a water bath to 141°F (60.5°C).

In a small bowl, combine the spices. Season the turkey breast with salt and pepper then sprinkle it with the spice mixture. Place the turkey breast in a sous vide bag then seal the bag. Place the bag in the water bath and cook for 2 to 4 hours.

PREPARE THE CURRY

In a pan over medium heat, heat the oil until hot. Add the onion, carrots, garlic, and cumin and cook until the onion softens and takes on some color. Add the curry paste and stir constantly for about 2 minutes. Add the coconut milk and $1/2$ cup water and bring to a boil. Add the beans then turn down the heat and simmer for 10 minutes.

Just before serving stir in the fish sauce, lime juice, and honey.

TO ASSEMBLE

Take the turkey breast out of the sous vide bag and pat the turkey breast dry. Sear the breast over high heat until just browned, 1 to 2 minutes per side. Remove the breast from the heat and cut into bite-size pieces.

Place the turkey breast pieces in individual bowls. Pour the curry over the top and garnish with the cilantro leaves.

TURKEY and COLESLAW

COOKS: **141°F (60.5°C) for 2 to 4 hours** · PREP: **10 minutes** · SERVES: **4**

This Asian-inspired coleslaw helps add a crisp texture and bold flavors to the turkey. The peas and bell peppers contribute a lot of sweetness, and the vinaigrette is full of umami. This is a favorite meal of mine to serve at summer BBQs when you need something lighter to go with heavier picnic sides like potato salad or macaroni and cheese.

PREPARE THE TURKEY

Preheat a water bath to 141°F (60.5°C).

Season the turkey breast with salt and pepper then sprinkle it with the ground ginger. Place the turkey breast in a sous vide bag then seal the bag. Place the bag in the water bath and cook for 2 to 4 hours.

PREPARE THE COLESLAW

Combine the cabbage, bell pepper, carrots, and snow peas in a large bowl.

PREPARE THE VINAIGRETTE

In a small bowl stir together the lemon juice, vinegar, soy sauce, ginger, and honey. Season with salt and pepper. Let sit for a few minutes. Slowly whisk in the peanut and sesame oils. Pour the vinaigrette over the coleslaw, tasting as you go to adjust the seasoning.

TO ASSEMBLE

Take the turkey breast out of the sous vide bag and pat the turkey breast dry. Sear the breast over high heat until just browned, 1 to 2 minutes per side. Remove the breast from the heat and slice into even slices.

Place the breast slices on individual plates and top with a large spoonful of the coleslaw. Garnish with the sesame seeds and serve.

FOR THE TURKEY

1 to 2 pounds turkey breast

1/2 teaspoon ground ginger

Salt and freshly ground
  black pepper

FOR THE COLESLAW

3 cups red cabbage, thinly
  sliced

1 red bell pepper, thinly
  sliced

2 large carrots, peeled and
  cut into matchsticks

1 cup snow peapods, cut
  into strips

FOR THE VINAIGRETTE

1 1/2 tablespoons fresh
  lemon juice

1 1/2 tablespoons rice wine
  vinegar

1 tablespoon soy sauce

2 tablespoons minced fresh
  ginger

1 tablespoon honey

3 tablespoons peanut oil

1 tablespoon sesame oil

TO ASSEMBLE

2 tablespoons sesame
  seeds, toasted

TURKEY with HERB BUTTER

COOKS: **141°F (60.5°C) for 2 to 4 hours** · PREP: **10 minutes** · SERVES: **4**

FOR THE TURKEY

1 to 2 pounds turkey breast

$1/2$ teaspoon garlic powder

$1/2$ teaspoon dried thyme

Salt and freshly ground black pepper

FOR THE BUTTER

1 stick unsalted butter, softened

1 tablespoon fresh thyme

2 tablespoons chopped fresh basil

$1/2$ tablespoon chopped fresh sage

$1/8$ teaspoon ground black pepper

This butter topping adds some great richness to the normally lean turkey. It also adds a lot of flavor with the herbs. You can serve this turkey with a side of rice and steamed vegetables for a healthy, complete meal.

PREPARE THE TURKEY

Preheat a water bath to 141°F (60.5°C).

Season the turkey breast with salt and pepper. Place the turkey breast in a sous vide bag and add the garlic powder and dried thyme then seal the bag. Place the bag in the water bath and cook for 2 to 4 hours.

PREPARE THE BUTTER

Place all the ingredients in a bowl and mash them together thoroughly using a fork.

TO ASSEMBLE

Take the turkey breast out of the sous vide bag and pat the turkey breast dry. Sear the breast over high heat until just browned, 1 to 2 minutes per side. Place the breast on a plate and place a spoonful or two of the butter on top.

BBQ TURKEY QUESADILLAS

COOKS: **141°F (60.5°C) for 2 to 4 hours** · PREP: **15 minutes** · SERVES: **4**

BBQ turkey is one of my favorite ingredients in quesadillas or on pizza. I add smoky bacon to it to pump up the flavors even more and give it some crunch. For even more flavor, you can caramelize the onion before adding it to the quesadilla.

Note: Usually turkey is best when cooked for 2 to 4 hours, but during the week you can get away with cooking it for up to 12 hours with just a minimal loss of moisture.

PREPARE THE TURKEY

Preheat a water bath to 141°F (60.5°C).

In a small bowl, combine the spices. Season the turkey breast with salt and pepper then sprinkle it with the spice mixture. Place the turkey breast in a sous vide bag then seal the bag. Place the bag in the water bath and cook for 2 to 4 hours.

TO ASSEMBLE

Take the turkey breast out of the sous vide bag and pat the turkey breast dry. Sear the breast over high heat until just browned, 1 to 2 minutes per side. Remove the turkey breast from the heat and cut into $1/2$-inch strips.

Lay out four of the tortillas and evenly divide the turkey and other ingredients among them. Top each with a remaining tortilla.

Brush the top of each tortilla with oil and place it, oil side down, on the grill or in the pan. Cover the tortilla while it is cooking. Once it turns golden brown on the bottom turn it and continue cooking until the cheese is melted and the quesadilla is browned on both sides.

Remove from the heat, cut into quarters, and serve.

FOR THE TURKEY

1 teaspoon garlic powder

$1/2$ teaspoon paprika

$1/2$ teaspoon ground cumin

$1/2$ teaspoon ground coriander

$1/2$ teaspoon ancho chile powder

1 to 2 pounds turkey breast

Salt and freshly ground black pepper

TO ASSEMBLE

8 flour tortillas

2 cups shredded Monterey Jack cheese

1 cup shredded cheddar cheese

1 sweet onion, thinly sliced

6 strips bacon, cooked and crumbled

BBQ Sauce, to taste

Canola or olive oil

SPICY TURKEY BREAST
with AVOCADO SALAD

COOKS: **141°F (60.5°C) for 2 to 4 hours** · PREP: **15 minutes** · SERVES: **4**

FOR THE TURKEY

1 teaspoon garlic powder

1 teaspoon chipotle chile powder or chile powder of your choice

1 teaspoon paprika

1 to 2 pounds turkey breast

Salt and freshly ground black pepper

FOR THE VINAIGRETTE

2 tablespoons fresh lemon juice

1 garlic clove, minced

$1/3$ cup olive oil

TO ASSEMBLE

7 cups arugula or baby spinach

1 avocado, sliced

Parmigiano-Reggiano cheese, for shaving

I really enjoy turkey for a light dinner, and it goes well with this avocado and arugula salad from *Beginning Sous Vide*. Here, I add some spice to the turkey in the form of chipotle chile powder, which is a great way to kick up the heat and flavor without overpowering the turkey.

PREPARE THE TURKEY

Preheat a water bath to 141°F (60.5°C).

In a small bowl, combine the spices. Season the turkey breast with salt and pepper then sprinkle it with the spice mixture. Place the turkey breast in a sous vide bag then seal the bag. Place the bag in the water bath and cook for 2 to 4 hours.

PREPARE THE VINAIGRETTE

Combine the lemon juice and garlic in a bowl, season with salt and pepper, and let sit for a few minutes. Slowly whisk in the oil until the mixture thickens.

TO ASSEMBLE

Take the turkey breast out of the sous vide bag and pat the turkey breast dry. Sear the breast over high heat until just browned, 1 to 2 minutes per side. Remove the breast from the heat and cut into strips.

Place the arugula in a serving bowl and add enough vinaigrette to flavor it, tossing to coat. Top the arugula with the avocado slices and turkey. Spoon a bit more vinaigrette over them and season with salt and pepper. Using a vegetable peeler, shave strips of Parmesan over the top, and serve.

PENANG TURKEY CURRY

COOKS: **148°F (64.4°C) for 4 to 8 hours** · PREP: **15 minutes** · SERVES: **4**

FOR THE TURKEY

1 pound turkey legs and thighs, cut in bite-size pieces

Salt and freshly ground black pepper

FOR THE CURRY

1 tablespoon oil

1 large onion, chopped

2 tablespoons Panang curry paste

1 cup coconut milk

1/4 cup heavy cream

2 tablespoons fresh lime juice

1 tablespoon fish sauce

1 tablespoon packed brown sugar

TO ASSEMBLE

1/2 cup roasted peanuts, chopped

1/2 cup chopped fresh basil leaves

1 cup chopped fresh pineapple

This is a salty, creamy, and nutty curry that really complements turkey. If you want more heat you can always add cayenne or hot sauce. It's best when served with rice or bread to soak up the flavors. You can also use green or red curry paste if you cannot find the Penang curry.

PREPARE THE TURKEY

Preheat a water bath to 148°F (64.4°C).

Season the turkey with salt and pepper and place it in a sous vide bag then seal the bag. Place the bag in the water bath and cook for 4 to 8 hours.

PREPARE THE CURRY

About 20 minutes before the turkey is done, begin the curry.

In a skillet over medium heat, heat the oil until hot. Add the onion and curry paste and stir for 3 minutes. Add the coconut milk and bring to a simmer. Reduce the heat and cook for 15 minutes, until it is reduced and thick.

Take the turkey out of the sous vide bag and set it aside. Add some of the juices from the bag to the pan and simmer for 5 more minutes. Add the cream, lime juice, fish sauce, and brown sugar then stir well to combine. Remove from the heat.

TO ASSEMBLE

Stir the turkey, peanuts, basil, and pineapple into the curry. Serve the curry with rice or crusty bread on the side.

CAPRESE SALAD with TURKEY SAUSAGE

COOKS: **141°F (60.5°C) for 2 to 3 hours** · PREP: **15 minutes** · SERVES: **4**

Caprese salad is light but satisfying. It is particularly flavorful when you can take advantage of the fresh tomatoes that show up at the farmers market. The tomatoes are so delicious there that I keep going back to it with regularity. In Caprese Salad with Turkey Sausage, I like to pair the tomatoes with turkey sausages for an unpretentious but filling meal that is especially great during the hot days of summer.

PREPARE THE SAUSAGE

Preheat a water bath to 141°F (60.5°C).

Place the sausages in a sous vide bag with the sage leaves then seal the bag. Place the bag in the water bath and cook for 2 to 3 hours.

TO ASSEMBLE

Take the sausages out of the sous vide bag and pat them dry. Sear the sausages over high heat until just browned, 1 to 2 minutes per side. Remove the sausages from the heat and cut into $1/4$-inch-thick slices.

Lay several tomato slices out on plates, place a slice of mozzarella on each one, then a slice or two of turkey sausage. Drizzle some oil and balsamic vinegar on top. Season with salt and pepper then sprinkle the basil over the top and serve.

FOR THE SAUSAGE

1 to 2 pounds turkey sausage links

4 sage leaves

TO ASSEMBLE

2 to 4 tomatoes, cut into $1/4$-inch- to $1/2$-inch-thick slices

1 or 2 balls mozzarella, cut into $1/4$-inch- to $1/2$-inch-thick slices

High-quality olive oil, such as extra virgin

High-quality balsamic vinegar, such as well-aged

1 bunch basil, 10 to 14 leaves, cut into thin strips

Salt and freshly ground black pepper

TURKEY with CRANBERRY BBQ SAUCE

COOKS: **148°F (64.4°C) for 2 to 12 hours** · PREP: **10 minutes** · SERVES: **4**

FOR THE TURKEY

1 to 2 pounds turkey legs and thighs

1 teaspoon garlic powder

4 sprigs thyme

Salt and freshly ground black pepper

FOR THE BBQ SAUCE

1 cup ketchup

$1/2$ cup cranberry sauce

$1/4$ cup apple cider vinegar

3 tablespoons Worcestershire sauce

2 tablespoons yellow mustard

2 tablespoons molasses

2 tablespoons packed brown sugar

1 tablespoon onion powder

$1/2$ teaspoon mustard powder

Turkey is a classic Thanksgiving food but sometimes you don't want to wait until the holiday to enjoy it. This is a family staple anytime that pairs the turkey with a sweet and sour cranberry BBQ sauce. It's especially satisfying when served with a chunky stuffing or mashed potatoes. The BBQ sauce can also be made ahead of time and stored in the refrigerator for later use.

PREPARE THE TURKEY

Preheat a water bath to 148°F (64.4°C).

Season the turkey with salt and pepper then sprinkle it with the garlic powder. Place the turkey in a sous vide bag with the thyme sprigs then seal the bag. Place the bag in the water bath and cook for 2 to 12 hours.

PREPARE THE BBQ SAUCE

Place all the BBQ sauce ingredients in a saucepan over medium-high heat and bring to a boil, stirring regularly to ensure all the ingredients are well blended. Reduce the heat and simmer, stirring regularly, for around 20 minutes, or until thickened.

TO ASSEMBLE

Take the turkey out of the sous vide bag and pat the turkey dry. Sear the turkey over high heat until just browned, 1 to 2 minutes per side. Place the turkey on a plate and place a spoonful or two of the BBQ sauce on top.

CHAPTER EIGHT

DUCK

ORANGE DUCK BREAST
with BERRY SALAD

COOKS: **131°F (55°C) for 2 to 4 hours** · PREP: **10 minutes** · SERVES: **4**

FOR THE DUCK

$^1/_2$ teaspoon garlic powder

$^1/_2$ teaspoon ground
coriander

2 duck breasts

Salt and freshly ground
black pepper

FOR THE ORANGE VINAIGRETTE

1 cup orange juice

$^1/_2$ teaspoon mustard

2 tablespoons red wine
vinegar

1 tablespoon honey

$^1/_2$ cup olive oil

TO ASSEMBLE

Mixed greens

1 sweet red bell pepper,
sliced

$^1/_2$ pint fresh raspberries or
blackberries

$^1/_2$ cup pecans

Hearty duck breast is complemented by a light and citrusy salad. The acid in the orange juice helps to cut the richness of the duck breast, and the berries and bell pepper add bursts of sweetness.

I prefer my duck breast medium rare, so I usually cook it at 131°F (55°C) until it is heated through or pasteurized, 2 to 4 hours. For a breast cooked to medium you can go up to 141°F (60.5°C).

PREPARE THE DUCK

Preheat a water bath to 131°F (55°C).

In a small bowl, combine the spices. Season the duck breasts with salt and pepper then sprinkle them with the spice mixture. Place the duck breasts in a sous vide bag then seal the bag. Place the bag in the water bath and cook for 2 to 4 hours.

PREPARE THE VINAIGRETTE

In a bowl, stir together the orange juice, mustard, vinegar, and honey then whisk in the oil until thoroughly combined. Season with salt and pepper.

TO ASSEMBLE

Take the duck breasts out of the sous vide bag and pat them dry. Lightly salt the outside of the duck breasts then quickly sear them until the outside has browned and the fat has begun to render. Cut the duck into slices.

To serve, place the mixed greens in individual bowls or on plates. Top with the bell pepper and berries. Add the duck slices and spoon the vinaigrette on top. Add the pecans and serve.

SPICY DUCK FRIED RICE

COOKS: **131°F (55°C) for 2 to 4 hours** · PREP: **15 minutes** · SERVES: **4**

FOR THE DUCK

1 teaspoon Chinese five-spice powder

$^1/_2$ teaspoon garlic powder

$^1/_4$ teaspoon cayenne pepper

2 duck breasts

Salt and freshly ground black pepper

FOR THE FRIED RICE

2 tablespoons canola oil

1 leek, rinsed and cut into thin slices

3 carrots, julienned or thinly sliced

1 hot red chile, thinly sliced

1 tablespoon grated fresh ginger

$2^1/_2$ cups cooked long-grain rice

1 cup diced fresh pineapple

$^1/_2$ cup cooked corn kernels

2 tablespoons soy sauce

1 tablespoon sherry vinegar

$^1/_2$ cup chicken stock

Fried rice adds a delicious base on which to enjoy this Asian-inspired duck. You can also add more vegetables, such as broccoli, peas, or bok choy.

PREPARE THE DUCK BREAST

Preheat a water bath to 131°F (55°C).

In a small bowl, combine the spices. Season the duck breasts with salt and pepper then sprinkle them with the spice mixture. Place the duck breasts in a sous vide bag then seal the bag. Place the bag in the water bath and cook for 2 to 4 hours.

PREPARE THE FRIED RICE

In a pan over medium heat, heat the oil until hot. Add the leek and carrots and cook for 10 to 15 minutes, or until the carrots begin to soften. Add the chile and ginger then cook for 1 to 2 minutes.

Add the rice and cook until it begins to crisp up. Stir in the pineapple, corn, soy sauce, sherry vinegar, and stock then warm thoroughly and reduce any liquids. Remove from the heat.

TO ASSEMBLE

Sesame seeds

Scallions, chopped

Peanuts, chopped

TO ASSEMBLE

Take the duck breasts out of the sous vide bag and pat them dry. Lightly salt the outside of the duck breasts then quickly sear them until the outside has browned and the fat has begun to render. Cut the duck into slices.

Place a spoonful of the rice onto a plate or in a bowl. Lay several strips of duck on top of each pile of rice, sprinkle with the sesame seeds, scallions, and peanuts, and serve.

SPICY DUCK with CUCUMBER SALAD

COOKS: **131°F (55°C) for 2 to 4 hours** · PREP: **15 minutes** · SERVES: **4**

FOR THE DUCK

$^1/_2$ teaspoon ground cumin

$^1/_2$ teaspoon ancho chile powder

$^1/_4$ teaspoon chipotle chile powder

2 duck breasts

4 sprigs rosemary

Salt and freshly ground black pepper

FOR THE CUCUMBER SALAD

1 cucumber, seeded and diced

2 tomatoes, diced

$^1/_4$ red onion, thinly sliced

$^1/_4$ cup finely chopped fresh mint leaves

$^1/_4$ cup plain whole yogurt

1 tablespoon fresh lemon juice

I'm a big fan of using two types of chile powder to add a base level of spiciness to Spicy Duck with Cucumber Salad. The richness of the duck holds up well to the peppery seasonings, which are ultimately cooled by the cucumbers and yogurt. The cucumber salad also adds a much-needed crunchy texture.

PREPARE THE DUCK

Preheat a water bath to 131°F (55°C).

In a small bowl, combine the spices. Season the duck breasts with salt and pepper then sprinkle them with the spice mixture. Place the duck breasts in a sous vide bag with the rosemary sprigs then seal the bag. Place the bag in the water bath and cook for 2 to 4 hours.

PREPARE THE CUCUMBER SALAD

In a large bowl, stir together all the ingredients until thoroughly combined.

TO ASSEMBLE

Take the duck breasts out of the sous vide bag and pat them dry. Lightly salt the outside of the duck breasts then quickly sear them until the outside has browned and the fat has begun to render. Cut the duck breasts into slices. Serve with the cucumber salad on the side.

HOT and SMOKY DUCK LEGS

COOKS: **156°F (68.9°C) for 6 to 12 hours** · PREP: **30 minutes** · SERVES: **4**

Rich duck legs hold up well to bolder flavors, and here I pair chipotle chiles with citrus juices to complement them. You can add more or less chipotle chiles to your desired heat level. These duck legs are great with a kale salad, rice pilaf, or a vegetable stir fry.

PREPARE THE MARINADE

Put the tomatoes, onion, and garlic on a rimmed baking sheet. Cook in an oven at 400°F (204°C) until the onions soften, 15 to 30 minutes. Set aside to cool.

Place the roasted vegetables and the remaining marinade ingredients in a blender and blend into a thick puree.

PREPARE THE DUCK

Preheat a water bath to 156°F (68.9°C).

Season the duck legs with salt and pepper then place them in a sous vide bag. Pour half the marinade into the bag then seal the bag. Reserve the rest of the marinade in the refrigerator. Place the bag in the water bath and cook for 6 to 12 hours.

TO ASSEMBLE

Take the duck legs out of the sous vide bag and pat them dry. Sear the duck legs over high heat in a pan or on a grill until just browned, 1 to 2 minutes. Serve with a spoonful of the reserved marinade on top.

FOR THE MARINADE

3 Roma tomatoes

1/2 onion, coarsely chopped

4 cloves garlic, peeled

1/2 cup fresh lime juice

3 tablespoons orange juice

2 tablespoons apple cider or red wine vinegar

3 canned chipotle chiles in adobo sauce

1 teaspoon dried oregano

1/2 teaspoon ground cumin

1/2 teaspoon ground coriander

FOR THE DUCK

2 pounds of duck legs

Salt and freshly ground black pepper

FIVE-SPICE DUCK

COOKS: **131°F (55°C) for 2 to 4 hours** · PREP: **20 minutes** · SERVES: **4**

FOR THE DUCK

3 whole star anise

2 cinnamon sticks

3 tablespoons Sichuan peppercorns

2 tablespoons fennel seeds

1 teaspoon whole cloves

2 duck breasts

Salt and freshly ground black pepper

Five-Spice Duck calls for freshly toasted and ground spices, which add a lot more depth and character than using preground spices. However, if you don't have the time or inclination to toast and grind your own spices, the dish is still excellent with the pre-ground spices, or even a premixed Chinese five-spice powder with some extra fennel seeds added.

I really like to serve this with roasted or stir-fried vegetables in a grain bowl.

PREPARE THE DUCK

Heat the water bath to 131°F (55°C).

In a pan over medium-low heat add the spices and toast for 3 to 5 minutes, or until they become fragrant. Remove from the heat and, once cooled, grind them in a spice grinder.

Season the duck breasts with salt and pepper then sprinkle them with the spice mixture. Place the duck breasts in a sous vide bag then seal the bag. Place the bag in the water bath to cook for 2 to 4 hours.

TO ASSEMBLE

Take the duck breasts out of the sous vide bag and pat them dry. Lightly salt the outside of the duck breast then quickly sear them until the outside has browned and the fat has begun to render. Cut the duck into slices and serve.

SHREDDED DUCK FRIED RICE

COOKS: **167°F (75°C) for 16 to 24 hours** · PREP: **15 minutes** · SERVES: **4**

Fried rice is a staple at Asian restaurants and making it at home is a pretty easy task. Here we pair it with shredded duck legs flavored with sweet spices for added flavor. The result is a very hearty dish that is full of flavor and really satisfying after a long day.

PREPARE THE DUCK

Preheat a water bath to 167°F (75°C).

In a small bowl, combine the spices. Season the duck legs with salt and pepper then sprinkle them with the spice mixture. Place the duck legs in a sous vide bag then seal the bag. Place the bag in the water bath and cook for 16 to 24 hours.

PREPARE THE FRIED RICE

Heat a pan over medium–high heat.

Add the oil to a pan. When the oil is hot, add the onion and carrots and cook for 10 to 15 minutes, or until the carrots begin to soften. Add the garlic, jalapeño, and ginger and cook for 1 to 2 minutes. Remove the vegetables from the pan and set aside.

Add the egg to the pan and scramble it, 1 to 2 minutes. Remove the egg then add the rice and cook until it just begins to get crispy. Stir in the remaining fried rice ingredients and let the liquid reduce, if needed. Remove from the heat.

TO ASSEMBLE

Take the duck legs out of the sous vide bag and pat them dry. Sear the duck legs in a hot pan until crispy. Remove the meat from the bones and shred.

Place a spoonful of the rice in a bowl. Lay some duck on top, sprinkle with the parsley, and serve.

FOR THE DUCK

1 teaspoon ground cinnamon

1/2 teaspoon cloves

1/2 teaspoon fennel seeds

1/2 teaspoon allspice

4 to 6 duck legs

Salt and freshly ground black pepper

FOR THE FRIED RICE

2 tablespoons canola oil

1 sweet onion, diced

3 carrots, diced

4 cloves garlic, diced

1 jalapeño chile, seeded and diced

1 tablespoon grated fresh ginger

1 egg

2 cups cooked long-grain rice

1/2 cup cooked corn kernels

1/2 cup cooked peas

2 tablespoons soy sauce

1 tablespoon rice vinegar

1/4 cup chicken stock

TO ASSEMBLE

1/4 cup chopped fresh parsley

DUCK SAUSAGE with ALMONDS and APRICOTS

COOKS: **131°F (55°C) for 2 to 3 hours** · PREP: **10 minutes** · SERVES: **4**

FOR THE SAUSAGES

4 to 8 duck sausages, about 1 inch in diameter

4 sage leaves

FOR THE SALAD

1 cup packed spinach

$1/2$ cup sliced almonds

$1/2$ cup dried apricots, diced

$1/2$ cup diced apple

1 tablespoon honey

1 teaspoon apple cider vinegar

1 tablespoon olive oil

Salt and freshly ground black pepper

Rich duck sausage pairs great with a salad of almonds, apricots, and apple. The salad adds a depth of flavor and many different textures. We also mix in some spinach for body and honey and vinegar to round out the flavors. It's very fast to put together and results in a satisfying meal.

PREPARE THE SAUSAGE

Preheat a water bath to 131°F (55°C).

Place the sausages and sage in a sous vide bag and seal the bag. Place the bag in the water bath and cook for 2 to 3 hours.

PREPARE THE SALAD

In a large bowl, toss together the spinach, almonds, apricots, apple, honey, vinegar, and oil until thoroughly combined. Season with salt and pepper.

TO ASSEMBLE

Take the sausages out of the sous vide bag and pat them dry. Quickly sear the sausages over high heat until just browned, 1 to 2 minutes per side.

Place some salad on a plate and top with the sausages and serve.

CHAPTER NINE

FISH and SHELLFISH

CATFISH TOSTADAS

COOKS: **130°F (54.4°C) for 15 to 45 minutes** · PREP: **10 minutes** · SERVES: **4**

FOR THE FISH

$1/2$ teaspoon garlic powder

$1/2$ teaspoon ground cumin

$1/2$ teaspoon ground coriander

1 pound catfish fillets

Salt and freshly ground black pepper

FOR THE SALSA

1 avocado, diced

1 mango, diced

1 jalapeño chile, seeded and diced

$1/2$ cucumber, diced

$1/4$ red onion, diced

2 tablespoons fresh lime juice

2 tablespoons olive oil

2 tablespoons chopped fresh basil

2 tablespoons chopped fresh oregano

TO ASSEMBLE

Oil, for frying (optional)

4 flour tortillas

Shredded Monterey Jack cheese

I love the crunch of tostadas paired with the flakiness of fish. Frying the tortilla shells doesn't add too much to the cooking time and can be done while the fish cooks. To test if the oil is hot enough, I usually have a spare tortilla around that I can rip pieces off of and add to the oil; they should puff and turn brown pretty quickly. But if you don't want to take the additional time to fry the tortillas, you can always use them as they are.

PREPARE THE FISH

Preheat a water bath to 130°F (54.4°C).

In a small bowl, combine the spices. Season the catfish fillets with salt and pepper then sprinkle them with the spice mixture. Place the fillets in a sous vide bag then seal the bag. Let the fish sit for 30 minutes for the dry brine to take effect then place the bag in the water bath and cook for 15 to 45 minutes.

PREPARE THE SALSA

Place all the ingredients in a bowl and stir to thoroughly combine.

TO ASSEMBLE

If frying the tortillas, take a pan large enough to fit one of the tortillas and add the oil to a depth of about a $1/2$ inch. Heat the oil over medium to medium-high heat until hot. Place one tortilla at a time in the pan and cook until golden brown. Transfer the tortilla to a paper towel or wire rack to drain. Repeat with the remaining tortillas.

Take the catfish out of the sous vide bag and pat it dry. Serve it on the tortillas topped with the salsa and cheese.

COD CHOWDER

COOKS: **130°F (54.4°C) for 15 to 45 minutes** · PREP: **15 minutes** · SERVES: **4**

I like a good thick chowder, especially when it has tender seafood in it. Here I use some liquid smoke and paprika to flavor the cod while it's cooking. The chowder itself is a simple mixture of aromatics, milk, and fish stock. You can add more or less flour or fish stock to control the thickness of the chowder. For an even richer chowder, you can substitute some of the milk with heavy cream.

PREPARE THE COD

Preheat a water bath to 130°F (54.4°C).

Brush the liquid smoke on the cod then lightly coat with salt and pepper. Sprinkle with the garlic powder and paprika. Place in the sous vide bag and seal. Let the fish sit for 30 minutes for the dry brine to take effect then place in the water bath and cook for 15 to 45 minutes.

PREPARE THE CHOWDER

Preheat a pot to medium-high heat.

Whisk the flour into the cold water.

Put the bacon in the pot and cook until the fat is rendered and it begins to crisp up. Remove the bacon and set aside, discarding all but 1 tablespoon of bacon fat. Add the potato, onion, carrot, and garlic to the pot and cook until the potato begins to turn tender. Add the mustard and Worcestershire sauce then stir well. Slowly whisk in the milk and the fish stock. Bring to a simmer then slowly mix in the flour-water mixture until it is the consistency you prefer.

TO ASSEMBLE

Remove the cod from the water bath and cut into portions. Spoon the soup into bowls and top with the cod, the reserved bacon, and the parsley.

FOR THE COD

$1/2$ teaspoon liquid smoke

1 pound cod

$1/2$ teaspoon garlic powder

$1/2$ teaspoon paprika

Salt and freshly ground black pepper

FOR THE CHOWDER

3 tablespoons all-purpose flour

3 tablespoons cold water

4 strips bacon, diced

1 red potato, diced

1 yellow onion, diced

1 carrot, peeled and diced

3 cloves garlic, coarsely chopped

1 teaspoon yellow mustard

$1/2$ teaspoon Worcestershire sauce

1 cup whole milk

3 cups fish stock

TO ASSEMBLE

3 tablespoons chopped fresh parsley

FLOUNDER with PEPPER and BEAN SALAD

COOKS: **130°F (54.4°C) for 15 to 45 minutes** · Prep:**10 minutes** · SERVES: **4**

FOR THE FISH

4 flounder portions

$1/2$ teaspoon ground cumin

2 tablespoons unsalted butter or olive oil

2 sprigs rosemary

Salt and freshly ground black pepper

FOR THE SALAD

Canola oil, for frying

$1/4$ cup red onion, finely diced

1 orange or red bell pepper, diced

1 poblano pepper, diced

2 cups corn kernels

1 (15-ounce) can black beans, drained and washed

1 (15-ounce) can pinto beans, drained and washed

$1/4$ cup chopped fresh cilantro

Flounder can sometimes be a bland fish so I try to spice it up here with a hearty bean salad with a spicy vinaigrette. I recommend ancho chile powder and poblano peppers but you can use any type of chile powder or hot pepper that you prefer and have on hand.

PREPARE THE FISH

Preheat a water bath to 130°F (54.4°C).

Season the flounder with salt and pepper then sprinkle it with the cumin. Place the flounder in a sous vide bag with the butter and rosemary sprigs then seal the bag. Let the fish sit for 30 minutes for the dry brine to take effect then place the bag in the water bath and cook for 15 to 45 minutes.

PREPARE THE SALAD

In a pan over medium to medium-high heat, heat the oil until hot. Add the red onion and cook until it begins to soften. Add the bell pepper and poblano pepper and cook until they are just tender. Stir in the corn and black and pinto beans and warm through. Remove from the heat and stir in the cilantro.

PREPARE THE VINAIGRETTE

Prepare the vinaigrette in a small bowl by combining the spices and lime juice. Season with salt and pepper. Slowly whisk in the oil. Add enough vinaigrette to the salad to thoroughly coat it.

FOR THE VINAIGRETTE

$1/2$ teaspoon ground cumin

$1/2$ teaspoon ancho chile powder

$1/8$ teaspoon cayenne pepper

3 tablespoons fresh lime juice

5 tablespoons olive oil

TO ASSEMBLE

Take the flounder out of the sous vide bag and pat the flounder dry. Sear one side over high heat just until browned, 1 to 2 minutes. Remove from the heat.

On each plate put a spoonful of the salad with the cod, seared side up, resting on the top and serve.

MOROCCAN GROUPER with GARBANZO BEANS

COOKS: **130°F (54.4°C) for 15 to 45 minutes** · PREP: **15 minutes** · SERVES: **4**

FOR THE FISH

1/2 teaspoon paprika

1/2 teaspoon ground ginger

1/2 teaspoon ground cumin

1/8 teaspoon turmeric

4 grouper fillets, cleaned

2 tablespoons unsalted butter or olive oil

Salt and freshly ground black pepper

FOR THE GARBANZO BEAN SALAD

1 can garbanzo beans, rinsed and drained

1/2 red bell pepper, diced

4 cloves garlic, minced

1 tablespoon ground cumin

1 tablespoon olive oil

1/4 teaspoon cayenne pepper or ground chile of your choice

This dish combines many of the flavors of traditional Moroccan cuisine into a rub for the grouper. I tend not to sear the fish before serving it, but if you want some extra flavor and texture you can sear it. The garbanzo beans add bursts of flavor and texture without overpowering the grouper.

PREPARE THE FISH

Preheat a water bath to 130°F (54.4°C).

In a small bowl, combine the spices. Season the grouper with salt and pepper then sprinkle them with the spice mixture. Place the grouper in a sous vide bag with the butter then seal the bag. Let the fish sit for 30 minutes for the dry brine to take effect then place the bag in the water bath and cook for 15 to 45 minutes.

PREPARE THE GARBANZO BEAN SALAD

In a large bowl, stir together all the ingredients until thoroughly combined.

TO ASSEMBLE

Take the grouper out of the sous vide bag and pat the grouper dry. Place some garbanzo bean salad on each plate and top with the grouper.

HALIBUT WITH TOMATOES and OLIVES

COOKS: **130°F (54.4°C) for 15 to 45 minutes** · PREP: **10 minutes** · SERVES: **4**

Adding a vinaigrette to a dish is an easy way to introduce additional flavors without overpowering the fish. Here, I use a mild vinaigrette in addition to tomatoes and olives to add depth of flavor. This dish is great when served over risotto, with creamy polenta, or mashed potatoes.

PREPARE THE FISH

Preheat a water bath to 130°F (54.4°C).

Season the halibut with salt and pepper then place it in a sous vide bag with the butter then seal the bag. Let the fish sit for 30 minutes for the dry brine to take effect then place the bag in the water bath and cook for 15 to 45 minutes.

PREPARE THE VINAIGRETTE

In a small bowl, combine the vinegar, lemon juice, and garlic. Season with salt and pepper. Slowly whisk in the oil.

TO ASSEMBLE

Take the halibut out of the sous vide bag and place the halibut on a plate, preferably with risotto or creamy polenta. Top with the tomato and olives. Spoon the vinaigrette over the top, sprinkle with the parsley and pine nuts, and serve.

FOR THE FISH

4 halibut portions

2 tablespoons unsalted butter or olive oil

Salt and freshly ground black pepper

FOR THE VINAIGRETTE

1 tablespoon red wine vinegar

1 tablespoon fresh lemon juice

1/2 teaspoon minced garlic

1/3 cup olive oil

TO ASSEMBLE

1/2 cup cherry tomatoes, halved

3 tablespoons olives, preferably Kalamata, pitted and coarsely chopped

1 tablespoon chopped fresh parsley

2 tablespoons pine nuts, toasted

HADDOCK with HERB VINAIGRETTE

COOKS: **130°F (54.4°C) for 15 to 45 minutes** · PREP: **10 minutes** · SERVES: **4**

FOR THE FISH

1½ pounds haddock, cut into 4 portions

1 tablespoon unsalted butter

Salt and freshly ground black pepper

FOR THE VINAIGRETTE

2 tablespoons white wine vinegar

½ tablespoon shallot, minced

1 clove garlic, minced

6 tablespoons olive oil

¼ cup chopped fresh basil

¼ cup chopped fresh parsley

An elegant vinaigrette dressing highlights the flavor of haddock. For variations in taste, you can also play around with the herbs in the vinaigrette, mixing and matching to your flavor preferences. Combined with steamed vegetables, this dish makes a light but satisfying meal.

PREPARE THE FISH

Preheat a water bath to 130°F (54.4°C).

Season the fish with salt and pepper then place it in a sous vide bag with the butter then seal the bag. Let the fish sit for 30 minutes for the dry brine to take effect then place the bag in the water bath and cook for 15 to 45 minutes.

PREPARE THE VINAIGRETTE

In a small bowl, combine the vinegar, shallot, and garlic. Season with salt and pepper. Let sit for 5 minutes then slowly whisk in the oil then stir in the herbs.

TO ASSEMBLE

Take the haddock out of the sous vide bag and pat the haddock dry. Sear one side over high heat just until browned, 1 to 2 minutes. Remove from the heat.

Serve the haddock with the vinaigrette spooned over it.

LOBSTER TAILS

COOKS: **131°F (55°C) for 20 to 40 minutes** · PREP: **20 minutes** · SERVES: **4**

Lobster cooked sous vide is tender and succulent and is showcased with a simple tomato and corn salad. I prefer my lobster cooked at 131°F (55°C), but 140°F (60°C) will give you a more traditional texture. For a much softer texture you can drop the temperature lower.

To remove the lobster from the shell, you can either cut the shell off with kitchen shears or boil the lobster for 1 to 2 minutes and chill it in an ice bath.

I usually serve this with traditional lobster dinner sides of corn on the cob and clam chowder. When I want to be fancy, I'll pair it with a simple salad of tomatoes, corn, and avocado.

PREPARE THE LOBSTER

Preheat a water bath to 131°F (55°C).

Place the lobster meat, butter, and the basil leaves in a sous vide bag. Season with salt and pepper then seal the bag. Place the bag in the water bath and cook for 20 to 40 minutes.

TO ASSEMBLE

Take the lobster out of the sous vide bag and place it on plates. Pour the juices from the sous vide bag into ramekins or dipping dishes. Squeeze some lemon over the top, sprinkle with the sea salt, and serve.

FOR THE LOBSTER

4 lobster tails, shells removed

4 tablespoons unsalted butter

8 basil leaves

Salt and freshly ground black pepper

TO ASSEMBLE

1 lemon, cut into 8 wedges

Sea salt

MACKEREL FILLETS
with CORN SALAD

COOKS: **130°F (54.4°C) for 15 to 45 minutes** · PREP: **20 minutes** · SERVES: **4**

FOR THE MACKEREL

1/2 teaspoon garlic powder

1/2 teaspoon onion powder

1/2 teaspoon paprika

1/4 teaspoon cayenne pepper, or more to taste

4 mackerel portions

Salt and freshly ground black pepper

FOR THE CORN SALAD

2 cups cooked corn kernels

1 red bell pepper, diced

Olive oil

1/2 pint cherry tomatoes, halved

2 tablespoons chopped fresh basil

FOR THE DRESSING

2 tablespoons fresh lime juice

1 teaspoon ancho chile powder

2 tablespoons olive oil

TO ASSEMBLE

1 lime, quartered, for garnish

1 tablespoon chopped fresh basil, for garnish

Mackerel is a full-flavored fish that can stand up to bolder ingredients. Here, I pair it with a corn salad and a lime vinaigrette laced with moderate heat. For a spicier dish, you can add sliced serrano or jalapeños to the dressing. For extra grilled flavor, you can half the lime and grill it for a few minutes until it caramelizes slightly.

PREPARE THE MACKEREL

Preheat a water bath to 130°F (54.4°C).

In a small bowl, combine the spices. Season the mackerel portions with salt and pepper then sprinkle them with the spice mixture. Place the mackerel portions in a sous vide bag then seal the bag. Let the fish sit for 30 minutes for the dry brine to take effect then place the bag in the water bath and cook for 15 to 45 minutes.

PREPARE THE CORN SALAD

In a large bowl, combine all the salad ingredients and stir to thoroughly combine. Season with salt and pepper.

PREPARE THE DRESSING

In a small bowl, whisk together all the dressing ingredients until thoroughly combined then pour the dressing over the corn mixture.

TO ASSEMBLE

Take the mackerel out of the sous vide bag and pat the mackerel dry. Sear one side over high heat just until browned, 1 to 2 minutes. Remove from the heat.

To serve, take a large spoonful of the corn salad and place it on individual plates. Place the mackerel on top of the corn salad then top with a lime wedge and the basil.

MAHI MAHI with CHIPOTLE BUTTER

COOKS: **130°F (54.4°C) for 15 to 45 minutes** · PREP: **10 minutes** · SERVES: **4**

The flavor of the mahi mahi is deepened and enhanced by this hot and smoky butter. You can add more or less of the chipotle peppers to get to the hotness you prefer. To make the chipotle puree, simply process a can of chipotle chiles in adobo sauce in a blender or food processor until smooth, freezing what you don't use for later use. This dish is enhanced when paired with roasted root vegetables or a salad of mixed greens.

PREPARE THE FISH

Preheat a water bath to 130°F (54.4°C).

In a small bowl, combine the spices. Season the mahi mahi portions with salt and pepper then sprinkle them with the spice mixture. Place the mahi mahi portions in a sous vide bag then seal the bag. Let the fish sit for 30 minutes for the dry brine to take effect then place the bag in the water bath and cook for 15 to 45 minutes.

PREPARE THE BUTTER

To make the butter, place all the butter ingredients in a bowl and mash them together thoroughly using a fork.

TO ASSEMBLE

Take the mahi mahi out of the sous vide bag and pat the mahi mahi dry. Sear one side over high heat just until browned, 1 to 2 minutes. Remove from the heat.

Place the mahi mahi on a plate with the seared side up and place a dollop or two of the butter on top.

FOR THE FISH

1 to 2 pounds mahi mahi, in 4 portions

$1/2$ teaspoon ground cumin

$1/2$ teaspoon ground coriander

Salt and freshly ground black pepper

FOR THE BUTTER

$1/2$ stick salted butter, softened

$1/4$ to 1 teaspoon chipotle puree (see headnote)

$1/2$ teaspoon paprika

$1/8$ teaspoon ground black pepper

MONKFISH and PUMPKIN SOUP

COOKS: **130°F (54.4°C) for 15 to 45 minutes** · PREP: **20 minutes** · SERVES: **4 to 6**

FOR THE MONKFISH

1 pound monkfish, cleaned

1 tablespoon unsalted
butter or olive oil

Salt and freshly ground
black pepper

FOR THE SOUP

2 yellow or white onions,
chopped

1 or 2 small red chiles, finely
chopped

1 teaspoon shrimp paste
(optional)

1 teaspoon granulated
sugar

1½ cups coconut milk,
divided

1 teaspoon tamarind paste
or puree, or 1 teaspoon
Worcestershire sauce

2 cups diced pumpkin,
seeds and skin removed

1 stem lemon grass (white
part only) (optional)

Monkfish and Pumpkin Soup is a rich, Asian-inspired soup full of deep flavor. Although many exotic ingredients are used, they can be left out and the soup will still taste delicious. I've marked the ones that aren't critical to the soup as optional, but I would try to add in as many as possible for the deepest flavor. For an additional garnish, you can roast the seeds from the pumpkin in a hot oven and serve them over the soup.

PREPARE THE MONKFISH

Preheat a water bath to 130°F (54.4°C).

Season the monkfish with salt and pepper. Place the monkfish in a sous vide bag. Add the butter to the bag then seal the bag. Place the bag in the water bath and cook for 15 to 45 minutes.

PREPARE THE SOUP

In a food processor, combine the onions, chiles, shrimp paste, if using, sugar and about half of the coconut milk and process until thoroughly combined. In a large pot, combine the onion mixture with the remaining coconut milk, the tamarind paste, and 1 cup of water.

Add the pumpkin and the stem of lemon grass, if using, to the pot and bring to a boil. Reduce the heat, cover, and simmer until the pumpkin begins to soften, 15 to 35 minutes. Remove the lemon grass.

TO ASSEMBLE

- ¹/₂ cup coconut cream or coconut milk
- 4 tablespoons fresh lime juice
- 1 tablespoon fish sauce
- 2 tablespoons chopped fresh Thai or Italian basil

TO ASSEMBLE

Take the monkfish out of the sous vide bag and pat the monkfish dry. Sear one side over high heat just until browned, 1 to 2 minutes. Remove from the heat.

Stir in the coconut cream, lime juice, fish sauce, and basil to the soup. Ladle the soup into bowls and top it with the monkfish. Serve with fresh, crusty bread.

SNAPPER with SAFFRON-CITRUS SAUCE

COOKS: **130°F (54.4°C)** for 15 to 45 minutes · PREP: **10 minutes** · SERVES: **4**

FOR THE FISH

4 red snapper fillets, cleaned

2 tablespoons unsalted butter or olive oil

Salt and freshly ground black pepper

FOR THE SAFFRON-CITRUS SAUCE

1 lemon

1 grapefruit

1 lime

3 oranges

2 tablespoons canola or olive oil

1 yellow onion, diced

1 zucchini, diced

1 teaspoon saffron threads

1 teaspoon diced chile, such as serrano or jalapeño

1 tablespoon granulated sugar

3 cups fish stock

1/2 cup all-purpose flour

1/2 cup cold water

3 tablespoons chopped fresh cilantro

This Moroccan flavored snapper still manages to stay light despite all the flavors in it. I tend not to sear the fish before serving it, but if you want some extra flavor and texture you can sear it. The flavors meld well with roasted fingerling potatoes or a Parmesan-pea risotto.

PREPARE THE FISH

Preheat a water bath to 130°F (54.4°C).

Season the fish fillets with salt and pepper then place them in a sous vide bag with the butter then seal the bag. Let the fish sit for 30 minutes for the dry brine to take effect then place the bag in the water bath and cook for 15 to 45 minutes.

PREPARE THE SAFFRON-CITRUS SAUCE

Before cutting the citrus fruits you can finely grate their peels and add them later in the cooking process or use them as a garnish for a more citrusy flavor.

Peel the citrus fruit and dice the flesh, removing all the white membrane.

In a large pan over medium heat, add the oil and sauté the onion and zucchini until just softened, about 10 minutes. Add the saffron, diced chile, and sugar and cook for 1 minute. Add the fish stock and bring to a boil. Simmer for 10 minutes then add the citrus pieces and simmer for 10 more minutes.

Whisk the flour and cold water together. Slowly whisk some of the flour and water mixture into the soup until it thickens to the desired consistency.

Remove from the heat and stir in the cilantro and some of the grated peels, if using. Set aside until ready to plate.

TO ASSEMBLE

Take the fish fillets out of the sous vide bag and place them on individual plates. Spoon the saffron-citrus sauce over the top and serve.

SALMON CARPACCIO

COOKS: **110°F (43.3°C) for 15 to 45 minutes** · PREP: **10 minutes** · SERVES: **4**

FOR THE FISH

1 pound salmon, skin and bones removed

1 tablespoon unsalted butter

2 sprigs thyme

Salt and freshly ground black pepper

FOR THE FENNEL CARPACCIO

1 fennel bulb

1$\frac{1}{2}$ tablespoons olive oil

1 lemon

TO ASSEMBLE

Zest from 1 lemon

The licorice flavor of fennel pairs well with the fatty flavors of salmon. I often serve Salmon Carpaccio as a starting course or at cocktail parties, but it is also great when served with a side of roasted potatoes or a hearty risotto to make a meal of it. The fennel salad can be used on many types of fish or even leaner meat like pork chops.

The salmon is cooked at only 110°F (43.3°C), so be sure to use salmon with a quality high enough to eat raw. The texture is almost sushi-like, but if you prefer a more cooked salmon you can increase the temperature as high as you prefer.

PREPARE THE FISH

Preheat a water bath to 110°F (43.3°C).

Season the salmon with salt and pepper. Place the salmon in a sous vide bag with the butter and thyme then seal the bag. Let the fish sit for 30 minutes for the dry brine to take effect then place the bag in the water bath and cook for 15 to 45 minutes.

PREPARE THE CARPACCIO

Remove any discolored outer layers, the core, and the stalks of the fennel bulb, reserving some of the fronds for garnish. Very thinly slice the fennel (using a mandolin is quicker and easier than using a knife); the thinner you cut the fennel the more tender it will taste.

Season the fennel with salt and pepper then drizzle it with the oil. Juice it with lemon and let sit for at least 15 minutes.

TO ASSEMBLE

Take the salmon out of the sous vide bag and thinly slice it. Fan the fennel carpaccio out on plates and top it with the salmon. Sprinkle with the lemon zest, top with the reserved fronds, and serve.

SALMON with CUCUMBER-DILL SALAD

COOKS: **130°F (54.4°C) for 15 to 45 minutes** · PREP: **10 minutes** · SERVES: **4**

Salmon is a classic sous vide beginner dish, and here I complement it with a cucumber and dill salad. The balsamic vinegar will give it some extra sweetness and tartness that helps the salmon to shine through while the cherry tomatoes add bursts of sweetness.

PREPARE THE SALMON

Preheat a water bath to 130°F (54.4°C).

Season the salmon with salt and pepper. Place the salmon in a sous vide bag then seal the bag. Place the sous vide bag in the water bath and cook for 15 to 45 minutes.

PREPARE THE SALAD

Place all the ingredients in a bowl and stir to thoroughly combine.

TO ASSEMBLE

Take the salmon out of the sous vide bag and pat the salmon dry. Sear it until browned, about 1 minute per side. Place the salmon on plates and top it with a spoonful or two of the salad.

FOR THE SALMON

4 salmon portions

Salt and freshly ground black pepper

FOR THE SALAD

1 cucumber, seeded and diced

3 tablespoons chopped fresh dill

1 teaspoon capers

12 to 15 cherry tomatoes, halved

1 tablespoon balsamic vinegar

2 tablespoons olive oil

SCALLOPS with MANGO-MINT SALSA

COOKS: **122°F (50°C)** for 15 to 35 minutes · PREP: **15 minutes** · SERVES: **4**

FOR THE SCALLOPS

1 pound large scallops

1 tablespoon unsalted
  butter

Salt and freshly ground
  black pepper

FOR THE SAUCE

1 tablespoon orange juice

2 tablespoons olive oil

TO ASSEMBLE

1 cup diced mango

1 serrano pepper, thinly
  sliced

1 tablespoon lime zest

1 tablespoon orange zest

2 tablespoons chopped
  fresh mint leaves

Sous vide scallops take on an interesting texture you don't get from just searing them. The sous vide lightly cooks them and then the searing finishes them off. I pair them with a sweet and spicy garnish of mango, mint, and a little hot pepper.

PREPARE THE SCALLOPS

Preheat a water bath to 122°F (50°C).

Season the scallops with salt and pepper. Place the scallops in a sous vide bag in a single layer. Add the butter then seal the bag. Place the sous vide bag in the water bath and cook for 15 to 35 minutes.

PREPARE THE SAUCE

In a small bowl, whisk together the sauce ingredients until thoroughly combined.

TO ASSEMBLE

Take the scallops out of the sous vide bag and pat them dry. Sear the scallops in a pan on one side until they just begin to brown. Remove from the heat and place on plates with the browned side up.

Drizzle the scallops with the sauce then place mango and pepper pieces on top. Garnish with lime zest, orange zest, and chopped mint leaves, and serve.

SEA BASS TOPPED with FENNEL COLESLAW

COOKS: **130°F (54.4°C) for 15 to 45 minutes** · PREP. **35 minutes** · SERVES: **4**

Coleslaw is often overlooked as a good side dish, and here I make a more upscale version with fennel, carrots, and pea-pods. The coleslaw adds a crunchy texture to the silky sea bass. It is all topped with an orange juice-based vinaigrette that adds some acidity without overpowering the fish or the coleslaw.

PREPARE THE SEA BASS

Preheat a water bath to 130°F (54.4°C).

Season the sea bass with salt and pepper then place it in a sous vide bag with the butter and seal the bag. Let the fish sit for 30 minutes for the dry brine to take effect then place the bag in the water bath and cook for 15 to 45 minutes.

PREPARE THE COLESLAW

In a small bowl, thoroughly combine all the coleslaw ingredients.

PREPARE THE VINAIGRETTE

In a small bowl, whisk together all the vinaigrette ingredients until thoroughly combined.

TO ASSEMBLE

Take the sea bass out of the sous vide bag and pat the sea bass dry. Sear one side over high heat just until browned, 1 to 2 minutes. Remove from the heat.

To serve pour the dressing over the coleslaw and stir to thoroughly combine. On each plate, put a spoonful of the coleslaw with the sea bass, seared side up, resting on the top. Top with the toasted almonds.

FOR THE SEA BASS

4 sea bass portions

2 tablespoons unsalted butter or olive oil

Salt and freshly ground black pepper

FOR THE COLESLAW

1 small fennel bulb, trimmed, cored, and shredded

5 large carrots, peeled and shredded

1 cup snow peapods, cut into long strips

$1/4$ red onion, minced

$1/2$ cup chopped fresh cilantro

FOR THE VINAIGRETTE

5 tablespoons orange juice

1 tablespoon white wine vinegar

2 teaspoons yellow mustard

3 tablespoons olive oil

$1/2$ teaspoon salt

$1/2$ teaspoon freshly ground black pepper

TO ASSEMBLE

$1/3$ cup sliced almonds, toasted

SCROD with HERB SALAD

COOKS: **130°F (54.4°C) for 15 to 45 minutes** · PREP: **10 minutes** · SERVES: **4**

FOR THE SCROD

4 portions of scrod

2 tablespoons unsalted butter

Salt and freshly ground black pepper

TO ASSEMBLE

1 cup mixed soft herbs such as basil, oregano, parsley, tarragon, chives, mint, and chervil

1 cup coarsely chopped frisée lettuce

1 tablespoon olive oil

1 lemon

The strong flavor of the herb salad helps to spruce up the mildly flavored scrod. This herb salad is great with many different kinds of fish and can even be used with a fattier cut of steak, like a ribeye. This dish makes for a nourishing meal when served with a side of sautéed vegetables.

PREPARE THE FISH

Preheat a water bath to 130°F (54.4°C).

Season the scrod with salt and pepper then place them in a sous vide bag with the butter then seal the bag. Let the fish sit for 30 minutes for the dry brine to take effect then place the bag in the water bath and cook for 15 to 45 minutes.

TO ASSEMBLE

Take the scrod out of the sous vide bag and place it on plates. Top with the herbs and frisée. Drizzle the oil over the top, squeeze on the lemon, and serve.

SHRIMP POMODORO
over LINGUINE

COOKS: **130°F (54.4°C) for 15 to 45 minutes** · PREP: **15 minutes** · SERVES: **4**

Pomodoro sauce is a very fast tomato sauce to make. It really highlights the flavor of the tomatoes and herbs in it. I like to serve this with fresh bread to really soak up all the sauce.

Here, I call for using canned diced tomatoes, which work well, but if you have extra time there's nothing like fresh, summer tomatoes. Just dice and cook them for an extra 5 minutes when you add them to the dish to break them down.

PREPARE THE SHRIMP

Preheat a water bath to 130°F (54.4°C).

Season the shrimp with salt and pepper, sprinkle them with the cayenne, then add them to a sous vide bag in a single layer. Add the butter then seal the bag. Place the sous vide bag in the water bath and cook for 15 to 45 minutes.

PREPARE THE POMODORO SAUCE

Heat a pan over medium to medium-high heat.

Add the oil to the pan and heat until hot. Add the garlic and cook for 1 minute then add the onion and cook until it begins to soften and turn translucent. Add the tomatoes and some of their juices to the pan and cook for 5 to 10 minutes. Whisk in the butter then remove from the heat and add the basil and oregano. Season with salt and pepper.

TO ASSEMBLE

Spoon the pasta into bowls and top with the pomodoro sauce. Take the shrimp out of the sous vide bag and place them on top of the pasta. Grate the Parmesan and sprinkle it along with the basil and lemon zest on top, and serve.

FOR THE SHRIMP

20 to 25 medium shrimp, shelled and deveined

$1/4$ teaspoon cayenne pepper or chile powder of your choice

1 tablespoon unsalted butter

Salt and freshly ground black pepper

FOR THE POMODORO SAUCE

2 tablespoons olive oil

4 cloves garlic, minced

$1/2$ yellow onion, diced

1 (28-ounce) can diced tomatoes

1 tablespoon unsalted butter

2 tablespoons chopped fresh basil

1 tablespoon chopped fresh oregano

TO ASSEMBLE

Cooked linguine or pasta of your choice

Parmesan cheese

1 tablespoon chopped basil

1 tablespoon grated lemon zest

SHRIMP BISQUE

COOKS: **130°F (54.4°C) for 15 to 45 minutes** · PREP: **20 minutes** · SERVES: **4 to 8**

FOR THE SHRIMP

1¹/₂ pounds medium
   shrimp, still in the shell

¹/₂ teaspoon paprika

Salt and freshly ground
   black pepper

FOR THE SEAFOOD STOCK

3 tablespoons olive oil

3 tablespoons unsalted
   butter

2 leeks, rinsed, roots
   trimmed, and the white
   section coarsely chopped

1 onion, coarsely chopped

2 celery stalks, coarsely
   chopped

2 carrots, peeled and
   coarsely chopped

4 sprigs thyme

1 bay leaf

3 tablespoons tomato paste

¹/₂ teaspoon sweet paprika

¹/₂ teaspoon chipotle
   pepper or cayenne
   pepper

Cooking the shrimp sous vide for this bisque ensures they will be perfectly cooked. You still get the classic bisque flavor by sautéing the reserved shells and making a quick seafood stock. Serve with warm rolls or bread for soaking up the bisque.

PREPARE THE SHRIMP

Preheat a water bath to 130°F (54.4°C).

Peel and devein the shrimp and set aside the shells for use in the stock. Sprinkle the shrimp with the paprika then season them with salt and pepper. Place the shrimp in a sous vide bag then seal the bag.

The bisque takes longer to make than the shrimp does to cook so set the shrimp aside in the bag. After about 30 minutes into making the bisque, add the shrimp to the water bath.

PREPARE THE SEAFOOD STOCK

You first want to make a simple seafood stock from the shrimp shells.

Heat the olive oil and butter in a large pot over medium-high heat until the butter melts. Add the shrimp shells, leeks, onion, celery, and carrots and cook for about 5 minutes, stirring every minute or so. Add the thyme, bay leaf, tomato paste, paprika, and cayenne and stir well. Cook for an additional 5 to 7 minutes, or until the vegetables begin to soften, stirring regularly.

Add enough water to cover the ingredients, about 3 cups. When adding the water, scrape the bottom of the pan with a wooden spoon to deglaze it. As soon as it boils, turn the heat to low and simmer for 30 to 35 minutes, or until the

FOR THE BISQUE

¼ cup brandy

3 cups heavy cream

1 cup whole milk

¼ cup all-purpose flour

¼ cup cold water

TO ASSEMBLE

1 tablespoon orange zest, preferably fresh

2 tablespoons chopped fresh basil

stock has reduced and thickened. Pour the stock through a strainer and into a clean pot.

PREPARE THE BISQUE

Add the bag with the shrimp to the water bath and cook for 15 to 45 minutes.

Add the brandy, cream, and milk to the seafood stock and bring to a simmer.

Whisk the flour and water together in a small bowl. Slowly whisk some of the flour-water mixture into the bisque until it reaches your desired thickness. Remove from the heat.

TO ASSEMBLE

Ladle the bisque into bowls, add the shrimp, top with the orange zest and fresh basil, and serve.

SHRIMP PICNIC SALAD

COOKS: **130°F (54.4°C) for 15 to 45 minutes** · PREP: **10 minutes** · SERVES: **4**

FOR THE SHRIMP

1 pound shrimp, shelled and deveined

1 tablespoon unsalted butter

Salt and freshly ground black pepper

FOR THE DRESSING

1 tablespoon fresh lemon juice

$1/4$ cup mayonnaise

3 tablespoons chopped fresh parsley

3 tablespoons chopped fresh basil

$1/4$ teaspoon chipotle chile powder or chile powder of your choice

TO ASSEMBLE

1 cup cooked corn kernels

1 celery stalk, finely diced

1 red bell pepper, diced

This is a great replacement for the shrimp salads that you find at grocery stores. The dressing is light and just coats the salad without overwhelming it. You can serve this salad as a side, on lettuce by itself, or even in a roll as a fresh and flavorful sandwich.

I usually use smaller shrimp or cut medium ones into bite-size pieces. However, it can be a dramatic presentation if larger, whole shrimp are used.

PREPARE THE SHRIMP

Preheat a water bath to 130°F (54.4°C).

Season the shrimp with salt and pepper then add them to a sous vide bag in a single layer. Add the butter then seal the bag. Place the sous vide bag in the water bath and cook for 15 to 45 minutes.

PREPARE THE DRESSING

In a small bowl, stir together all the dressing ingredients until thoroughly combined. Season with salt and pepper.

TO ASSEMBLE

Take the sous vide bag out of the water bath and place it in an ice bath for 15 minutes. Take the chilled shrimp out of the sous vide bag and coarsely chop them. Add the shrimp to the dressing along with the corn, celery, and bell pepper. Season with salt and pepper and serve.

FISH TACOS with CORN SALSA

COOKS: **130°F (54.4°C) for 15 to 45 minutes** · PREP: **15 minutes** · SERVES: **4**

These fish tacos are inspired by some made for me by a friend I was visiting in Denver. Avocado and corn always go great together, and they form the base for this flavorful salsa. If you can't find mahi mahi you can use any flaky, white fish.

PREPARE THE TILAPIA

Preheat a water bath to 130°F (54.4°C).

In a small bowl, combine the spices. Season the tilapia with salt and pepper then sprinkle it with the spice mixture. Place the tilapia in a sous vide bag then seal the bag. Let the fish sit for 30 minutes for the dry brine to take effect then place the bag in the water bath and cook for 15 to 45 minutes.

PREPARE THE CORN SALSA

In a large bowl, stir together all the salsa ingredients until thoroughly combined.

TO ASSEMBLE

Take the tilapia out of the sous vide bag and pat the tilapia dry.

Add some tilapia to a tortilla, top with the corn salsa, and serve.

FOR THE TILAPIA

2 teaspoons garlic powder

$1/2$ teaspoon paprika

$1/4$ teaspoon chipotle powder or chile powder of your choice

1 pound tilapia

Salt and freshly ground black pepper

FOR THE CORN SALSA

1 cup cooked corn kernels

2 tomatoes, diced

1 avocado, diced

$1/2$ cup black beans, either canned or cooked

2 tablespoons chopped red onion

$1/4$ cup chopped fresh cilantro

4 cloves garlic, diced

2 tablespoons olive oil

1 teaspoon fresh lime juice

TO ASSEMBLE

4 to 8 soft corn tortillas

LEMON-TARRAGON SWORDFISH

COOKS: **130°F (54.4°C) for 15 to 45 minutes** · PREP: **10 minutes** · SERVES: **4**

FOR THE FISH

4 swordfish portions

1 tablespoon unsalted butter

Salt and freshly ground black pepper

FOR THE BUTTER

$1/2$ stick unsalted butter, softened

2 tablespoons finely chopped fresh tarragon

1 teaspoon grated lemon zest

$1/8$ teaspoon ground black pepper

Swordfish is my wife's favorite fish, and this is one of the preparations she likes best. The flavor of the swordfish is brightened by the lemon-tarragon butter and it is also a very quick and easy dish to make. Serving this dish with steamed vegetables or a light risotto rounds out the meal.

PREPARE THE FISH

Preheat a water bath to 130°F (54.4°C).

Season the fish with salt and pepper. Place the swordfish in the sous vide bag with the butter then seal the bag. Let the fish sit for 30 minutes for the dry brine to take effect then place the bag in a water bath and cook for 15 to 45 minutes.

PREPARE THE BUTTER

Place all the butter ingredients in a bowl and mash them together thoroughly using a fork.

TO ASSEMBLE

Take the swordfish out of the bag and pat the swordfish dry. Sear one side over high heat just until browned, 1 to 2 minutes. Remove from the heat.

Place the swordfish on plates and place a dollop or two of the butter on top.

CHAPTER TEN

FRUITS and VEGETABLES

GARLIC MASHED POTATOES

COOKS: **183°F (83.9°C) for 30 to 60 minutes** • PREP: **20 minutes** • SERVES: **4 as a side**

FOR THE POTATOES

2 pounds potatoes, large dice

1 tablespoon fresh thyme leaves

2 tablespoons salted butter

Salt and freshly ground black pepper

FOR THE ROASTED GARLIC

6 cloves garlic, peeled

Olive oil, for coating

Salt

TO ASSEMBLE

4 tablespoons unsalted butter, softened

$1/2$ cup whole milk or heavy cream

3 tablespoons chopped fresh basil

2 tablespoons chopped fresh parsley

Garlic Mashed Potatoes is one of my favorite side dishes. Cooking the potatoes sous vide removes all the guesswork from the process and reduces your cleanup. The roasted garlic adds a pungent bite and also a sweetness from the roasting process. These are also enhanced with some freshly grated Parmesan cheese on top.

PREPARE THE POTATOES

Preheat a water bath to 183°F (83.9°C).

Place the potatoes in a sous vide bag and lightly season them with salt and pepper. Add the thyme and butter then seal the bag. Place the bag in the water bath and cook for 30 to 60 minutes, or until the potatoes are tender.

PREPARE THE ROASTED GARLIC

As soon as the potatoes go into the water bath, begin roasting the garlic. Lightly coat the garlic in the oil and wrap them in foil. Season with salt and place in a 400°F (204°C) oven until soft, 30 to 45 minutes. Remove and set aside to cool slightly.

TO ASSEMBLE

Take the potatoes out of the sous vide bag and place them in a large bowl. Add the roasted garlic, butter, milk, basil, and parsley; mash the potatoes with a potato masher or large fork; do not over mash or the potatoes will take on a tacky texture. Season with salt and pepper and serve.

SPICY CAULIFLOWER and GARBANZO BEANS

COOKS: **183°F (83.9°C) for 20 to 30 minutes** · PREP: **15 minutes** · SERVES: **4 as a side**

Cauliflower can sometimes be bland, so in this dish I use some spicy garbanzo beans to add bold flavors. I really like garbanzo beans, but you can use any canned beans you have as each kind will add its own flavor component to the dish. The sous vide process tenderizes the cauliflower without making it too tough to eat.

PREPARE THE CAULIFLOWER

Preheat a water bath to 183°F (83.9°C).

Place the cauliflower in the sous vide bag with the butter. Season the cauliflower with salt and pepper then seal the bag. Place the bag in the water bath and cook for 20 to 30 minutes, or until the cauliflower is soft.

PREPARE THE VINAIGRETTE

In a small bowl, combine the lemon juice and serrano pepper. Season with salt and pepper and let sit for 3 to 5 minutes then slowly whisk in the oil.

TO ASSEMBLE

Take the cauliflower out of the sous vide bag and put it in a large serving bowl. Add the garbanzo beans, tomatoes, bell pepper, red onion, and cilantro and stir thoroughly to combine. Add some vinaigrette to the bowl then toss to lightly coat but not overpower the mixture.

FOR THE CAULIFLOWER

1 head cauliflower, cut into florets

2 tablespoons salted butter or olive oil

Salt and freshly ground black pepper

FOR THE VINAIGRETTE

3 tablespoons fresh lemon juice

1 serrano pepper, seeded and diced

1/4 cup olive oil

TO ASSEMBLE

1 cup canned garbanzo beans, rinsed and drained

1 cup halved cherry tomatoes

1/2 cup diced red bell pepper

1/4 red onion, thinly sliced

1/2 cup chopped fresh cilantro

GLAZED CARROTS

COOKS: **183°F (83.9°C) for 45 to 60 minutes** · PREP: **10 minutes** · SERVES: **4 as a side**

FOR THE CARROTS

4 large carrots, peeled and chopped into ¾-inch pieces

1 tablespoon salted butter

1 tablespoon granulated sugar

Salt and freshly ground black pepper

TO ASSEMBLE

1 tablespoon chopped fresh parsley

Coarse sea salt and freshly ground black pepper

Sous vide carrots are many people's go-to vegetable. Glazed Carrots is easy to make and also works remarkably well for many other vegetables, including radishes, turnips, parsnips, or pearl onions. You can also try different herb combinations, such as rosemary and thyme for a more savory dish or tarragon and mint for a sweeter combination.

PREPARE THE CARROTS

Preheat a water bath to 183°F (83.9°C).

Combine all the carrot ingredients in a sous vide bag then seal the bag. Place the bag in the water bath and cook for 45 to 60 minutes.

TO ASSEMBLE

Once the carrots are tender, take them out of the bag and place them in a pan over high heat and cook for 2 minutes, stirring constantly. Once glazed, place them directly on plates. Top with the parsley, sprinkle on some coarse salt, and ground black pepper, on top and serve.

PAPRIKA and CHILE CARROTS

COOKS: **183°F (83.9°C) for 45 to 60 minutes** · PREP: **15 minutes** · SERVES: **4 as a side**

While simple glazed carrots are delicious, sometimes I like to cook them with paprika and chile powder to add a punch of savoriness to the dish. If you prefer a glazed version, you can add the sous vided carrots, along with their juices, to a saucepan and slightly reduce the juice, but I often just eat them right out of the bag.

PREPARE THE CARROTS

Preheat a water bath to 183°F (83.9°C).

Combine all the carrot ingredients in a sous vide bag then seal the bag. Place the bag in the water bath and cook for 45 to 60 minutes.

TO ASSEMBLE

Once the carrots are tender, take them out of the sous vide bag and transfer them immediately to plates. Top with the parsley and a sprinkle of coarse sea salt and serve.

FOR THE CARROTS

4 large carrots, peeled and chopped into $1/2$-inch pieces

1 tablespoon salted butter or olive oil

1 teaspoon white vinegar

1 tablespoon honey

2 teaspoons sweet paprika

1 teaspoon chile powder

1 teaspoon salt

TO ASSEMBLE

4 tablespoons chopped fresh parsley

Coarse sea salt

MASHED SWEET POTATOES

COOKS: **183°F (83.9°C) for 45 to 60 minutes** · PREP: **10 minutes** · SERVES: **4 as a side**

FOR THE SWEET POTATOES

2 large sweet potatoes, peeled and cut into 1- to 2-inch pieces

4 tablespoons salted butter, cut into $1/4$-inch-thick pieces

$1/8$ teaspoon ground nutmeg

$1/8$ teaspoon cayenne pepper

TO ASSEMBLE

1 tablespoon bourbon

Kosher salt and freshly ground black pepper

This home-style mashed sweet potato dish is a delicious combination of sweet potatoes, butter, and bourbon. I love it when it is served as a side with duck or a fattier cut of steak such as ribeye. Sometimes I'll also puree the dish at the end for a more refined presentation.

PREPARE THE SWEET POTATOES

Preheat a water bath to 183°F (83.9°C).

Place the sweet potatoes in a sous vide bag along with the butter. Add the nutmeg and cayenne then seal the bag. Place the bag in the water bath and cook for 45 to 60 minutes, or until the potatoes are very soft.

TO ASSEMBLE

Take the sweet potatoes and butter out of the sous vide bag and place them in a bowl. Add the bourbon and mash the potatoes using a potato masher or large fork. Season with kosher salt and pepper and serve.

BROCCOLI with CRISPY PARMESAN and LEMON

COOKS: **183°F (83.9°C) for 30 to 60 minutes** · PREP: **10 minutes** · SERVES: **4 as a side**

This dish uses sous vide to perfectly cook the broccoli then the broiler to melt the Parmesan and add a crispy texture and deeper flavor. This approach works well with many different vegetables, and I'll often include cauliflower or asparagus in the mix for some variety.

PREPARE THE BROCCOLI

Preheat a water bath to 183°F (83.9°C).

Cut the broccoli into large pieces and place them in a sous vide bag. Season the broccoli with salt and pepper then seal the bag. Place the bag in the water bath and cook for 30 to 60 minutes.

TO ASSEMBLE

Preheat the oven broiler.

Take the broccoli out of the sous vide bag and place it in a roasting pan. Sprinkle the Parmesan over the top. Place the pan in the oven until the cheese melts and begins to crisp up. Take the broccoli out of the oven and place it in a serving bowl. Squeeze the lemon over the top and serve.

FOR THE BROCCOLI

1 head broccoli

Salt and freshly ground black pepper

TO ASSEMBLE

$1/2$ cup freshly grated Parmigiano-Reggiano cheese

1 lemon

FINGERLING MUSTARD POTATO SALAD

COOKS: **183°F (83.9°C) for 30 to 60 minutes** · PREP: **20 minutes** · SERVES: **4 as a side**

FOR THE POTATOES

3 pounds small fingerling potatoes, halved or quartered

1 tablespoon fresh thyme leaves

Salt and freshly ground black pepper

FOR THE SALAD

¼ pound bacon, cut crosswise into strips

2 carrots, diced

2 cloves garlic, diced

3 shallots, diced

1 celery stalk, diced

FOR THE DRESSING

¼ cup mayonnaise

2 tablespoons apple cider vinegar

2 tablespoons Dijon mustardTo Assemble

2 tablespoons chopped fresh parsley

1 tablespoon chopped fresh tarragon

Potato salad is a popular side dish and this one has a unique mustard-vinegar dressing with a tartness not found in the typical heavy mayonnaise-based potato salads. The vinegar also helps this dish complement fattier main courses, such as ribeye or duck breast.

PREPARE THE POTATOES

Preheat a water bath to 183°F (83.9°C).

Place the potatoes in a sous vide bag with the thyme. Season the potatoes with salt and pepper then seal the bag. Place the bag in the water bath for 30 to 60 minutes, or until the potatoes are tender.

PREPARE THE SALAD

In a pan over medium heat, sauté the bacon until it begins to crisp and the fat is rendered. Remove the bacon from the pan and discard half of the bacon fat, leaving the rest in the pan. Add the carrots, garlic, and shallots to the pan and cook until the garlic and shallots soften, about 5 minutes. Remove from the heat and place the cooked vegetables and bacon in a large bowl with the celery.

PREPARE THE DRESSING

In a small bowl, stir together the mayonnaise, vinegar, and mustard until thoroughly combined. Season with salt and pepper.

TO ASSEMBLE

Take the cooked potatoes out of the sous vide bag and pour them into the bowl with the bacon mixture. Add the dressing and stir to thoroughly combine. Plate the potato salad, sprinkle the parsley and tarragon on top, and serve.

SPICY SWEET POTATO SALAD

COOKS: **183°F (83.9°C) for 45 to 60 minutes** · PREP: **20 minutes** · SERVES: **4 as a side**

Sweet potatoes pair really well with spicy chipotle peppers to form a savory salad. I like to add corn and black beans to bulk it up and add a spicy vinaigrette that is full of flavor. You can use as much chipotle pepper in adobe as you prefer.

PREPARE THE POTATOES

Preheat a water bath to 183°F (83.9°C).

Peel the sweet potatoes and cut them into ¾- to 1-inch pieces. Place the potatoes in a sous vide bag with the butter and the spices then seal the bag. Place the bag in the water bath and cook for 45 to 60 minutes, or until the potatoes are soft.

PREPARE THE VINAIGRETTE

Place the chipotle, garlic, and ketchup In a blender and blend until smooth. Add the lime juice and honey then blend again. With the blender still running, slowly drizzle in the oil and blend until the mixture is smooth. Season with salt and pepper.

TO ASSEMBLE

Take the potatoes out of the sous vide bag and place them in a large serving dish. Add the corn, black beans, shallots, and cilantro, and stir well to combine. Spoon the vinaigrette over the salad, tossing and tasting as you go so that you don't over dress it, and serve.

FOR THE POTATOES

2 sweet potatoes

3 tablespoons salted butter

½ teaspoon ground cumin

½ teaspoon ground coriander

½ teaspoon ground cloves

½ teaspoon ancho chile powder

½ teaspoon kosher salt

FOR THE VINAIGRETTE

1 chipotle chile from a can of chipotles in adobo

2 cloves garlic, chopped

2 tablespoons ketchup

6 tablespoons lime juice

1 tablespoon honey

½ cup olive oil

Salt and freshly ground black pepper

TO ASSEMBLE

2 cups cooked corn kernels

2 cups canned black beans, rinsed and drained

3 shallots, diced

½ cup chopped fresh cilantro

CREAMY GREEN BEAN SALAD

COOKS: **183°F (83.9°C) for 30 to 45 minutes** · PREP: **20 minutes** · SERVES: **4 as a side**

FOR THE GREEN BEANS

1 pound green beans, washed and trimmed

Salt and freshly ground black pepper

FOR THE CREAMY DRESSING

¾ cup sour cream

$1/4$ cup heavy cream

Juice from 1 lemon

$1/4$ cup olive oil

2 teaspoons chopped fresh dill

Salt and freshly ground black pepper

TO ASSEMBLE

$1/4$ cup pitted Kalamata olives

Several sprigs dill, for garnish

Crisp green beans and a creamy sour cream-based sauce make a hearty side dish. Dill is added to round out the flavor and some Kalamata olives are added for bursts of salty savoriness. These beans are a heavy side dish, as far as beans go, and should be served with a boldly flavored main course so that they don't overpower the meal. They can also be made ahead of time and served cold.

PREPARE THE GREEN BEANS

Preheat a water bath to 183°F (83.9°C).

Place the green beans in a sous vide bag and season them with salt and pepper then seal the bag. Place the bag in the water bath and cook for 30 to 45 minutes, or until tender.

PREPARE THE CREAMY DRESSING

Place the sour cream, cream, lemon juice, oil, and dill in a blender and blend until smooth. Season with salt and pepper.

TO ASSEMBLE

Take the green beans out of the sous vide bag and place them in a bowl. Add the olives and dill. Pour the creamy dressing over the green beans, stir to combine, and serve.

ASPARAGUS and BEAN SALAD

COOKS: **183°F (83.9°C) for 10 to 30 minutes** · PREP: **15 minutes** · SERVES: **4 as a side**

Asparagus is everywhere in spring, and I like to take full advantage of it. Cooking the asparagus sous vide and then combining it with white beans and a light vinaigrette is a playful way to turn it into a flavorful side dish. It goes really well with mahi mahi or seared tuna and also complements poultry, like turkey or chicken.

PREPARE THE ASPARAGUS

Preheat a water bath to 183°F (83.9°C).

Cut the bottoms off the asparagus then cut them into 1-inch pieces. Place the asparagus in a sous vide bag, add the butter, season with salt and pepper and then seal the bag. Place the bag into the water bath and cook for 10 to 30 minutes, or until tender.

PREPARE THE VINAIGRETTE

In a small bowl, combine the vinegar and shallot. Season with salt and pepper then let sit for 3 to 5 minutes. While whisking, slowly drizzle in the oil just until the mixture comes together then stir in the basil.

TO ASSEMBLE

Take the asparagus out of the sous vide bag and place it in a serving bowl. Add the beans and bell peppers and toss. Add enough vinaigrette to coat the salad, season with salt and pepper, and serve.

FOR THE ASPARAGUS

$1/2$ pound asparagus

1 tablespoon salted butter or olive oil

Salt and freshly ground black pepper

FOR THE VINAIGRETTE

2 tablespoons apple cider vinegar

1 shallot, minced

6 tablespoons olive oil

10 basil leaves, coarsely chopped

TO ASSEMBLE

1 (14-ounce) can white beans

2 roasted red bell peppers, diced

GREEN BEAN and RADICCHIO SALAD

COOKS: **183°F (83.9°C) for 30 to 45 minutes** · PREP: **20 minutes** · SERVES: **4 as a side**

FOR THE GREEN BEANS

1 pound fresh green beans, ends trimmed

1 tablespoon unsalted butter or olive oil

Salt and freshly ground black pepper

FOR THE RADICCHIO

1 radicchio, thinly sliced

FOR THE VINAIGRETTE

1 tablespoon fresh lemon juice

2 small cloves garlic, minced

1 shallot, diced

4 tablespoons olive oil

TO ASSEMBLE

$1/3$ cup pecans

Feta cheese, crumbled

Sweet green beans are always taking over the farmers market in summer. Cooking them simply with some butter and serving them with some bitter radicchio and a citrusy vinaigrette allows the sweetness to stand out. These beans can either be served warm or as a chilled side. They go great with steak or pork chops.

PREPARE THE GREEN BEANS

Preheat a water bath to 183°F (83.9°C).

Place the green beans in a sous vide bag with the butter. Season them with salt and pepper then seal the bag. Place the bag in the water bath for 30 to 45 minutes, or until tender.

PREPARE THE RADICCHIO

Soak the radicchio slices in cold water for 10 to 15 minutes; this will help to remove some of the bitterness. Drain then pat dry.

PREPARE THE VINAIGRETTE

In a small bowl, stir together the lemon juice, garlic, and shallot. Season with salt and pepper. Let sit for 3 to 5 minutes. While whisking, slowly drizzle in the oil just until the mixture comes together.

TO ASSEMBLE

Take the green beans out of the sous vide bag and place them in a bowl. Add the radicchio. Coat with the vinaigrette and toss. Place a spoonful of the salad on plates, top with the pecans and cheese, and serve.

SESAME BOK CHOY

COOKS: **183°F (83.9°C) for 15 to 30 minutes** · PREP: **10 minutes** · SERVES: **4 as a side**

Bok choy cooked sous vide always ensures a well-cooked meal. Sesame Bok Choy uses several common Asian ingredients, such as ginger, soy sauce, and sesame seeds, to create a complex sauce that coats the bok choy. There is no clean-up either, since you don't need to use a pan for any part of the process. For a spicier dish, you can add some sriracha or other hot sauce to the sous vide bag.

PREPARE THE BOK CHOY

Preheat a water bath to 183°F (83.9°C).

Combine all ingredients in a bowl and toss to thoroughly combine. Pour the mixture into a sous vide bag and arrange it in a single layer then seal the bag. Place the bag in the water bath and cook for 15 to 30 minutes, or until tender. Once the bok choy is tender remove the bag from the water bath.

TO ASSEMBLE

Take the bok choy out of the sous vide bag and place it in a bowl. Drizzle with the sesame oil, sprinkle with the sesame seeds, and serve.

FOR THE BOK CHOY

4 baby bok choy

1 tablespoon olive oil

1 tablespoon grated fresh ginger

1 tablespoon minced garlic

2 teaspoons soy sauce

Salt and freshly ground black pepper

TO ASSEMBLE

Sesame oil

Sesame seeds

CHILLED LEEKS

COOKS: **183°F (83.9°C) for 30 to 60 minutes** · PREP: **20 minutes** · SERVES: **6 as a side or starter**

FOR THE LEEKS

9 leeks

2 tablespoons fresh thyme

1 tablespoon grated lemon zest

2 bay leaves

2 tablespoons dry white wine

FOR THE DRESSING

1 teaspoon Dijon or country mustard

2 tablespoons apple cider vinegar

6 tablespoons olive oil

Salt and freshly ground black pepper

TO ASSEMBLE

1 tablespoon chopped fresh tarragon

This unique, savory leek salad ramps up any meal as a starter or side course for a poached fish or roasted chicken. Cooking the leeks sous vide renders them very tender and mild. The Dijon vinaigrette adds a touch of sharpness to the leeks while the tarragon brightens them up.

PREPARE THE LEEKS

Preheat a water bath to 183°F (83.9°C).

Wash and trim the leeks by cutting off the top green portion and the bottom strings. Cut the root ends in half and add to a sous vide bag. Add the thyme, lemon zest, bay leaves and white wine to the bag and seal. Place in the water bath and cook for 30 to 60 minutes.

Take the leeks out of the water bath and place the bag in an ice water bath to cool off.

PREPARE THE DRESSING

In a small bowl, stir together the mustard and vinegar. Season with salt and pepper and stir to combine. While whisking, slowly drizzle in the oil just until the mixture comes together.

TO ASSEMBLE

Take the leeks out of the sous vide bag and arrange them on the plates. Spoon the dressing on top, season with salt and pepper, sprinkle on the tarragon, and serve.

CHAPTER ELEVEN

EGGS and CUSTARDS

BACON CHEDDAR
EGG-CUP BITES

COOKS: **170°F (76.6°C) for 1 hour** · PREP: **20 minutes** · SERVES: **4**

FOR THE EGGS

6 eggs

$1/2$ cup shredded cheddar cheese

$1/2$ cup heavy cream

$1/2$ cup diced cooked broccoli

$1/2$ cup crumbled cooked bacon

$1/2$ cup cooked shallots

Sous vide egg-cup bites were initially popularized by Starbucks but are very easy to make at home. You can use any ingredients to flavor them, but my favorites are broccoli, cheddar cheese, and bacon. For a lighter egg, you can replace the cream with milk. For a denser egg, replace the cream with $1/4$ cup cream cheese.

You can make them in any glass container, but the quarter pint or half pint work really well if you finger-tighten the lids so they're closed but not too tight. I've also made them in ramekins, which shapes the eggs nicely.

PREPARE THE EGGS

Preheat a water bath to 170°F (76.6°C).

Whisk together the eggs, cheese, and cream. Stir in the broccoli, bacon, and shallots. Pour the mixture into four Mason jars and tighten the lids using your fingers. Place the jars in the water bath and cook for 60 minutes.

Remove the jars from the water bath, run a knife along the inside of the jar to loosen the egg, and serve.

FRENCH-STYLE SCRAMBLED EGGS

COOKS: **167°F (75°C) for 18 minutes** · PREP: **20 minutes** · SERVES: **4**

FOR THE EGGS

8 eggs

4 tablespoons heavy cream

Parmesan cheese, for grating

4 tablespoons unsalted butter

Salt and freshly ground black pepper

TO ASSEMBLE

6 strips bacon, cut into lardons (thick-cut small strips)

2 tablespoons chopped fresh basil

Parmesan cheese, for grating

Sous vide scrambled eggs is one of the more interesting dishes to cook. The resulting texture is much more like a custard than the rubbery scrambled eggs often found in American cooking.

Here, I use bacon lardons and basil chiffonade for garnish, along with some freshly grated Parmesan. This dish is wonderful when served with a fresh baguette or toast. Preparing scrambled eggs in this way couldn't be easier.

PREPARE THE EGGS

Preheat a water bath to 167°F (75°C).

Whisk together the eggs and cream until well blended. Season with salt and pepper. Grate a few tablespoons of the Parmesan into the mixture then pour the mixture into a sous vide bag. Add the butter then seal the bag lightly, shutting off the vacuum when the eggs get close to the opening (a good way to help with this is to hang the sous vide pouch off the edge of your counter when sealing it). Add the bag to the water bath and cook for about 10 minutes.

TO ASSEMBLE

While the eggs are cooking, cook the lardons in a skillet over medium heat until crispy. After 10 minutes of cooking time, take the sous vide bag out of the water bath and massage it to break up the eggs. Return it to the water bath and cook for another 5 to 8 minutes, or until the mixture begins to firm up.

Take the sous vide bag out of the water bath and massage it once more to break up the eggs. Evenly divide the scrambled eggs between two bowls and adjust the seasoning as needed. Add the lardons and basil to the bowls. Grate some Parmesan over the top and serve.

SOUS VIDE HARD-BOILED EGG

COOKS: **165°F (73.8°C) for 40 to 60 minutes · Makes: 6 eggs**

With the precision of sous vide, eggs can be cooked to any degree of desired doneness. Hard-boiled eggs are usually cooked for 40 to 60 minutes, depending on the size of the egg. You can use these eggs In any way you want, from mashing them up into egg salad or halving them to place on salads.

PREPARE THE HARD-BOILED EGGS

Preheat a water bath to 165°F (73.8°C).

Gently place the eggs, in their shells, directly into the water bath and cook for 40 to 60 minutes.

TO ASSEMBLE

Remove the eggs from the water bath and let cool. Just before using, remove the shells.

FOR THE HARD-BOILED EGGS

6 eggs

POACHED EGGS on SPINACH SALAD

COOKS: **145°F (62.8°C) for 40 to 60 minutes** · PREP: **10 minutes** · SERVES: **4**

FOR THE EGGS

4 eggs

FOR THE SALAD

4 bacon slices, cut across into thin strips

1 onion, sliced

3 cloves garlic, coarsely chopped

2 tablespoons honey

1 tablespoon balsamic vinegar

TO ASSEMBLE

1 bag baby spinach

1 tomato, diced

1 tablespoon olive oil

Freshly ground black pepper

1 wedge fresh Parmesan cheese

The eggs, especially the yolks, add a ton of flavor to this salad, and the eggs go great with the bacon and cheese. Sous viding the eggs allows you to accurately determine how hard or soft you would like them. Moving a few degrees in either direction results in dramatic changes.

PREPARE THE EGGS

Preheat a water bath to 145°F (62.8°C).

Gently place the eggs, in their shells, directly into the water bath and cook for 40 to 60 minutes.

PREPARE THE SALAD

In a large pan over medium heat, cook the bacon for 5 to 6 minutes to render the fat. Remove the bacon from the pan and set aside. Pour out and discard half the bacon fat, leaving the rest of the fat in the pan. Add the onion and garlic to the pan and cook until the onion turns soft. Add the honey and vinegar and cook until the onion begins to caramelize, 5 to 6 more minutes.

TO ASSEMBLE

When the eggs are almost done (after 50 to 60 minutes of cooking time), add the spinach to the pan with the onion and garlic; stir until the spinach is just wilted, about 1 minute. Remove from the heat and divide among four individual bowls. Top with the bacon and tomato.

Take the eggs out of the water bath using a slotted spoon or tongs. One at a time, gently crack the eggs on the counter and remove the top quarter or half of the shell. Turn the shell upside down to remove the egg. Add 1 egg to the top of each salad. Drizzle oil on each salad, season with pepper, grate the Parmesan on top, and serve.

AVOCADO TOAST WITH 13-MINUTE POACHED EGG

COOKS: **167°F (75°C) for 13 minutes** · SERVES: **4**

Hearty, whole-grain toast combined with a runny sous vide egg is a simple, rich and creamy meal. Be sure to use a high-quality bread and a ripe avocado because the flavors will shine through.

The 13-minute egg is one of the most popular ways to cook eggs because it's easy and fast with consistently great results. I first heard of the 13-minute egg from *Ideas in Food*, but many other chefs use this technique as well. The timing is critical because of the high heat.

PREPARE THE 13-MINUTE EGG

Preheat a water bath to 167°F (75°C).

Gently place the eggs, in their shells, directly into the water bath and cook for 13 minutes. Once cooked, remove them from the water bath and set aside.

PREPARE THE AVOCADO SPREAD

Remove the flesh from the avocado and mash it together with the oil. Add the lime juice and season with salt and pepper, just until the spread is slightly tangy and well-balanced in flavor.

TO ASSEMBLE

Slather some of the avocado spread on each piece of toast. Crack a 13-minute egg over the top then sprinkle with the fresh cracked pepper and sea salt.

FOR THE 13-MINUTE EGG

4 eggs

FOR THE AVOCADO SPREAD

2 avocados

2 tablespoons olive oil

Lime juice

Salt and freshly ground black pepper

TO ASSEMBLE

4 slices whole-grain bread, toasted

Fresh cracked pepper

Sea salt

SOUS VIDE YOGURT

COOKS: **110°F (43.3°C) for 5 to 10 Hours** · SERVES: **4**

FOR THE YOGURT

4 cups half-and-half or
   whole milk

1/2 cup plain yogurt with live
   and active cultures

To make yogurt, milk or cream is heated to above 180°F (82.2°C), cooled, mixed with a starter culture, then incubated at 100°F to 120°F (37.8°C to 48.9°C) for several hours. A sous vide machine allows you to easily maintain these specific temperatures.

Sous vide yogurt is typically made in glass Mason jars with the lids either off or not fully tightened. The starter bacteria will give off gasses as they create the yogurt, so a tightly sealed container can leak or explode. The yogurt is also usually made in the container in which it will be stored or served because transferring it to a new container can change its consistency.

To start the incubation, add 1/2 cup of yogurt that contains live and active cultures (this will be indicated on the package). The length of the incubation time, which can range from 3 to 24 hours, determines the tanginess of the yogurt.

PREPARE THE YOGURT

Fill a water bath to about 1 inch below the height of the Mason jars and preheat the water to 110°F (43.3°C).

Heat the half-and-half in a saucepan to at least 180°F (82.2°C). Remove it from the heat and let it cool to at least 120°F (48.9°C) then whisk in the yogurt. Pour the mixture into the Mason jars and seal each with plastic wrap secured with rubber bands. Place the jars into the water bath and let incubate for at least 5 hours.

After 5 hours, remove the jars from the water bath and refrigerate until chilled. Once the yogurt is cold, seal with the Mason jar lids. The yogurt will last in the refrigerator for 1 to 2 weeks.

CINNAMON-VANILLA CRÈME BRÛLÉE

COOKS: **190°F (87.8°C) for 60 to 90 Minutes** · SERVES: **4**

FOR THE CRÈME BRÛLÉE

2 cups whipping or heavy whipping cream

1 vanilla bean

1 cinnamon stick

4 egg yolks

1 pinch salt

$1/3$ cup granulated sugar

TO ASSEMBLE

Sugar

Mint leaves

Creme brûlée is a fancy dish but is very simple to make at home, especially when you are using a sous vide machine. This is a classic crème brûlée recipe that makes a good base that you can take in a variety of directions, depending on the flavors you prefer.

Crème brûlée cooks best if you pour the mixture a little less than 1-inch-high in the dish, otherwise the inside might not cook all the way through. For crème brûlées prepared in deeper dishes, you may need to increase the cooking time. If your ramekins are touching in the water bath, rotate them half way through the cooking process to ensure even cooking.

PREPARE THE CRÈME BRÛLÉE

Place an upside-down strainer or bowl with a flat bottom in the empty water bath container. Place a sheet pan or plate on top of the bowl. Set the ramekins on the sheet pan and fill the water bath two-thirds of the way up the ramekins; remove the ramekins. Preheat the water bath to 190°F (87.8°C).

Pour the cream into a saucepan. Split the vanilla bean lengthwise in half and scrape out the seeds then add the seeds and the empty pod to the cream. Add the cinnamon stick. Bring just to a simmer, stirring regularly. Turn off the heat and let it infuse for 10 minutes. Strain the cream.

In a separate bowl, whisk together the egg yolks then slowly whisk in the salt and sugar (the mixture should turn glossy and thicken slightly). Slowly whisk in the infused hot cream. Evenly divide among the ramekins, cover each ramekin with plastic wrap and use a rubber band to hold the plastic wrap

in place. Place the ramekins back in the sous vide bath on top of the sheet pan and cook for 60 to 90 minutes, depending on how thick you prefer your crème brûlée.

Remove the ramekins from the water bath and let cool for 15 to 20 minutes. Refrigerate until cold, preferably overnight.

TO ASSEMBLE

Spread a thin layer of sugar over the entire top of the chilled crème brûlées (cover the tops completely) and quickly torch the sugar until it melts and begins to brown. Add a few mint leaves and serve.

HAM and PEPPER
EGG-CUP BITES

COOKS: **170°F (76.6°C) for 1 hour** · PREP: **10 minutes** · SERVES: **4**

FOR THE EGGS

6 eggs

$1/2$ cup shredded mozzarella cheese

$1/2$ cup whole milk

$1/2$ cup diced ham

$1/2$ cup diced red bell pepper

$1/4$ cup diced green bell pepper

This version of the egg-cup bites emulates a Denver omelet by using ham and bell peppers. I like to include mozzarella cheese to tie it together. I've also replaced the heavy cream with whole milk to make a lighter version of this dish.

PREPARE THE EGGS

Preheat a water bath to 170°F (76.6°C).

Whisk or blend together the eggs, cheese, and milk. Stir in the ham and bell peppers. Pour the mixture into four Mason jars and tighten the lids using your fingers. Place the jars in the water bath and cook for 60 minutes.

TO ASSEMBLE

Remove the jars from the water bath. Loosen the egg by running a knife along the inside of the jar. Serve in the Mason jar for a fun presentation.

CHAPTER TWELVE

INFUSIONS

ORANGE-PASSION FRUIT TEA VODKA

COOKS: **160°F (71.1°C) for 1 to 3 hours** · PREP: **10 minutes** · Makes: **1¹/₂ Cups**

FOR THE PASSION FRUIT
VODKA

3 tablespoons orange-
passion fruit tea mix,
preferably Harney & Sons,
or other fruity tea mix

1¹/₂ cups vodka

One of the easiest ways to flavor infusions is to use pre-made blends, especially herbal and dried fruit teas. The resulting infusion is sweet, fruity, and tropical with a lovely red color. My friend Fran Rotella recommends serving the infusion over ice with a splash of club soda, or mixed with a little Prosecco for an upscale drink.

PREPARE THE PASSION FRUIT VODKA

Preheat a water bath to 160°F (71.1°C).

Combine the tea mix with the vodka in a sous vide bag or a Mason jar then seal it and place it in the water bath to infuse for 1 to 3 hours.

Prepare an ice bath with half ice and half water. Remove the bag or Mason jar from the water bath and place it in the ice bath for 15 to 20 minutes. Strain, then store in a sealed container.

SPICED PUMPKIN PIE VODKA

COOKS: **131°F (55°C) for 1 to 3 hours** · PREP: **45 minutes** · Makes: **1¹/₂ Cups**

Spiced Pumpkin Pie Vodka brings a holiday favorite to your cocktail glass, saving plenty of room for other desserts and Thanksgiving traditions! This infusion recreates the flavors of pumpkin pie in a wonderfully complex vodka that enhances cocktails, especially when mixed with sugar and a splash of club soda. It's also a party favorite when enjoyed on its own.

PREPARE THE PUMPKIN PIE VODKA

Preheat an oven to 400°F (204°C) and preheat a water bath to 131°F (55°C).

Place the pumpkin pieces on a sheet pan and bake until just starting to brown, 20 to 30 minutes. Remove from the heat and combine with the remaining ingredients in a sous vide bag or Mason jar then seal it and place it in the water bath to infuse for 1 to 3 hours.

Prepare an ice bath with half ice and half water. Remove the bag or Mason jar from the water bath and place it in the ice bath for 15 to 20 minutes. Strain, then store in a sealed container.

FOR THE PUMPKIN PIE VODKA

- 2 cups coarsely chopped pumpkin (from 1 small pumpkin)
- 1 cinnamon stick
- 5 whole cloves
- ¹/₂ teaspoon freshly grated nutmeg
- ¹/₂ teaspoon freshly grated ginger
- 1¹/₂ cups vodka

VANILLA ORANGE VODKA

COOKS: **140°F (60°C) for 1 to 3 hours** · PREP: **15 minutes** · Makes: **1¹/₂ Cups**

FOR THE VANILLA ORANGE
VODKA

2 oranges

1 vanilla bean, split
lengthwise

1¹/₂ cups vodka

Vanilla goes great with oranges, and this infusion takes full advantage of that. The resulting vodka is citrusy with a deep-vanilla backbone. It is awesome in a martini or simply over ice. I also like to make a "creamsicle" by mixing it with a little bit of cream and orange juice then serving it over ice.

PREPARE THE VANILLA ORANGE VODKA

Preheat a water bath to 140°F (60°C).

Lightly scrub the outside of the oranges then remove the zest with a vegetable peeler or zester. Make sure little to no pith (the white membrane) came off as well; use a paring knife to remove any that is attached to the zest. The orange sections can be reserved for garnishing the drink.

Combine all the ingredients in a sous vide bag or a Mason jar then seal it and place it in the water bath to infuse for 1 to 3 hours.

Prepare an ice bath with half ice and half water. Remove the bag or Mason jar from the water bath and place it in the ice bath for 15 to 20 minutes. Strain, and store in a sealed container.

BLACK CHERRY RYE

COOKS: **160°F (71.1°C) for 1 to 3 hours** · PREP: **15 minutes** · Makes: **1^1/$_2$ Cups**

Peppery rye and sweet black cherries come together in this flavorful infusion. The fruity cherry notes complement the spicy rye and tone down its bite. The cinnamon and clove contribute background notes to round out the infusion. I like to use Bulleit Rye because it has a strong, peppery flavor that holds up to the cherries and spices, plus it's very affordable. You can substitute the rye of your choice, or use a bourbon for more sweetness and less peppery notes.

FOR THE BLACK CHERRY RYE

20 to 30 black cherries

^{1}/$_2$ stick cinnamon

6 cloves

1^1/$_2$ cups rye

PREPARE THE BLACK CHERRY RYE

Preheat a water bath to 160°F (71.1°C).

Remove the stems from the cherries. Place the cherries in a sous vide bag or a Mason jar. Lightly crush or muddle the cherries. Add the remaining ingredients to the cherries then seal the bag or jar and place it in the water bath to infuse for 1 to 3 hours.

Prepare an ice bath with half ice and half water. Remove the bag or Mason jar from the water bath and place it in the ice bath for 15 to 20 minutes. Strain, then store in a sealed container. The cherries can be reserved for a garnish or boozy snack

APPLE PIE BOURBON

COOKS: **140°F (60°C) for 1 to 3 hours** · PREP: **15 minutes** · Makes: **2 Cups**

FOR THE APPLE PIE BOURBON

2 Gala apples or other sweet apples

2 cinnamon sticks

1 vanilla bean, split lengthwise

1 teaspoon freshly grated nutmeg

1 teaspoon ground allspice

1 teaspoon grated fresh ginger

2 cups bourbon

The only thing more American than warm apple pie is bourbon, so why not combine the two? This is always a crowd favorite and is the first infusion to disappear at parties. The bourbon is flavored with fresh apples and classic apple pie spices like cinnamon, ginger, and nutmeg. It's a perfect bourbon to sip with dessert or to make into a liqueur. The quantities below fit best in a quart-size jar because the apples take up so much space, but you can halve the quantity, if desired.

PREPARE THE APPLE PIE BOURBON

Preheat a water bath to 140°F (60°C).

Lightly scrub the outside of the apples then core and coarsely chop them. Combine the apple pieces with the remaining ingredients in a sous vide bag or a Mason jar then seal it and place it in the water bath to infuse for 1 to 3 hours.

Prepare an ice bath with half ice and half water. Remove the bag or Mason jar from the water bath and place it in the ice bath for 15 to 20 minutes. Strain, then store in a sealed container.

BLUEBERRY COMPOTE

COOKS: **183°F (83.9°C) for 30 to 60 minutes** · PREP: **10 minutes** · SERVES: **4 as a topping**

Fresh blueberries combine with bright citrus juice and sharp cinnamon and ginger to form a full-flavored blueberry compote that makes a great topping for oatmeal, toast, or even ice cream. I prefer a chunkier compote so I usually just smash the blueberries through the sous vide bag, but for a smoother compote, you can puree the blueberries once cooked.

PREPARE THE BLUEBERRIES

Preheat a water bath to 183°F (83.9°C).

Combine all the ingredients in a sous vide bag then seal the bag. Place the bag in the water bath and cook for 30 to 60 minutes.

Once cooked, smash or puree the blueberries and serve.

FOR THE BLUEBERRIES

8 ounces blueberries

2 tablespoons orange juice

1 teaspoon fresh lemon juice

$1/8$ teaspoon ground cinnamon

$1/8$ teaspoon ground ginger

1 tablespoon packed brown sugar

1 tablespoon granulated sugar

STRAWBERRY BASIL RUM

COOKS: **131°F (55°C) for 1 to 3 hours** · PREP: **10 minutes** · Makes: **1¹/₂ Cups**

FOR THE STRAWBERRY
BASIL RUM

8 large strawberries

14 basil leaves

1¹/₂ cups rum

In early summer you can find strawberries at all the markets but they tend to go bad quickly. Strawberry Basil Rum infusion is a terrific way to preserve them for later enjoyment. The basil adds a nice hint of spice to the infusion. This rum is delicious in mojitos and rum punch, but I really like it in a fizz to cool me off on a warm summer day.

PREPARE THE STRAWBERRY BASIL RUM

Preheat a water bath to 131°F (55°C).

Coarsely chop the strawberries and the basil leaves. Combine the strawberries, basil, and rum in a sous vide bag or a Mason jar then seal it and place it in the water bath to infuse for 1 to 3 hours.

Prepare an ice bath with half ice and half water. Remove the bag or Mason jar from the water bath and place it in the ice bath for 15 to 20 minutes. Strain then store in a sealed container.

APPLE and CRANBERRY VINEGAR

COOKS: **140°F (60°C) for 1 to 2 hours** · PREP: **15 minutes** · Makes: **1¹/₂ Cups**

Fruits and spices are easily infused into vinegars that can be used in vinaigrettes or sauces. Apple and Cranberry Vinegar is a tart, sweet, and fruity mixture that uses the combination of apples and cranberries to add wonderfully complex flavors to dishes. Infusing the fruit into the vinegar makes it easy to add these flavors to salads, as a vinaigrette, or to create a refreshing shrub cocktail by combining it with sugar and club soda.

PREPARE THE APPLE AND CRANBERRY VINEGAR

Preheat a water bath to 140°F (60°C).

Lightly scrub the outside of the apples then core and coarsely chop them. Lightly crush the cranberries with a rolling pin or the back of a knife. Combine the apple pieces, cranberries, and vinegar in a sous vide bag or a Mason jar then seal it and place it in the water bath to infuse for 1 to 2 hours.

Prepare an ice bath with half ice and half water. Remove the bag or Mason jar from the water bath and place it in the ice bath for 15 to 20 minutes. Strain then store in a sealed container.

FOR THE APPLE AND CRANBERRY VINEGAR

2 Granny Smith apples

¹/₂ cup cranberries

1¹/₂ cups apple cider vinegar

VANILLA and CHERRY BALSAMIC VINEGAR

COOKS: **140°F (60°C) for 1 to 2 hours** · PREP: **15 minutes** · Makes: **1^1/$_2$ Cups**

FOR THE VANILLA AND
CHERRY BALSAMIC VINEGAR

16 cherries

1 vanilla bean, split
lengthwise

1^1/$_2$ cups balsamic vinegar

The sweet and tart tastes of cherries go wonderfully with the earthy flavor notes of vanilla. Cherries and vanilla are both strong flavors and hold up well to naturally deep flavors of balsamic vinegar. If you want a vinegar where the cherry and vanilla flavors shine more brightly, try using a white balsamic or white wine vinegar instead.

Note: Cherries stain easily so be sure to cover your cutting board with parchment paper or plastic wrap.

PREPARE THE VANILLA AND CHERRY BALSAMIC VINEGAR

Preheat a water bath to 140°F (60°C).

Remove the stems from the cherries and place them in a sous vide bag or a Mason jar. Lightly crush or muddle the cherries. Add the vanilla bean to the cherries. Pour the vinegar over top then seal the bag or jar and place it in the water bath to infuse for 1 to 2 hours.

Prepare an ice bath with half ice and half water. Remove the bag or Mason jar from the water bath and place it in the ice bath for 15 to 20 minutes. Strain, then store in a sealed container.

SAGE and ROSEMARY OIL

COOKS: **131°F (55°C) for 1 to 2 hours** · PREP: **10 minutes** · Makes: **1¹/₂ Cups**

Many different ingredients can be infused into oils, such as sage and rosemary used here. Since I want to emphasize their subtle flavors, I call for a neutral oil. This combination results in a woody, herby oil that I often use to finish fish dishes or to add extra herbal notes to vinaigrettes and other sauces.

PREPARE THE SAGE AND ROSEMARY OIL

Preheat a water bath to 131°F (55°C).

Combine the oil, rosemary, and sage in a sous vide bag or a Mason jar then seal it and place it in the water bath. Heat the infusion for 1 to 2 hours.

Prepare an ice bath with half ice and half water. Remove the bag or Mason jar from the water bath and place it in the ice bath for 15 to 20 minutes. Strain, then store in a sealed container. It will last for a week or two in the refrigerator.

FOR THE SAGE AND ROSEMARY OIL

1¹/₂ cups canola, grapeseed, or other neutral oil

5 large sprigs rosemary

25 sage leaves

DRIED CHILE PEPPER OIL

COOKS: **160°F (71.1°C) for 4 to 5 hours** · PREP: **15 minutes** · Makes: **1¹/₂ Cups**

FOR THE DRIED CHILE
PEPPER OIL

3 ancho dried chile peppers

3 guajillo dried chile
    peppers

2 chipotle dried chile
    peppers

1¹/₂ cups canola,
    grapeseed, or other
    neutral oil

This oil picks up the spice and smoke from the peppers, making it quicker and easier to add those flavors to other dishes. You can use any dried chile peppers you like, but I prefer a combination of ancho, guajillo, and chipotle. The ancho contributes fruitiness, the chipotle adds heat, and the guajillo complements the smokiness of the other peppers.

PREPARE THE DRIED CHILE PEPPER OIL

Preheat a water bath to 160°F (71.1°C).

Remove the stems from the peppers and lightly chop the flesh. Combine the oil and peppers in a sous vide bag or a Mason jar and seal it. Heat the infusion for 4 to 5 hours.

Prepare an ice bath with half ice and half water. Remove the bag or Mason jar from the water bath and place it in the ice bath for 15 to 20 minutes. Strain then store in a sealed container. It will last for a week or two in the refrigerator.

RHUBARB and ROSEMARY SIMPLE SYRUP

COOKS: **165°F (73.8°C) for 2 to 4 hours** · PREP: **10 minutes** · Makes: **1¹/₂ Cups**

You can infuse simple syrups with many different combinations of fruits, herbs, and spices–and Rhubarb and Rosemary Simple Syrup is one of my favorites. It is an herby, minty, and tangy syrup that adds complexity to cocktails or can even be fermented into a carbonated beverage. It is also a delicious addition to iced tea for an easy-to-make drink that impresses guests.

PREPARE THE RHUBARB AND ROSEMARY SYRUP

Preheat a water bath to 165°F (73.8°C).

Combine all the ingredients with 1 cup of water in a sous vide bag or a Mason jar then seal it. Heat the infusion for 2 to 4 hours, shaking vigorously twice during the infusion process to keep the sugar evenly distributed.

Prepare an ice bath with half ice and half water. Remove the bag or Mason jar from the water bath and place it in the ice bath for 15 to 20 minutes. Strain the simple syrup, squeezing out any liquid, and store it in a sealed container. It will last for several months if stored in a cabinet or cupboard.

FOR THE RHUBARB AND ROSEMARY SYRUP

1¹/₂ cups granulated sugar

2 sprigs rosemary

2 stalks rhubarb

AROMATIC BITTERS

COOKS: **140°F (60°C) for 2 to 4 hours** · PREP: **20 minutes** · Makes: **1 Cup**

FOR THE AROMATIC BITTERS

1 orange

1 lemon

1 cup vodka

4 green cardamom pods, cracked

2 cinnamon sticks

1 tablespoon gentian root

2 teaspoons quassia bark

1 teaspoon ground allspice

$1/2$ teaspoon cracked peppercorns

12 whole cloves

Artisanal bitters are currently all the rage, and they are actually very easy to make at home with sous vide. Classic bitters add flavor-enhancing aromas to cocktails, subtly tweaking the flavors found in each drink in different directions. The bitters have notes of cinnamon, clove, and cardamom while using several bittering agents to round out the flavors. Some of the ingredients can be hard to find locally, but they can all be found online.

PREPARE THE AROMATIC BITTERS

Preheat a water bath to 140°F (60°C).

Lightly scrub the outside of the orange and lemon then remove the zest with a vegetable peeler or zester. Make sure little to no pith (the white membrane) came off as well; us a paring knife to remove any attached to the zest.

Combine all the ingredients in a sous vide bag or a Mason jar then seal it and place it in the water bath to infuse for 2 to 4 hours.

Prepare an ice bath with half ice and half water. Remove the bag or Mason jar from the water bath and place it in the ice bath for 15 to 20 minutes. Strain the bitters, squeezing any liquid out, and store in a sealed container. They will last for several months if stored in a cabinet or cupboard.

COCOA NIB and ORANGE CREAM

COOKS: **150°F (65.5°C) for 1 to 2 hours** · PREP: **15 minutes** · Makes: **1 1/2 Cups**

Bitter and chocolaty cocoa nibs combine with rich cream and a hint of vanilla for an infused cream that is perfect for making fancy whipped cream. This cream also works great when used in White Russian cocktails or gelled into a panna cotta.

FOR THE COCOA NIB CREAM

1 orange

1 1/2 cups whipping or heavy whipping cream

1/2 cup cocoa nibs

1 vanilla bean, split lengthwise

PREPARE THE COCOA NIB CREAM

Preheat a water bath to 150°F (65.5°C).

Lightly scrub the outside of the orange then remove the zest with a vegetable peeler or zester. Make sure little to no pith (the white membrane) came off as well; use a paring knife to remove any attached to the zest.

Combine all the ingredients in a sous vide bag or a Mason jar then seal it and place it in the water bath to infuse for 1 to 2 hours.

Prepare an ice bath with half ice and half water. Remove the bag or Mason jar from the water bath and place it in the ice bath for 15 to 20 minutes. Strain then store in a sealed container in the fridge until ready to use.

MIXED MUSHROOM BROTH

COOKS: **150°F (65.5°C) for 1 to 2 hours** · PREP: **20 minutes** · Makes: **1 Cup**

FOR THE WILD MUSHROOM BROTH

1 1/2 cups dried mushrooms

1 tablespoon fresh thyme leaves

1 shallot, diced

Dried mushrooms are full of concentrated flavors. Infusing them into water creates a rich, flavorful broth that is a wonderful base for savory dishes, such as soups or pan sauces or as a cooking liquid for rice or risotto. I usually press the mushrooms to extract all the liquid from them, but if you want a clearer broth you can skip that step or just use a finer strainer to better clarify it.

PREPARE THE WILD MUSHROOM BROTH

Preheat a water bath to 150°F (65.5°C).

Combine all the ingredients in a sous vide bag or a Mason jar with 1 1/2 cups of water then seal it and place it in the water bath to infuse for 1 to 2 hours.

Prepare an ice bath with half ice and half water. Remove the bag or Mason jar from the water bath and place it in the ice bath for 15 to 20 minutes. Strain the broth, pressing the mushrooms with a wooden spoon or the back of a spatula to release all their juices. Store in a sealed container in the fridge until ready to use.

SPICED RUM-INFUSED RAISINS

COOKS: **150°F (65.5°C) for 1 to 2 hours** · PREP: **20 minutes** · Makes: **$^2/_3$ Cup**

Traditionally, infused raisins are made by placing them in the cupboard to soak for several days, or even weeks, until they plump up. Since I normally don't plan that far ahead, I like to use a sous vide machine instead, which speeds up the process to only few hours. And if rum isn't your thing, you can also make these with bourbon.

Both the raisins and the resulting rum have a sweet flavorful taste and can be used together or separately. The rum is wonderful in any traditional spiced rum cocktail or in a Rum Old Fashioned. The raisins can be used as garnish on desserts, in bread puddings, on top of ice cream, or as an adornment on drinks. I've even used the raisins and rum in a caramel sauce for sticky rolls to start my morning off right!

PREPARE THE SPICED RUM INFUSED RAISINS

Preheat a water bath to 150°F (65.5°C).

Combine all the ingredients in a sous vide bag or a Mason jar then seal it and place it in the water bath to infuse for 1 to 2 hours.

Prepare an ice bath with half ice and half water. Remove the bag or Mason jar from the water bath and place it in the ice bath for 15 to 20 minutes.

The raisins can be kept in the rum to continue absorbing flavor and plumping up or they can be strained out of the rum and stored in the refrigerator. The raisin-infused rum should also be reserved and can be used in many drinks.

FOR THE SPICED RUM INFUSED RAISINS

$^2/_3$ cup raisins

1 cup spiced rum

MARASCHINO CHERRIES

COOKS: **165°F (73.8°C) for 2 to 3 hours** · PREP: **20 minutes** · **Makes: 2 Cups**

FOR THE MARASCHINO
CHERRIES

2 cups sweet cherries

$^1/_2$ cup Luxardo liqueur

$^1/_2$ cup brandy

$^3/_4$ cup granulated sugar

Cherries, brandy, Luxardo liqueur, and sugar come together for a garnish that is full of cherry flavor and boozy after-notes. Maraschino cherries are nothing like the fluorescent red, syrupy sweet cherries that are sold in the grocery store. If you prefer a less boozy cherry, you can add more sugar or replace the brandy with more Luxardo or water.

PREPARE THE MARASCHINO CHERRIES

Preheat a water bath to 165°F (73.8°C).

Combine all the ingredients in a sous vide bag or a Mason jar. If the liquid does not fully cover the cherries, add some more Luxardo or brandy to cover them. Seal the jar or bag, and shake well to combine. Place in the water bath and heat the infusion for 2 to 3 hours.

Prepare an ice bath with half ice and half water. Remove the bag or Mason jar from the water bath and place it in the ice bath for 15 to 20 minutes.

The cherries can be stored in the liquid in the refrigerator for several weeks.

INDEX